ENTERTAINMENT LAW

IN A NUTSHELL

THIRD EDITION

By

SHERRI BURR

Dickason Professor of Law
University of New Mexico

WEST®

A Thomson Reuters business

Mat # 41256043

© West, a Thomson business, 2004
© 2007 Thomson/West
© 2013 Thomson Reuters

      610 Opperman Drive
      St. Paul, MN 55123
      1-800-313-9378

Printed in the United States of America

ISBN: 978-0-314-28061-9

DEDICATION

I hereby dedicate this book to voice teacher Jennie Proctor Schwoebel, whose careful tutelage expanded my vocal range by illuminating many high notes. Teachers like Jennie have long inspired my work.

Sherri Burr
September 2012

ACKNOWLEDGMENTS

In addition to those who were interviewed for previous editions, the third edition of *Entertainment Law in a Nutshell* has benefitted from interviews with John Corbett, Tony Duarte, Giancarlo Esposito, José Fragoso, Martin Katz, Tony Mark, Jacques P. Mer, Brigitte Monneau, Sophia Nieves, Paulo Pereira, Eduardo Pinto, Paul Sanderson, José Pedro Ribeiro, Julia Sereny, Susanne Vaas, and Miguel Valverde, and Pedro Vasconcellos. The author was also fortunate to attend American Pavilion lecture events at the Cannes International Film Festival with Col Needham, Terry Gilliam and Ryan Gosling. The author also thanks Stavros Lambrinidis for introducing her to Ignasi Guardans who provided interview leads in Portugual and David Burt and Brigitte Monneau for introductions in Canada.

The author thanks the University of New Mexico, Dean Kevin Washburn, Attorney Robert St. John for the Dickason Professorship that enabled her to travel to conduct research for this book. The author expresses gratitude to UNM Law School students Caroline Seigel and Shelby Carlson for their research assistance, and to Kelli Grady and Lawrence Kemp for proofreading the manuscript.

For the second edition, the author interviewed the following individuals: Sabine Aigner, Robyn Ayres, Jan-Holzer Arndt, Klaus Beucher, Mat Boggs, Stephen Boyle, Sam Bray, Bruno Charlesworth, Frank I. Davis, Nelson De Sousa, Michael Emerson, Lori Flesker, Chris Gallagher, Terry Gruber, Margo Holt, Cyril Jost, Andrew Laurence, Helen Leake, Dick Marks, Anja Metzger, Jason Miller, Christopher Mills, Fess Parker, Doris Petrevcic, Dee Dee Phelps, Tony Shaloub, Rebel Steiner, Marc Vlessing, Nancy Wilson, Morgan Woodward, Mark Woods, and Toby Wright.

For the first edition, she interviewed Wally Amos, Diane Bloom, Greg Brooker, Johnnie Cochran, Max Evans, Chris Eyre, Guillermo Figueroa, Stephen Frears, John Carlos Frey, Walon Green, Bob Guiney, Tony Hillerman, Matt Jackson, Jonathan Miller, Shirley MacLaine, Jon Moritsugu, Duncan North, Keali'i Reichel, Jim Rogers, Sam Wong, and Frank Zuniga.

OUTLINE

TABLE OF CASES

References are to Pages

TABLE OF CASES

TABLE OF AUTHORITIES

References are to Pages

ENTERTAINMENT LAW

IN A NUTSHELL

THIRD EDITION

INTRODUCTION

Hollywood is a place, but more importantly an industry based in Los Angeles with national offshoots in New York and Nashville, and global components around the world. The entertainment business is central to the lives of most Americans and to the United States economy. According to a Variety Magazine article, entertainment supplanted food as this country's greatest export in 2004. [Crabtree, *Casting Against Type*.] The table below was constructed from the various sources indicated in the Table of Authorities and shows both domestic and global sales figures for five major sectors of the industry. [Table, Global Sales]

TABLE: ENTERTAINMENT INDUSTRY		
INDUSTRY	*2011 DOMESTIC SALES*	*2011 GLOBAL SALES*
Film	$10.2 billion	$32.6 billion
Television	$131.8 billion	$373.2 billion
Music	$7 billion	$168 billion
Publishing	$44 billion	$244.4 billion
Video game Software	$13.1 billion	$38.394 billion

Because of the globalization of the United States entertainment industry, other countries are routinely exposed to U.S. culture. Their citizens often seek to emulate what they read, see on big and small screens, hear on the radio or their smart devices, or play on video game consoles.

The many players within the entertainment business rely on the law and lawyers to look after their interests. Lawyers who do not understand how the entertainment business works are at a disadvantage when it comes to protecting their clients. It is not enough for a lawyer to read a contract and advise clients on its context if he does not understand the intricacies of the agreement's special meanings. Clients come to lawyers seeking advice on seemingly incomprehensible legal language. Many smart lawyers make assumptions about entertainment related issues that are wrong. As a consequence, they bring misfortune to their clients and sometimes themselves.

Similarly, numerous talented individuals have become so thrilled when a Hollywood person comes knocking on their door that they unwittingly sign anything placed before them. By reading this book, film artists, television talent, musicians, authors, video game creators, and other talented individuals will appreciate the value of consulting well-versed attorneys before inking their name on the dotted line.

Because of this necessity to understand how the entertainment business works in order to comprehend the law that applies to it, this book's first four chapters provide an overview of the film, television, music, and video game industries. Chapters 1 – 4 discuss the process of creating film, television, music, and video game products, as well as the major players who have different interests. These chapters also converse about particularized components of the four businesses.

Chapter 5 scrutinizes the efforts of entertainers to protect their products from censorship. During the McCarthy era, entertainers had their free speech rights curtailed for political reasons. Other entertainment products have been accused of touting obscenity, which does not enjoy the protection of the First Amendment. Still other creative output has been labeled excessively violent and charged as contributing to the tortious and violent behavior of third parties.

Chapter 5 explores censoring efforts that have succeeded and failed. It demonstrates that censorship brings more attention and often more resources to the author(s) of the sought-to-be-banned articles. Indeed, film and other artists have come to relish the attention, as patrons queue to see films others tell them not to see or buy music certain groups urge them to avoid.

Chapter 6 highlights intellectual property law by revealing how the laws of ideas, copyrights, trademarks, patents, and trade secrets protect products like films, games, music, television shows, theater plays, and books. Over the decades, fiction authors have accidentally lost the rights to their characters or have found themselves in legal quicksand by producing material based on the copyrighted characters of other professionals. This chapter discusses not only how to protect all authors' works, but also details the elements of infringement cases. Chapter 6 provides a synopsis of several problematic cases.

Chapter 7 focuses on representing entertainers, particularly the importance of agents, managers, lawyers, and unions to the successful career. Talented individuals sometimes find themselves in a paradox. When they need assistance they cannot get it, and to obtain aid requires a certain level of verifiable talent. Chapter 7 describes some of the legal issues involved in acquiring representation.

Chapter 8 discusses the issues concerning the relationship between credits and compensation. Credits acknowledge the contribution of the talented individual to a particular project. An individual's compensation increases with the success of the projects attributed to him. Thus talent and their attorneys need to understand the nature of credits, how they are acquired, and their links to receiving revenue. In the film and television industry, for example, contracts often contain references to guaranteed, deferred, and contingent compensation. Many individuals have misunderstood these terms to their regret, as they subsequently watched the hit they helped create generate hundreds of millions of dollars in profits for others and nothing more for themselves beyond the revenue that was initially guaranteed to them. Chapter 8 also contains information important to musicians.

Chapter 9 analyzes different types of contracts and their peculiarities in the entertainment industry, including some of the fine points that make them similar yet different. Film and television contracts, for example, include clauses that are set by union regulation, whereas music contracts for most bands do not. The exceptions are symphony orchestra contracts negotiated between the American Federation of Musicians and the management of the orchestra. Even so, classical musicians have watched their earnings barely keep up with inflation as conductor and management salaries skyrocket.

By reading chapters 7, 8 and 9, the attorney and law student should understand the difference between what talent has already obtained through union negotiated agreements and what can still be bargained for. The distinction is critical so that talent and their lawyers do not waste energy and time asking for items, like breaks, that the individual already has. Instead, they should concentrate on augmenting the minimum pay and other perks to make the talent's life more bearable on set or on stage.

Chapter 10 covers issues associated with celebrity status. An individual may attain this rite of passage through enormous ability or due to notoriety associated with infamous behavior. Either way, the newfound celebrity status can be exploited to generate additional revenue for the individual. This chapter discusses the advantages and disadvantages to possessing celebrity status, including the actions of ordinary folks and the media that lead to violations of the entertainer's right to privacy. Celebrities may also exploit their right of publicity. This form of intellectual property permits entertainers and sports stars to profit commercially from the popularity of their names and images.

Chapter 10 also discusses estate planning, which has gained in importance because many entertainers make more money after their deaths than during their lives. Minding their estate finances enables them to ably support family members left behind or to create charitable institutions to impact social concerns they care about. Chapter 10 reviews the legal issues associated with dying intestate, or without a will, versus testate, or with a will. It also reviews issues associated with creating trusts.

This book concludes with a discussion of the globalization of the entertainment industry and the changes that have taken place as producers seek to create products that cross cultural boundaries in the international marketplace. Film and television industries have arisen in countries throughout the world, along with unique musical sounds. This globalization process means more Americans have been exposed to Indian weddings and Brazilian music and vice versa. Chapter 11 examines issues associated with foreign production, intercontinental markets, global piracy, and the availability of appropriate forums to resolve disputes between nationals of different countries.

This book covers all of the above and more. As *American Idol* judges say to successful television contestants, "Welcome to Hollywood."

CHAPTER 1
THE FILM INDUSTRY

The film business comprises a vibrant component of the entertainment industry. On a weekly, monthly and yearly basis, millions of individuals in the United States and abroad flock to view the products produced in Hollywood. In 2009, the top film, *Avatar*, sold $2,771,500,000 worth of tickets. Only $750 million of that total, or 27.1%, was earned in the United States. The remaining $2 billion was accumulated worldwide. In 2011, the top film was *Harry Potter and the Deathly Hallows Part 2*, which earned $1,328,100,000 worldwide, with only 28.7% of that total from United States' sales. By September 2012, *Marvel's The Avengers* had collected a global box office total of $1,503,100,000, with 41.3% (or $620,800,000) coming from United States' sales, according to Box Office Mojo.

Nevertheless, video games are now sometimes besting film sales. *Call of Duty: Modern Warfare 3* made its first billion in sales in 16 days, which exceeded *Avatar's* first billion in sales by one day.

Tinseltown amazes and excites as it attracts talented people from countries around the world to Los Angeles to pursue their dreams. The goal of entertainment law practitioners is to keep aspirations from turning into nightmares.

A. THE FILM PROCESS

The process of creating a film consists of pre-production, production, and post-production periods.

1. PRE-PRODUCTION

The pre-production stage often begins with a pitch. Agents, managers, actors, and producers routinely make brief presentations on their projects to people in a position to provide resources or ultimately green-light the film. "Green-light" is an industry term referring to the ability of someone with power to give the final approval to send the movie into production.

Typically, producers will be accorded three minutes and writers will receive 45 minutes to pitch their ideas. The writer is expected to outline the story, including the beginning, middle, and end. She should be able to provide character and story arcs, indicating how both the main character and the overall plot will develop.

Immediately following the pitch meeting, an interested studio executive might ask a screenwriter to turn over his or her entire script and a producer to prepare and submit a treatment. A treatment can range from a page or two to several dozen pages. The treatment provides an overview of the film, including plotlines, essential characters, sometimes locations and settings, and an estimate of what it would take to make the movie work financially. The purpose of the treatment is to give the reader a sense of how this project might develop on screen and sometimes the cost.

This pre-production process also involves preparing and submitting scripts, hiring talent (actors and directors) and the production crew, scouting locations, and obtaining financing. Some directors may rehearse their actors during this phase. This gives actors a sense of the overall emotional development of their characters. Location availability, weather, and other variables determine the order of production. The ending could be shot before the middle, and thus actors must be prepared to emotionally deliver where their characters are at any given point in the film.

2. PRODUCTION

With all aspects of pre-production settled, the film moves into the production phase, during which principal photography commences and the movie is shot. The production supervisor prepares daily call sheets to indicate which scene will be shot on a particular day and which actors and technicians are expected to be on set. The call sheets also indicate arrival times and the make-up schedule.

3. POST-PRODUCTION

Post-production encompasses editing and putting together all the pieces of the film, including video, dialogue, and sound tracks. Sidney Lumet, the director of more than 40 films, including *12 Angry Men*, *The Verdict*, and *Serpico*, describes the mix as the only dull part of moviemaking. With this component, the filmmakers put all the tracks together to make the final soundtrack of the movie. [Lumet, *Making Movies*, at 186.] The last stage is to color balance the film and produce the answer print, which will be used to print the film shown in theaters.

Since anything can go wrong in the pre-production, production, and post-production phases, it is important for lawyers to have a sense of the overall process, as well as the players and the types of films.

B. THE PLAYERS

Filming is a collaborative enterprise, requiring the aid of many individuals and groups to bring a final product to completion. The film then goes to the theater where an audience can view it. Some films deemed un-commercial for theaters may go straight to DVD or Blu-ray and end up in a local Redbox distributor, which purports on its website www.redbox.com to make renting films and games easier. Others may be played on airlines or streamed over the Internet on large and small screens. Many more will ultimately receive cable, satellite, and network television broadcasts.

Several players contribute to the final product and their roles are discussed in turn.

1. PRODUCERS

The general public may not recognize producers because they operate behind the scenes. They often set the wheels in motion with an idea or a book and then hire the talent and secure financing. They may actively shape the project from embryo stage (an idea) to adulthood (when the full film is released in theaters). These producers often operate on the word of individuals, or obtain written agreements to lock-in talent to a particular project.

Producer Lynda Obst says in her book, *Hello, He Lied*, that producers "breathe life into [a] movie—from its infancy as [an article or book] through its adolescence as a script being written against a tight time clock, and finally into its adulthood—by finding a director and choosing and securing the cast." She describes the greatest crisis for a producer as "the threat of watching your baby die." [Obst, *Hello, He Lied*.]

A motion picture producer often does the following activities:

(1) Generates enthusiasm among the various creative elements and brings them together;

(2) Searches out locations that would be proper for the artistic side of the production and from the logistical physical production side;

(3) Creates a budget that would be acceptable from the physical point of view, as well as satisfactory from the point of view of implementing the requirements of the script;

(4) Makes arrangements with foreign government(s) where photography would take place;

(5) Supervises the execution of the script and the implementation of it onto film;

(6) Supervises the editing of all the production work, down through the dubbing process and the release printing process, at least through the answer print process with Technicolor;

(7) Consults with studio people on advertising and publicity;

(8) Arranges casting;

(9) Engages the interest of the kind of star or stars that ... [the studio people] would find sufficiently attractive to justify an investment; and

(10) Develops the interest of a proper director.

[*Blaustein v. Burton,* 9 Cal.App. 3d 161, 167, 88 Cal.Rptr. 319 (Cal.App. 2 Dist. 1970)] The main producer takes on these roles during the pre-production and production process.

Producers supervise the creative and physical aspects of making motion pictures. [Knopf v.

Producers Guild of America, 40 Cal.App.3d 233, 114 Cal.Rptr. 782 (1974)] Martin Katz, a producer of *A Dangerous Method* and executive producer of *Hotel Rwanda*, says much of what producers do is about spotting issues to be resolved. "I am constantly negotiating and renegotiating." [Author Interview with Katz.]

Tony Mark, the executive producer of *The Hurt Locker*, which won the 2010 Academy Award for best picture, describes producing as one of the film industry's toughest jobs. Nevertheless, he says, "it is enormously satisfying. You are deeply engaged behind the scenes. You interact with the director, studio, fundraisers, as well as keep the blue collar people happy so they want to go to work." [Author Interview with Mark.] He adds, "When a producer is associated with an Oscar winner, it creates the perception of being more valuable. Some people will translate that into bigger paychecks. But for me, I hope it creates a greater ability to get my projects paid attention to."

Some producers are primarily money men. As outside investors, their chief function is to finance the picture themselves or obtain financing from others. This can be a chicken and egg process, as the bigger the name of the talent (such as Tom Hanks or Will Smith), the easier it is for producers to secure financing and to sell the film's foreign and ancillary rights. They may also oversee the budget.

These money-men producers have often made their fortune elsewhere before entering the film business. Bob Yari, a real estate developer who established two production companies and a film financing company, and Jeff Skoll, co-founder of eBay, exemplify this breed, according to the New York Times. [Nussenbaum, *New Producers Have Fat Wallets*.]

Even before the film is completed, producers must also secure domestic and foreign box office distribution. They contract and negotiate with distributors to arrange key aspects of distributing the movie to the general public. This includes the release date, the release pattern, the selection of theaters to exhibit the picture, the advertising budget, and the terms of the contracts with exhibitors. [United States v. Tracinda Investment Corp., 477 F.Supp. 1093, 1104 (C.D. Cal. 1979)]

Producers also seek sales agents and distributors to sell the film for airplane viewing, DVD and Blu-ray players, cable, satellite, and broadcast television, and Internet streaming on computers and smart devices. Producers may strive to merchandise the film's characters into video game products and other store goods. In some foreign countries, they may obtain government investment through the co-venture process to be discussed in Chapter 11.

2. SCREENWRITERS

Writers often launch the film process. Writers may be inspired to craft a screenplay from an original idea, or a producer may bring them a book or theatrical play and ask them to adapt it for the big screen. Walon Green, who received an Oscar® nomination for *The Wild Bunch* and is credited with 13 feature films, says, "The first obligation a writer has is to make sure he's not going to be sued, that he didn't steal the idea from someone." [Author Interview with Green.]

Greg Brooker, who received co-credit for writing *Stuart Little* with M. Night Shyamalan, says, "A lot of writers can make a good living writing screenplays in Hollywood, even if ... [the screenplays] don't see the light of day." [Author Interview with Brooker.] Brooker adds, "Writers tend to keep on the periphery of the business. You don't see a lot of writers hanging out at parties because they're home writing." [*Id.*]

In her article "Separation of Rights for Screen and Television Writers," Grace Reiner discusses the most recent addition to the separated rights possessed by writers—the right of reacquisition. Reiner says the writer has the right to buy back original material not based on any preexisting material that has not been produced within five years. She says that "[t]he writer may do so as long as the material is not in active development.... To reacquire the material, the writer must pay the company the amount the writer was paid for the purchase and/or writing services." Further, Reiner opines that the writer must obligate the new buyer to pay the balance of direct literary material costs plus interest, which is "due upon commencement of principal photography." [Reiner, *Separation of Rights*.]

3. DIRECTORS

Directors are responsible for the entire look and feel of the physical product. Sidney Lumet, the director of dozens of films, calls what he does "the best job in the world." [Lumet, *Making Movies*, at 3.] Depending on the complications associated with the physical production of the movie, Lumet says he is in preproduction "anywhere from two and a half to six months. And, depending on how much work must be done on the script, perhaps for months before preproduction began.... There are no minor decisions in movie making." [*Id*. at 7.]

In describing his contributions to *Dr. Zhivago*, David Lean said that he works with the writer to obtain an acceptable shooting script, rehearses the actors, and gives direction to the cameraman, set designer, costume designer, sound men, editor, composer, and even the laboratory that prepares the final print. [Caro, *The Director or the Writer: Whose Film is It?*]

Independent directors of small-budget films often get involved in producer-like activities, such as raising money, luring talent, securing gun permits, enforcing child labor laws, and negotiating with film commissions. John Carlos Frey, the director of *The Gatekeeper*, shot his film in 18 days at a cost of $200,000. To do so, he said, required that "the actors work for nearly free, the crew works nearly for free, your locations get donated, your food gets donated, and you go begging, basically, to pull it off." [Author Interview with Frey.] Frey financed his film by taking out a second mortgage on his home, borrowing from family members, draining his savings account, and running up credit card debt. [*Id.*]

After casting a child actor in a major role, Frey familiarized himself with child labor laws, which limit the hours that a child can work, and labor union laws that regulate adult hours. He even needed to secure gun permits for the fake guns in the film in case police officers drove by. When he needed to blow up a building, he contacted the San Diego Film Commission, which ran interference between him and the fire department. For all this trouble, Frey made a story close to his heart, which won numerous awards at independent film festivals. [*Id.*]

Another director of independent films, John Moritsugu, also makes movies about things that matter to him. Moritsugu says he directed the 1999 *Fame Whore* to call attention to "people who seek fame at any cost.... There is a naïve view that once you're famous, that everything will fall into place. Fame can be a particularly deadly drug." [Author Interview with Moritsugu.] He says, "[f]rom the time you start to the time you finish, it can take up to five or ten years to make a movie.... With my movies, I have a voice in society. It gives me a chance to put a little bit of my money and all of my time and [all] of my friends' time and energy into a project that ... ultimately will ... say something and will hopefully affect something." [Id.]

Many famous actors, such as Barbra Streisand, Clint Eastwood, and Robert Redford, have taken up the director's chair. Tony Shaloub, who is best known for starring in the film *Big Night* and the television show *Monk*, premiered his film *Made-up* at the 2002 Taos Talking Pictures festival. He said he used dolls to stage the scenes before he filmed them and received help from the screenwriter, producer, and co-star of *Made-up*, Lynne Adams. [Burr, *Taos films bring lessons*.]

That said, producer-director Michael Emerson believes that it may be a negative to be multi-talented. He says that Hollywood likes "to compartmentalize" and thus "it's better to be just a producer, a director, a writer." [Author Interview with Emerson.] Depending on the client, lawyers may end up representing someone with only one talent or those who crossover to other areas.

4. ACTORS

Actors must master voice, movement, and physical skills to create memorable characters on large and small screens. Many attend fine arts colleges or independent film classes or both to hone their craft. Actors give physical embodiment to screenwriters' words and the director's instructions. They may find work in film, television, music videos, radio, interactive games, and theatrical plays. In animated films, put together by illustrators or with computers, actors lend their voices to fictional characters. Brad Pitt, for example, voiced the animated character Sinbad in the 2003 film by the same name and Antonio Banderas voiced the character Puss in Boots in the *Shrek* films and in 2011 film by the same name. Computers can similarly generate characters that look alive, and are voiced by real actors.

Some actresses, like Meryl Streep, are particularly adept at voicing accents, dialects, and unique speech patterns such as when she recreated Dame Margaret Thatcher's intonations in *The Iron Lady*. Streep dubbed her own voice into several foreign languages for the film *Sophie's Choice*, which won her an Academy Award for Best Actress. Streep's films have also been financially successful; her top 10 films have earned approximately $1.3 billion in total box office revenue. [Freierman, *Popular Demand: Meryl Streep Movies*.]

Actors in the theater must be able to project to the last row of the house. Radio actors must portray nuanced roles that create mental and emotional images of their characters for their listening audience. Their voices may be clear or fuzzy, strong or weak, depending on the demands of the character portrayed. In the 1950s, actress Hattie McDaniel, who is best known for her Academy Award-winning performance as Mammy in *Gone with the Wind*, gained even more fame when her radio show *Beulah* was projected into millions of homes.

Should actors strive for lead, supporting, or character roles? The choice can make a difference on the longevity of their career. According to producer-director Michael Emerson, a leading man may work for six to seven years whereas character actors work for 50 years. [Author Interview with Emerson.] Character actors can be thought of as individuals whose faces the audience may recognize, but whose names are rarely learned.

Morgan Woodward, who played character roles on stage, film, and television for nearly 50 years, proves Emerson's point. Woodward says, "A character actor lends himself to a wide range of roles through the use of make-up and props. The primary tricks of a character actor include the ability to employ body language and dialects to varied effects." [Author Interview with Woodward.]

Woodward holds the record for having guest starred nineteen times on *Gunsmoke*, television's longest running drama. To play the bad guy, Woodward says, "You've got to go toe-to-toe, eyeball-to-eyeball, and not blink." On film, Woodward is perhaps best recognized for playing Boss Godfrey, the menacing "man with no eyes," in *Cool Hand Luke*, which starred Paul Newman in the title role. Woodward describes his character as a "walking Mephistopheles," the evil spirit in the Faustian legend to whom Faust signs away his soul in return for assistance. [*Id.*]

Giancarlo Esposito demonstrated how a talented actor can turn a dramatic character into a legend when he played drug dealer Gustavo "Gus" Fringe in 26 episodes of the award-winning television show *Breaking Bad* between 2009 and 2011. Esposito, who began his acting career in the Broadway musical *Maggie Flynn* at the age of 10 and has since acted in numerous film and television productions, said he agreed to play Gus because the character showed "the devastation of meth in the West. I let roles speak to me, and draw on their organic nature. Gus was unpredictable. Gus was graceful, caring, and polite. He cared about people. He ran a business, an illegal business. He took care to choose people with integrity. That went to the success of Gus."

It can be challenging for an actor to leave behind a character. After Gus was killed off in the "Face Off" episode at the end of season four, Esposito found he would catch himself walking like Gus and speaking like Gus. He finally accepted that excising Gus was like a journey and that he needed to compartmentalize the character from his soul. [Author Interview with Esposito.] Esposito's work was recognized by Emmy Association when he was nominated for Best Supporting Actor in 2012.

Webster's Dictionary defines a starlet as "a young movie actress being coached or publicized for starring roles." Depending on whether the individual possesses talent, she may fade quickly from public view, become a character actress, or graduate to leading roles.

For some actors, their portrayals of memorable characters attract stardom and superstardom. Stars are actors who have reached a certain level of recognition in their profession. William Goldman describes a star as "whoever *one* studio executive with 'go' power *thinks* is a star and will underwrite with a start date." Goldman defines a superstar as "someone they'll all kill for." [Goldman, *Adventures in the Screen Trade*, at 13.]

Stars and superstars come and go with the popularity of their films. Goldman says an actor reaches stardom invariably by mistakes committed when another name with bigger box office draw potential passes on a picture that becomes the breakthrough hit for the successor actor. [Goldman, *Adventures in the Screen Trade*, at 13-14.] For examples, he cites how Montgomery Clift turned down "the William Holden part in *Sunset Boulevard*, the James Dean part in *East of Eden*, the Paul Newman part in *Somebody Up There Likes Me*, and the Brando part in *On the Waterfront*." [*Id*. at 14.] These roles all helped these actors become stars, and Marlon Brando win his first Oscar for Best Actor.

Stars and superstars provide the shorthand for a picture, as industry insiders may pitch an "Angela Jolie action flick" or "Eddie Murphy comedy" to studio executives seeking financing for their films. Because star names are instantly recognizable, producers have easier times raising revenue if stars or superstars are attached to their pictures.

While actors may be essential to 95% of film products, some have questioned whether they actually add value at the box office. In 2003, for example, major Hollywood studios spent $63.8 million on average to make a film and another $39 million to advertise it. [Diorio, *Tentpole teeter-totter*.] By 2010, the average advertising budget for a wide-release Hollywood movie had declined to $32 million, according to http://thehollywoodeconomist.blogspot.com. Yet a review of outrageously successful films over the last several decades reveals fewer than 50 percent that were star vehicles. Instead, many, like the *Harry Potter* or *Shrek* series, were fantasy or animated flicks. As fewer films earn back their costs, studios sometimes cancel star-driven vehicles when their budgets increased significantly beyond the original projection. Other times, like with the *Lone Ranger* starring Johnny Depp, they may force a revamping of the budget to lower the cost.

5. TECHNICAL STAFF

The technical staff makes the production work. They are involved in the preproduction process and several arrive on location before the actors to position the set and lights. Editors fashion raw footage into an understandable product during post-production.

The art director is responsible for the overall look and feel of the set. Art directors can make a picture feel as luminous as a painting by an old master, as Christina Schaffer achieved with the 2003 film *Girl with a Pearl Earring*, or as an impressionist canvas, as Thomas Voth and Christian Wintter accomplished with the 1998 film *What Dreams May Come*.

The costume designer creates the clothes that the actors wear. Edith Head was nominated for 35 Oscars between 1948 and 1977 for best costume design. She won so many times that director John Huston once joked that an Academy Award was written into her contract. [Scott, *Personality Parade*.]

The makeup director creates the character's look. Lee Grimes and Toni G. turned Charlize Theron, an actress noted for her beauty, into an unattractive serial killer for her feature role as Aileen Wuornos in *Monster*. Makeup artists have also transformed men into women, as when Robin Williams played Mrs. Doubtfire in a film by the same name and two African-American men, Marlon and Shawn Wayans, became Caucasian females for the 2004 film *White Chicks*. They create alien looks for films as diverse as *Star Wars* or *John Carter*, which featured a Civil War veteran transplanted to Mars.

The director of cinematography is responsible for photographing the entire film process in moving imagery. For the film *Glory,* Freddie Francis received the 1989 Academy Award for Best Cinematography by capturing a gritty and realistic vision of the horrors of the Civil War from the perspective of black soldiers who fought on the side of the North. An excellent cinematographer can make or break an epic adventure whose story sweeps the audience along. Independent directors, like John Carlos Frey, are sometimes able to hire excellent cinematographers from abroad to work for very little in return for acquiring a U.S. film credit. [Author Interview with Frey]

Gaffers are the lighting technicians who bestow ambiance on the set. By appropriately illuminating the actors, gaffers create mood and can make the talent look older or younger, as the situation requires.

The drivers are members of the Teamsters Union. They transport talent and crew material from location to location. Production assistants are usually recent college graduates who do whatever is needed, from making coffee and picking up dry cleaning to chaperoning visitors to the set.

Editors are critical to the post-production process, as they take the raw footage and turn it into a story. Certain types of films, like documentaries, can be editorially intense, requiring an editor to pull together the story line, says Craig Serling, who has edited documentaries and episodes of the reality TV shows *Survivor* and *Amazing Race*. [Author Interview with Serling.]

The music composer creates the film's score. At the Academy Award ceremonies, they frequently show composers working on a keyboard as the movie plays on a screen. The job of the composer is to match the mood the director is trying to depict on film. The score can foreshadow dread or foretell a happy ending. Perhaps the most highly regarded music composer is John Williams, a symphony orchestra conductor who has won five Oscars and 18 Grammy Awards. He is best known for scoring *Jaws*, *Star Wars*, and *E.T., the Extra-Terrestrial*. [Burlingame, *Why Stop at 43 Nominations*.] He combined Japanese music with Western music to score *Memoirs of a Geisha*, and created a memorable score to open the London Summer Olympics in 2012.

Musicians also perform and write original music for films. Cellist Yo-Yo Ma and violist Itzhak Perlman contributed solo performances to *Memoirs of a Geisha*. At the 78th annual Academy Awards ceremony, Jordan Houston, Cedric Coleman, and Paul Beauregard won the best original song Oscar® for "It's Hard Out There For a Pimp," which was featured in the 2005 film *Hustle and Flow*.

These are only a few of the many talented individuals who lend their expertise to the making of a film. Their positions and names scroll down the screen at the end of the picture. Depending on the type of picture, such as with an action flick, the names of those who created special effects may be listed. Sometimes, the credits for films, such as those in the *Star Wars* series, may list upwards of a thousand people in the credits. For his 2004 documentary *Fahrenheit 9/11*, Michael Moore listed all the production assistants, interns, and law firms who contributed to his film.

6. STUDIOS

Studios are corporations with the power and resources to underwrite a film. Goldman describes studio executives as ex-agents, who "are intelligent, brutally overworked men and women who share one thing in common with baseball managers: They wake up every morning ... with the knowledge that sooner or later they're going to get fired." [Goldman, *Adventures in the Screen Trade*, at 39.] The reason for this, Goldman says, is that in Hollywood, "Nobody Knows Anything." [*Id.*] Because they can never predict "what's going to work," Goldman maintains that every time out is a guess—and if they're lucky, "an educated one." [*Id.*]

Michael Ovitz and Ron Meyer, founders of Creative Artist Agency (CAA), are examples of two agents who transitioned into studio executives. Ovitz spent 14 months at Disney before parachuting out with a golden $140 million, the equivalent of nearly 10 percent of Disney's earnings in 1996. In

1995, Meyer began a longer and more successful tenure as the head of Universal Studios. The role of agents will be discussed in more detail in Chapter 6.

Studio executives are the individuals with the power to make the picture a go. Joe Roth ran two major Hollywood studios before starting an independent company to create quality movies with modest budgets in 2000. [Holson, *The Rise and Fall of Revolution*.] Roth's Revolution experiment lasted six years and accumulated a 47-film library before collapsing. Roth's adventures in filmmaking prove that it may be even more difficult to start a studio than to run one.

7. FILM COMMISSIONS AND COUNCILS

Film commissions and councils increasingly play important roles in the film-making process. Internationally, over 300 film commissions belong to the Association of Film Commissions International (AFCI). According to its website, www.afci.org, these film commissions and councils attract "filmmakers and videographers to their respective regions by providing services that an out-of-town producer would be hard-pressed to acquire without their assistance." These commissions, found throughout the globe, may assist filmmakers in a variety of functions, from scouting locations in their area to offering financial incentives to encourage production featuring local casts and crews.

California, which tops P3 Update's list of "The Top 10 Locations in the Universe," expected its incentives to bring $2.8 billion in direct spend. [http://www.p3update.com/preproduction/locations/1 264-the-top-10-locations-in-the-universe-]   Other states have sought to pull away some of this entertainment production revenue by adopting incentives to encourage filming in their locales.

In the article, "Top 10: United States of Production," P3 Magazine ranks the states of Louisiana, Illinois, Florida, Georgia, California, Connecticut, New York, Utah, New Mexico, and Michigan as its top 10 for filmmaking. [http://www.p3update.com/ preproduction/locations/1199-top-10-united-states-of -production] According to P3 Update, "Louisiana's success is largely due to the state's ability to attract repeat business with its attractive incentive programs, deep crew base and abundance of studio facilities." [Id.] "Louisiana offers motion picture productions a 30-percent transferable credit to put towards total in-state expenditures, with no cap and a minimal spending requirement of $300,000. At the same time, the state promotes the use of domestic labor through an additional 5-percent labor-tax credit on the payroll of Louisiana residents employed by a production." [Id.] These incentives permit producers and studios to recoup a significant portion of their production budgets.

New Mexico exemplifies what can happen when a state tampers with its incentive program. New Mexico was listed as the second most desirable place to film in 2006, but its ranking fell to number nine after the state changed the program to limit individual film rebates and to create an overall rolling cap of $50,000,000 a year. In the fiscal year ending July 2011, New Mexico issued over $102 million rebates. By the close of the 2012 fiscal year, the amount declined to $19.2 million. [Boyd, *Film Rebates Plunged*.]

Illinois incentivizes film production with "a 30-percent tax credit on all qualified local expenditures, including postproduction. An additional 15 percent is available on salaries for individuals living in an economically disadvantaged area." [*Id.*] Florida, which rounds out the top three destinations, with a 20-percent transferable tax credits that increases to 30 percent for Florida qualified production expenditures.

Not all states are inclined to hitch their economic resources to Hollywood bandwagons. While Illinois and Florida augmented their incentives, other states, like Arizona and Colorado, cut funding for their film commissions. Ohio and Wisconsin closed their film commission offices after developing budget woes. [*Id.*] None of these states were ranked in P3 Magazine's top 10.

C. FILM TYPES

Unlike books, where nonfiction works far outnumber fiction, feature films are predominantly fictional. Even when based on a true story, components will be fictionalized. For example, composite characters were created for *Amadeus*, a film about the life of classical composer and musician Mozart.

Films may be dramatic, comical, or musical. *Amadeus* featured all the above, although it was not a full-scale musical like the adaptations of Broadway musicals *The Sound of Music* and *Chicago*, which respectively took home Oscars® for Best Picture in 1965 and 2002.

Movies may also elicit terror in the viewing audience. They can make people laugh, or cry. Documentaries may be short or feature film length.

Shorts can range in screen time from 5 to 30 minutes. They are more often shown in groups at film festivals or in a special theatrical exhibition. Screenwriter Greg Brooker made the short *Nosferatu L.A.-02* as a story that imagines Dracula coming to live in Los Angeles and experiencing loneliness because people react negatively to his appearance. Brooker envisioned having *Nosferatu L.A.* become his "calling card to get directing work." [Author Interview with Brooker.]

Most feature films run approximately 100 minutes. Some may be limited to 80 minutes and others, like *Gone With the Wind*, screen nearly four hours. That Civil War drama was originally shown with an intermission. Next follows brief discussions

on action flicks, animated treasures, and documentaries.

1. ACTION FLICKS

Action films can be based on comic book heroes,
such as *Batman, Spiderman*, or *Superman*, or on
best-selling fantasy books like the *Harry Potter* series. They may also derive from a writer's imagination, such as *Rambo* or *Rocky*. Action films are likely
to be seen over and over again by under 25-year-old
males, who comprise the biggest segment of the
film-purchasing audience.

The other three box office segments are over 25-
year-old males, over 25-year-old females, and under
25-year-old females. *Titanic,* a romantic drama
based on a renowned tragedy, was the first film to
make nearly $2 billion dollars in revenue at the
global box office. It became a major hit because under 25-year-old females repeatedly purchased tickets to re-experience the film's fictionalized love story. Over 35 females are a subset of the feminine audience that made hits of *Julia and Julie* in 2009,
and of the *Sex and the City* movies.

Action films are highly sought after by studios as
they are most likely to generate gold at domestic
and global box offices and through subsidiary sales.
However, they are often expensive and sometimes
dangerous to make. Several action films have
brought death to the set. Special effects caused a
helicopter to crash on the set of *Twilight Zone: The*

Movie, killing actor Vic Morrow and two children. The director John Landis was charged with involuntary manslaughter, although he was eventually acquitted. On the set of *The Crow*, a real bullet was loaded into a gun and used to shoot actor Brandon Lee. His father, Hong Kong action star Bruce Lee, also met an untimely death. Studios and producers purchase insurance, which will be discussed in more detail in Chapter 9, to ensure against such risks.

Studios also like action films because they travel well to foreign countries and translate easily into different languages. Action films need less dialogue to make them understandable to audiences and are less culturally nuanced. In contrast, comedies generate most of their revenue in the country of origin where the audience more easily understands the jokes.

2. ANIMATED TREASURES

Many animated films become blockbusters. *Beauty and the Beast*, *Shrek*, and *Finding Nemo* respectively spawned over $100 million, $200 million, and $300 million in box office ticket sales. Disney was long the king of animated films with classics such as *Snow White* and *The Lion King*. Other studios, such as Pixar and Dreamworks, have successfully released animated films and challenged Disney's crown.

Animated treasures are less expensive to make, and yet they resonate with kids who beg their parents to take them to the theater and later purchase the DVD or Blu-ray version of the film, along with all kinds of character merchandise. While Broadway has long been a source of inspiration for films, it is only recently that films, such as *Beauty and the Beast* and *The Lion King*, have been turned into theatrical hits.

3. DOCUMENTARIES

Documentaries supply an increasingly popular film type. They are the film equivalent of nonfiction books. As their production costs decline and their box office value increases, they are more likely to be financed and distributed as feature films. Further, television networks like PBS and HBO have also financed original documentaries for their audiences.

Filmmakers Mat Boggs and Jason Miller obtained sponsors to finance a country-wide tour to shoot *Project Everlasting*, their film featuring interviews with couples married 40 years or longer. They then distributed *Project Everlasting* DVDs through their website www.projecteverlasting.com.

Morgan Spurlock's *Super Size Me*, which chronicles the effects of a 30-day McDonald's diet on the director's health, cost $65,000 to create and yet became a top-10 film while screening on 230 screens, barely 6% of the 3855 screens reserved for 2004 blockbuster *Harry Potter and the Prisoner of Azkaban*. *Super Size Me* made over $10 million.

Perhaps the best indication of a film's impact is the response. When *Super Size Me* opened in Australia to the best documentary debut in that country's history, McDonald's Australia countered with an advertising campaign to discredit Spurlock's action of eating three meals a day at McDonald's for 30 days as "stupid." [Dabkowski, *Splitting Chips*.]

Filmmaker Michael Moore's 2002 documentary *Bowling for Columbine* made over $21.3 million at the box office while playing at approximately 230 theaters. *Bowling for Columbine* set a box office record for documentaries until Moore released *Fahrenheit 9/11* on June 25, 2004. The latter film cost $6 million to make and $10 million to distribute, yet generated $21.8 million in domestic ticket revenue during its first weekend and $38.9 million throughout its first week at the box office. *Fahrenheit 9/11* won the Palme d'Or at the 2004 Cannes Film Festival two weeks before it opened at 868 theaters in the United States, a record number of engagements for a documentary. It eventually grossed over $119 million in domestic box office revenue and took in approximately $250,000,000 in total global box office. The controversial nature of *Farhenheit 9/11* will be discussed in Chapter 5, which focuses on censorship.

The successes of Spurlock and Moore have led to the production and distribution of more feature-length documentaries, such as *March of the Penguins* and *An Inconvenient Truth*. For newcomers to the film industry, documentaries can be a great way to begin, but they are not without their headaches.

Diane Bloom, who possesses a Ph.D. in psychology, made her first documentary without ever talking to a lawyer. *An Unlikely Friendship* uncovers an amiable relationship that developed between a black female civil rights activist and the leader of the Durham, North Carolina, Ku Klux Klan. Bloom did not obtain release agreements from her subjects, the person she retained to host the documentary, or those who provided equipment. Once the film became a hit, several individuals came forward and claimed an ownership interest in the film. She said afterwards, "I would [now] hire a lawyer at the beginning. I could have saved myself a lot of grief." [Author Interview with Bloom.]

Whatever the type, what resonates most with audiences are good films. High quality flicks generate word of mouth and create legs to generate sound box office potential.

The next chapter will consider business and legal issues peculiar to the television industry.

CHAPTER 2

THE TELEVISION INDUSTRY

The first television set was invented in the 1920s. It consisted of a small screen (anywhere from three to twelve inches wide diagonally) inside a big box displaying black and white imagery when plugged in and turned on. [Burr, *Television and Societal Effects*.] Programming was limited at a time when radio was the most popular form of entertainment. It wasn't until the 1950s that television came into its own, helped along by the popularity of *I Love Lucy* and other beloved shows of the decade.

Currently, a television, ranging from ordinary boxes to high definition plasma sets, can be found in approximately 90% of American homes. According to Nielsen Media Research, there are 2.55 people and 2.73 TV sets in the typical American home, with more than half of these dwellings possessing three or more TVs. [Bauder, *TVs Outnumber People in Most U.S. Homes*.] Nielsen says that a television set is turned on eight hours, 14 minutes in the average home, whereas the average person watches four hours, 35 minutes a day. [*Id.*] It also reported on its website that the average American spends 20% of their day watching television.

This chapter explores the legal issues involved in the television industry. The chapter begins by discussing the process of creating a television show from an idea. It then addresses television cultural issues related to society and diversity, and the rise of cable and satellite television as an alternative to network programming.

A. THE TELEVISION PROCESS

Similar to the film process, television shows begin with someone pitching an idea to a person with the power to "green-light" the show. The pitch season has traditionally been in the fall, when new shows would begin. This has changed as networks now seek new material for their schedules throughout the entire year.

1. THE PITCH

Pitches for TV shows can be simply stated. Imagine finding an ordinary construction worker to masquerade as a millionaire and surrounding him with beautiful women who do not know the secret. The camera and the audience will then observe whether the women fall in love with him for his imagined millions or his true self. Effectively told and well cast with common individuals, this simple idea became *Joe Millionaire*, which drew 40 million viewers for its final episode on February 17, 2003.

High ratings and low production costs made shows like *Joe Millionaire* popular with studio executives. However, William Goldman's gripe about the film process, "Nobody Knows Anything," also applies to television. When the Fox network followed up with *The Next Joe Millionaire,* set in Europe, it slumped in the ratings game. That didn't stop ABC, however, from setting its *Bachelor* series in Rome during the fall 2006 season. ABC featured an Italian prince, who had been raised in the United States and barely spoke his native language, in the title role.

Pitches can also be tailor-made to fulfill fantasies. The late Brandon Tartikoff had such green-light power as an executive at NBC. In his book, *The Last Great Ride,* he described his favorite pitch. Legendary actor Marlon Brando walked into his office and outlined the show he wanted to do based on his life in Tahiti. Brando smiled and said, "Well, it's my home movies of Tahiti, of myself in the water, over a number of years, with all these beautiful native women."

Brando continued, "I've got thousands of minutes of this stuff. And I think I can get the Tahitian government to come in with me on the deal so the price won't be prohibitive. I think it would be a success." He urged Tartikoff, "You put this thing on in February and it's fifteen below with the windchill factor, how can the guy in Pittsburgh *not* watch naked Tahitian women in the water and Marlon Brando when it comes on at ten p.m.?"[Tartikoff, *Last Great Ride*, at 22]

Brando was unable to obtain the proper permissions from the Tahitian government and his idea never made it on the air, but it did illustrate a quality that Tartikoff valued in pitching ideas—enthusiasm. [*Id.* at 25.] Tartikoff believed there had to be passion at the beginning to sustain five years "when the show is a hundred episodes old and staggering." The other qualities that Tartikoff looked for were a connection to real life, storytelling ability, and the actor's roles. [*Id.* at 24-25.]

2. THE SEASON

While the traditional television season commences after Labor Day, networks will often replace shows mid-season in January and offer special summer shows. The Fox network implemented year-round scheduling beginning in June 2004 to keep its "offerings fresh and compelling" and its viewers engaged "continually throughout the year." [The Fulton Critic Staff, *Fox Releases Summer 2004 Schedule*.] The other broadcast, cable, and digital networks have followed suit with new material appearing throughout the year.

3. THE SCHEDULE

At any given time, four major television networks —ABC, CBS, FOX, and NBC—may have a program schedule comprised of dramas, game shows, news, reality TV shows, situation comedies, sports, and talk shows. Some cable channels focus all their programming on one type of show, such as sports on ESPN, ESPN2, and ESPN News. Cable networks may seek to appeal to a particular gender, such as

Spike TV for men or Lifetime, whose slogan is "television for women," or a particular race, such as BET, Black Entertainment Television, or Univision, a popular Spanish network.

The popularity of show genres varies through the years. Westerns were once ubiquitous on network schedules. In the late 1950s, there were 30 different westerns on three network channels. [Nusbaum, *The Lone Gunman*.] *Gunsmoke*, which premiered in 1955 and ran until 1975, became the most popular of the genre and still holds the record as the longest-running television show with 633 episodes produced. *Gunsmoke* was set in a raw frontier town in Kansas and featured the 6-foot, 7-inch James Arness as Matt Dillon, the lawman who, as Emily Nusbaum described, pulled "his pistol one second slower than his opponent, but with better aim." [*Id.*]

The western later declined in popularity and resurfaced after a long absence on television when HBO launched *Deadwood* in March 2004. [Martel, *Resurrecting the Western*.] In 2012, A&E premiered *Longmire* as a modern-day western set in Wyoming and starring Robert Taylor as a grieving widowed lawman whose deputy runs against him for sheriff.

a. Scripted TV

Scripted shows are fictional creations that may be humorous or dramatic, or both. For scripted shows, executives may first order a pilot, and later purchase three, six, or 13 episodes as a mid-season replacement or the current full-season order of 22 episodes. An order for a cable show may encompass 12 or 13 episodes, such as for the HBO series *Big Love* or the AMC series *Mad Men*. The executives seek shows with legs; that is, those that could potentially last five seasons and generate approximately 100 episodes. Once this magic number has been reached, the show can be syndicated. Syndication permits the network and production company to sell all the show's episodes in bulk, and generate tremendous revenue.

For example, the Desilu Company realized $60 million between 1955 and 1965 from licensing its television film library, which included *I Love Lucy* and *The Lucy-Desi Show*. [Desilu Productions, Inc. v. C.I.R., 1965 WL 1076 (U.S. Tax Ct. 1965)] *I Love Lucy* featured a Cuban bandleader and his wacky redheaded wife who was dying to get into show business. Because CBS did not believe that *I Love Lucy* had much chance of success, it gave the Desilu Company the copyrights. Desi Arnaz, an excellent negotiator with fine-tuned business acumen, insisted on taping the show instead of broadcasting live, as was customary in the 1950s. He thereby created an extensive library of 179 episodes. Due to syndication, *I Love Lucy* has never been off the air and continues to generate revenue.

Fictional shows like comedies, dramas, and children's television are not immune from lawsuits brought by ordinary people. Michael Constanza sued comedian Jerry Seinfeld, claiming that the fictional character of George Constanza was based on him. Michael Constanza alleged in *Constanza v. Seinfeld*, 181 Misc.2d 562, 693 N.Y.S.2d 897 (N.Y.Sup. 1999), that Seinfeld placed him in "a negative, humiliating light" by attributing a "self-centered nature and unreliability" to the character of George Constanza, who is short, fat, and bald like Michael. Observing that New York courts had rejected such claims for decades, the court dismissed the case as frivolous and awarded sanctions of $2,500 each against the plaintiff and his attorney. [*Id.* at 567.] On appeal, the Appellate Division agreed that plaintiff's lawsuit warranted dismissal, but vacated the awarding of sanctions against the plaintiff and his attorney. [Costanza v. Seinfeld, 279 A.D.2d 255, 719 N.Y.S.2d 29 (N.Y.A.D. 1 Dept. 2001)].

b. Reality Television

Reality television shows, like *American Idol* and *Dancing with the Stars*, are the most recent phenomena to capture and hold the interest of the viewing public. Reality TV resembles nonfiction books and documentaries, all of which are based or purport to be based on truth. Americans tune in to watch shows like *Survivor*, *The Bachelor*, and *The Apprentice* to observe ordinary participants compete for money, love, or employment. One reality TV show called *For Love or Money*, which aired during the summers of 2003 and 2004, required contestants to choose between their love interest and checks worth up to $2 million.

The Apprentice, starring real estate developer Donald Trump, became the first reality show to be featured within a network's signature nightly lineup. *The Apprentice* premiered on a Thursday in January 2004, crouched between *Friends* and *ER* on NBC. It immediately received good reviews and excellent ratings. Its 16 contestants vied to receive a $250,000 job running one of Trump's companies. On Thursday, 15 April 2004, *The Apprentice* became the number one show of that week when 28 million viewers tuned in to see who Donald Trump would hire. Not without detractors, Trump's competitors accused him of using the show to advertise his conglomerate.

Audience participation versions of reality TV shows ask the public to call in to vote on who should be eliminated from a musical competition show (*American Idol*, *Dancing with the Stars*) or selected to become the husband of a particular female who came with a $1 million dowry (*Cupid*). Other programs, such as *Extreme Makeover* and *Queer Eye for the Straight Guy*, alter the appearance or living quarters, and sometimes both, of volunteers. The shows also present family and friends' reactions to the person's vast changes.

Customarily, networks order a pilot episode to test the concept. With reality TV, they must order the complete series because the execution of the full work is critical. Reality TV shows are shot in their entirety before they are edited and massaged into a story line. Thus, network executives who were comfortable ordering a pilot episode of a new comedy or game show now find themselves ordering the entire four to fifteen episodes of a reality TV show from a pitched idea.

While syndicated reality TV shows are rare, network executives are attracted to these shows for the initial profits generated from not having to pay professional actors or staff wages and benefits negotiated by unions. Indeed, some reality TV stars have been asked to forgo joining a union until after they have appeared on the show. Seeking to increase their audience appeal, networks will sometimes share their reality TV shows with sister networks related through corporate structures.

Other reality TV stars have received some form of payment, either as appearance fees to compensate for their loss of time at their jobs, or more likely because they won the prize money. Trista Rehn received only $10,000 for appearing on both the inaugural *Bachelor* and *Bachelorette*, but then she and her chosen bachelor Ryan Sutter were paid $1 million to wed on television. Donald Trump collected $100,000 per episode for his Spring 2004 appearance on *The Apprentice*. Without revealing details, he indicated that he would earn "a lot more" in subsequent seasons. [Naughton and Peyser, *The World*

According to Trump.] Trump's spinoff *The Appren-tice: Martha Stewart* flopped in the ratings, while his *Celebrity Apprentice* has been a continuing success.

Contestants who win prize money or receive payments are required to pay taxes on their earnings. Richard Hatch, the winner of the first *Survivor* contest, failed to pay taxes on his winnings. He claimed he thought *Survivor*'s producers would pay the taxes or alternatively that he just forgot to mention his television earnings to his accountants. He was convicted of tax evasion and condemned to serve 51 months in prison. In sentencing Hatch, Judge Torres said he issued a harsher punishment because it became clear to him "that Hatch lied." [Tucker, *"Survivor" Champ Gets 51 Months in Prison*]

The doctors, lawyers, accountants, teachers, and airline pilots who win placement on reality TV shows must take several weeks off from their day jobs to film or appear live on a reality TV show. Because *Survivor* requires 39 days of filming, casting director Lynne Spillman says that one-third of its participants quit their jobs to participate. Spillman told Newsweek, "The people who apply are at a crossroads." [Newsweek Mag., *The lure of shows like Apprentice.*]

Newsweek Magazine also reported that investment banker Kwame Jackson quit Goldman Sachs to appear on *The Apprentice*, attorney Alex Michel resigned from the Boston Consulting Group to star as the initial *Bachelor*, and educator Randi Coy was forced to leave her teaching job after taking too much time off to star *in My Big Fat Obnoxious Fiancé*. Michel, who subsequently became a spokesman for the Internet dating service www.match.com, said, "Anyone who'd take a two-month leave is putting their career progress at risk." [*Id.*]

Further, reality shows often mandate that participants sign agreements releasing producers from liabilities. The reality show *Survivor* required participants to sign a "Confidentiality and Life Story Rights Agreement" in which they (1) relinquished their right to disclose any trade secrets obtained or learned as a result of participating in the series; (2) were forbidden from disclosing any information about the series prior to broadcast; and (3) agreed that the producer could seek injunctive relief, return of the prize, and recovery of attorneys' fees if the agreement was breached. In *SEG, Inc. v. Stillman*, 2003 WL 21197133 (Cal.App. 2 Dist. 2003), a contestant unsuccessfully challenged this agreement.

c. Game and Quiz Shows

Game and quiz shows tests participants' knowledge in particular subjects. The Game Show Network (GSN) shows both classic shows such as *Password* and reboots with new hosts such as *Family Feud* with Steve Harvey and *The Newlywed Game* with Sherri Sheppard. These shows regularly seek contestants through their websites.

In 2010, GSN premiered the dating game show *Baggage* with Jerry Springer hosting contestants seeking love by revealing three levels of baggage. After the selector chooses one contestant, the table turns and the selector reveals baggage that the contestant can choose to accept or discard with the jocular phrase "You have too much baggage for me." Examples of rejected female baggage include "I was locked up in a mental institution" and "I used to be a man and still am."

Some quiz shows limit the number of appearances contestants can make on other shows. In *Winston v. NBC*, 231 Cal.App.3d 540, 282 Cal.Rptr. 498 (Cal.App. 2 Dist. 1991), the California Court of Appeals upheld NBC's right to disqualify a contestant who was not forthcoming about the number of other game shows that he appeared on and to force a forfeiture of the cash he won as a contestant on *Sale of the Century*.

Quiz show contracts specify that the TV series has the right to determine the answers to questions. In *Gelbman v. Valleycrest Productions, Ltd.*, 189 Misc.2d 403, 732 N.Y.S.2d 528 (N.Y. Sup. 2001), Robert Gelbman sued ABC, claiming that a question on *Who Wants to be a Millionaire* was ambiguous, and thus he was entitled to additional funds because the show provided two possible answer choices that were both correct. The court upheld the signed release agreement, which stated that decisions by the producers and ABC were final.

In *Rosner v. Valleycrest Productions*, Ltd., 2004 WL 1166175 (Cal.App. 2 Dist.2004), Richard Rosner sued after he missed the $16,000 question as a contestant on *Who Wants to Be a Millionaire*. He was asked: "What capital city is located at the highest altitude above sea level?" Of the four choices, Rosner picked the city with the lowest altitude. The capital city located at the highest altitude, La Paz, Bolivia, was not a choice. Rosner alleged that the $16,000 question without La Paz as a possible answer constituted human error pursuant to paragraph 7 of official rules, which require defendants to take action to preserve integrity of show, and that he should have been invited back to compete again.

The trial court disagreed, finding that he has no actionable claim against producers of the show. His signed contract gave *Millionaire* producers the sole and exclusive right to interpret questions and answers, plus the sole and exclusive right to determine who is invited back to the show in the event of error. Rosner had also signed a valid release of liability, releasing the show producers from all claims arising from his appearance on show. According to the court, the language was clear, unambiguous and not unconscionable.

What happens when a contestant suffers an injury as a result of participating in a show? This question arose in *Wright v. Sony Pictures Entertainment*, 394 F.Supp.2d 27 (Dis. D.C. 2005) after a participant alleged that he was injured during a taping of *Wheel of Fortune* at Constitution Hall in Washington, D.C. on Oct. 14, 2000. After Wright won, he alleged that show host Pat Sajak approached Wright, jumped on Wright, and "kind of like bounced." Shortly afterwards, Wright claimed he experienced lower back pain, which he attributed to the actions of Sajak.

Wright had signed "Contestant Release Form," but argued that public policy forbids waivers of personal injury claims. The contract stated: "I agree that I will not bring... any legal action or claim against the released parties, ... based upon or arising out of my participation on... the program, on any legal theory (including, but not limited to personal injury...)". The court held that the Contest Release Form barred Wright's claim based on alleged negligent conduct, but allowed his claim based on reckless or intentional conduct. The district court cited the Restatement (Second) of Contracts, which provides that waivers which release party from tort liability or harm caused intentionally or recklessly are unenforceable as matter of public policy. Thus Wright was permitted to pursue his claims based on reckless and intentional conduct.

d. Talk Shows

Talk shows also have participants sign release agreements. Many of them pay for transportation and housing costs for their guests, and some pay appearance fees. In *Campoverde v. Sony Pictures Entertainment*, 2002 WL 31163804 (S.D.N.Y. 2002), attorney Susan Chana Lask and her client Juan Campoverde sued the producers of *The Ricki Lake Show* after their scheduled visit did not conform to the negotiated terms. Further, the producers insisted that they sign a union agreement prior to their appearance. When they refused, they were held against their will. The court denied the defendant's motion to dismiss Lask and Campoverde's claims for breach of contract, false imprisonment, and assault and battery.

A participant sued *The Jerry Springer* show after his archenemy bursts from behind the scene and beat him about the head and shoulders. He claimed the show promised his archenemy would not be invited to the studio during the taping. Before appearing on the show, Pemerton signed a release agreement that said disputes would be resolved by arbitration. In *Pemerton v. Springer*, 1995 WL 579465 (Dis. Ill. 1995), the court granted the TV show's motion to compel arbitration because Pemerton's claims arose out of the production of the show and his appearance on it.

e. Network News

News is competitive in local arenas, while broadcast news faces increasing competition from the Internet for breaking news. The news is one of the few shows produced by affiliate stations, which ordinarily obtain a significant percentage of their programming from their respective national conglomerates. In their search for ratings, both local and broadcast news shows must also honor people's privacy and are required to follow the legal rules governing employment.

In *Miller v. NBC*, 187 Cal.App.3d 1463, 232 Cal.Rptr. 668 (Cal.App. 2 Dist. 1986), Brownie Miller successfully sued NBC after its television camera crew followed Los Angeles Fire Department paramedics into her home and filmed the futile attempt to rescue her husband Dave. NBC did not obtain a release agreement. Brownie Miller saw the footage of her husband weeks after his death while flipping channels. The court held that she had a cause of action for trespass, invasion of privacy, and intentional infliction of emotional distress.

In addition to trying to attract audiences with sensational programming, network news shows have tried to capture audiences by choosing attractive anchors. Nevertheless, they must be careful not to commit employment discrimination based on age.

David Minshall successfully sued the McGraw-Hill Broadcasting Company, which does business as

KMGH in Denver, Colorado, for age discrimination after it decided not to renew his contract when he was over the age of 50. When news director Melissa Klinzing decided to reach a younger demographic, she moved individuals over 40 years of age to the ten o'clock nightly news and increasingly gave other individuals over 40 less favorable job assignments. Eventually KMGH instructed Klinzing not to renew the contract of anyone over the age of 40. The court found in *Minshall v. McGraw Hill Broadcasting Co.*, 323 F.3d 1273 (10th Cir. 2003), that Klinzing and KMGH had engaged in age discrimination. Klinzing had urged Minshall to adopt "a more youthful presentation." She also said one person was "too fucking old" for the news format, and said "old people should die" in reference to her own father.

In 2001, a group of 50 television writers sued 51 studios, network television companies, and talent agencies for age discrimination, claiming that they had been grey-listed. [Langton, *'Greylisted" Hollywood Writers to Sue.*] The class action lawsuit alleged a "systematic and pervasive pattern of age discrimination" against writers over 40 and sought damages of $200 million. [*Id.*]

After the initial class action was dismissed, approximately 150 television writers filed 23 separate class action lawsuits in Los Angeles Superior Court in 2002. The lawsuits claimed that in the 1997-98 season, two-thirds of prime-time series did not employ a single writer over the age of 50. The writers cited remarks from Marta Kauffmann, the co-creator of NBC's *Friends*, who said, "Once you hit 40, you can't do it anymore." Gary David Goldberg, the producer of ABC's *Spin City*, was quoted as saying his program had "no writers on the set over the age of 29—by design." [www.writerscase.com.]

In January 2005, the 23 class actions were reinstated in Los Angeles Country Superior Court. The parties settled the cases in January 2010 when 17 major networks and production studios and seven talent agencies agreed to pay $70 million to thousands of writers to resolve 19 claims.[Verrier, Hollywood Writers.]

In a different case, a 61-year-old sales manager for a television station claimed age discrimination after she was discharged following a merger of two stations. The District Court granted summary judgment for the combined company in the case of *Woodman v. WWOR-TV.* The sales manager offered no evidence that the defendants were aware of her age at the time she was discharged. Discrimination cases require knowledge of protected status, which the District Court said "can be assumed based on personal contact between the parties or review of the employee's personnel record." [*Id.* at 386.] Here, each Fox executive who participated in the decision to terminate Woodman's employment affirmed that he or she had no knowledge of her age. The Court of Appeals affirmed the District Court's opinion in

Woodman v. WWOR-TV, Inc., 411 F.3d 69 (2nd Cir. 2005).

When TV writers use of sexually coarse and vulgar language, have they committed sexual harassment within the meaning of the Fair Employment and Housing Act (FEHA)? In *Lyle v. Warner Bros. Television Productions,* 38 Cal.4th 264 (2006), a writers' assistant for the television show *Friends* sued three male comedy writers and others, alleging sexual harassment and a hostile work environment. Warner Brothers said Lyle was fired because of problems with her typing and transcription. The California Supreme court held that the TV writers' use of sexually coarse and vulgar language and conduct in Plaintiff's presence was not sexual harassment under FEHA.

To avoid succumbing to age discrimination or "greylisting," talented individuals have been known to lie about their age or remove older credits from their resume in order not to date themselves by their work. Discrimination issues merit further consideration, particularly since it is not as easy to fabricate race or ethnicity. Diversity issues will be addressed in more detail in the section on "television and society."

B. TELEVISION AND SOCIETY

Given the pervasive nature of television, it is not surprising that it has had and continues to have a profound impact on society. In the United States, television reaches a broad array of ethnic groups and homes.

Television programming can be educational, teaching its young viewers how to read and adults how to cook. Because several shows focus on the law, some Americans learn about their legal rights from watching television. Nevertheless, some people have claimed that television has had a negative impact on their lives, making them dumb, delinquent, fat, lethargic, and sometimes pathological. Children may be particularly susceptible to television's subtle impacts.

1. IMPACT ON CHILDREN

The Karl Miller study in American Family Physician tested the impact of television viewing on children's behavior. The study divided school children participants into three groups: "group 1 watched television for two hours or less per day; group 2, for two to four hours per day; and group 3, for more than four hours per day." [Miller, *Children's Behavior Correlates with Television Viewing.*] The Miller study determined that "[o]verall viewing time had a negative relationship with social and school achievement scores." The Miller study further found that increased viewing time correlated with "social problems, thought problems, attention problems, delinquent behavior, aggressive behavior, and externalization." The Miller study recommended that "parents limit their children's television viewing time to two hours or less per day." [*Id.*]

Despite the Miller study's recommendations and urgings from the American Academy of Pediatrics, few Americans heed warnings to limit television watching. Nineteen percent of babies under 2 have a television in their room, and eight in 10 of these young children watch two hours of television a day. [Neergaard, *TV Looms Large in Tots' Lives*.] A different study found that preschoolers who watch lots of television are more likely to become bullies later on, with the risk of antisocial behavior increasing with each hour watched. [Sommerfeld, *Study Links TV to Bullying*.]

The parents of Ronny Zamora sued NBC, CBS, and ABC after their son killed their 83-year-old neighbor Elinor Haggart. The parents charged that Ronny became involuntarily addicted to and subliminally intoxicated by the excessive violence on television from the age of five until 15 when he shot Haggart. The parents contended that Ronny was stimulated and incited to duplicate the atrocities he saw on television.

The District Court, however, dismissed *Zamora v. CBS*, 480 F.Supp. 199 (D.C.Fla. 1979), because the parents failed to state a cognizable claim. The court expressed concern that the complaint did not cite a particular program or distinguish among the networks in Ronny's viewing pattern. The court was reluctant to expand Florida tort law to create a duty on the part of the networks to anticipate a minor's voracious, yet voluntary, intake of violence, his parents' acquiescence, and that the minor would respond with a criminal act.

This court sent a message that urges parents to take responsibility to limit the television viewing of their children, particularly if it is having a negative impact on their development.

Children are also exposed to diversity issues through watching television. A 1998 study conducted on behalf of Children Now, a nonprofit children's advocacy group, revealed that children "more often associate positive qualities such as financial and academic success, leadership, and intelligence with White characters, and negative qualities such as law breaking, financial hardship, laziness, and goofy behavior with minority characters." [Burr, *Television and Societal Effects*, at 180.] Fifty-eight percent of the children said they see Caucasians on television as having a lot of money, but only eight percent perceived minority characters as having a lot of money. Conversely, 47% reported seeing minority characters break the law but only six percent reported seeing Caucasians break the law. The children also observed how often they saw their own race depicted: 71% of Caucasian children saw their race portrayed very often compared with only 42% of African-Americans and 22% of Hispanic-Americans. [*Id.*]

Hae-Kyong Bang and Bonnie B. Reece analyzed the content of 813 commercials in children's television programs and found that minorities were "more likely than Caucasians to have minor roles and to be portrayed in certain product categories, settings, and relationships." [Burr and Henslee, at 565.] Bang and Reece found that Blacks and Asian Americans were over-represented and Hispanics were somewhat underrepresented in these commercials, but that they were less likely to appear in major roles, and less likely to appear as a group compared to Caucasians. Bang and Reece postulated that these portrayals could potentially harm children's self-perception and recommended that conscious efforts "be made to portray all ethnic groups fairly and in a non-stereotypical manner so that minority groups are seen as valued consumers well integrated into the society." [*Id.* at 571-572.]

2. TELEVISION DIVERSITY

Television also impacts how adults in a diverse society perceive ethnic groups other than their own. It was several years after the first TV set was invented in the 1920s before African-Americans and other ethnic groups began to make appearances on television. In 1939, Clarence Muse became the first African-American to appear on television when he was featured on Los Angeles station W6XAO. Bob Howard was the first African-American to have his own network program, which ran between 1948 and 1949. [Burr, *Television and Societal Effects*, at 160-161.] From the 1950s through the 1990s, more Americans of diverse backgrounds made appearances in a variety of network shows, from musical variety to dramas and comedies. With the opening up of television to more ethnic groups came criticism that the programming was stereotypical, and thus reinforced negative group images.

Several efforts were made to diversify television programming and images by encouraging the hiring of more producers, actors, and crews from a variety of racial and ethnic backgrounds. In the 1970s and 1980s, the Federal Communications Commission (FCC) adopted programs to encourage minority ownership of television stations and increase the number of minorities who appear in front of and behind the camera.

In *Metro Broadcasting v. FCC*, 497 U.S. 547, 110 S.Ct. 2997 (1990), a few Caucasians challenged these programs as violating the equal protection component of the Fifth Amendment. The Supreme Court upheld the programs, finding that the interest in enhancing broadcast diversity is "an important governmental objective and is therefore a sufficient basis for the Commission's minority ownership policies." The Court noted that these minority ownership policies were "appropriately limited in extent and duration, and subject to reassessment and reevaluation by the Congress prior to any extension or reenactment."

The Supreme Court overruled this decision five years later in *Adarand Constructors v. Pena*, 515

U.S. 200, 115 S.Ct. 2097 (1995), holding that strict scrutiny governs whether race-based classifications violate the equal protection component of the Fifth Amendment's Due Process Clause. In the subsequent case of *Adarand Contractors v. Mineta*, 534 U.S. 103, 122 S.Ct. 511 (2001), the Supreme Court confirmed that the strict scrutiny standard "should be addressed in the first instance by the lower courts."

For the fall 1999 season, the major networks announced that their lineups would consist of twenty-six new shows, not one of which featured a lead character who was African American, Asian American, Native American, or Latino. [Williams, *Don't Try to Adjust Your Television*.] After a threatened boycott and numerous meetings between Hollywood executives and the NAACP, the networks made adjustments to their schedules. They added more minority characters to their planned shows and augmented the number of shows that featured minority story lines. [*Id.*]

In March 2004, ABC and Touchstone TV announced a pact with the Directors Guild of America to place women and minority directors behind the camera on at least 20 television episodes during the 2004-2005 season. [Schneider, *Diversity Directive*.] The plan assigned a diverse group of at least 10 directors to 10 half-hour comedy episodes and 10 hour-long drama segments of new and returning series.

By 2006, most scripted shows, such as *CSI*, *Desperate Housewives*, *Grey's Anatomy*, and *Without a Trace*, featured minority characters in significant roles. Indeed, the top rated show during the week of 26 September 2006, *Grey's Anatomy*, was created by African American Shonda Rhimes. About her multiracial cast, Rhimes said, "We had everyone of every color read for every single part, and it was about casting the best actor in the room." [Ogunnaike, *'Grey's Anatomy' Creator Finds Success in Surgery*.]

Native Americans have faced issues that differ from other groups on television. Because of the early popularity of westerns, they were regularly featured on television as well as in films. Chris Eyre, the first Native American director to produce a nationally released film, bemoans "the lack of representation of Indian people in the mainstream media." He thinks that a "politically correct romanticism of what Indians should be" gets depicted, but not "the average Joes of Indian country who are not romantic." [Author Interview with Eyre.] Eyre once told The New York Times that "the only thing that has been more detrimental to Indians than religion has been John Ford movies" because he believes John Ford focused on the period of Indian wars and never investigated the culture that grew out of that period. Eyre says that he is less interested in portraying positive images, than he is in "depicting accurate images." [*Id.*]

3. TELEVISION ADDICTION

A study by Robert D. McIlwraith determined people could become addicted to television. The indicators of dependence on television were (1) television consumed large amounts of their time; (2) they watched TV longer or more often than they intended; (3) they made repeated unsuccessful efforts to cut down their TV watching; (4) they withdrew from or gave up important social, family, or occupational activities in order to watch television; and (5) they reported "withdrawal" like symptoms of subjective discomfort when deprived of TV. [McIlwraith, *I'm Addicted to Television.*] The McIlwraith study postulated that television addiction had "similarities to pathological gambling."

Robert Kubey and Mihaly Csikszentmihalyi revealed in the journal Scientific American that people tend to turn on the television out of boredom, and yet their study using electroencephalograph (or EEG) found that people watching television "showed less mental stimulation, as measured by alpha brain-wave production, during viewing than during reading." [Kubey and Csikszentmihalyi, *Television Addiction Is No Mere Metaphor*] Further, they discovered that the sense of relaxation "ends when the set is turned off, but the feelings of passivity and lowered alertness continued." [*Id.*]

All of these studies should alert audience members to pay attention to television's subtle and overt effects.

C. CABLE AND SATELLITE TELEVISION

The increasing availability of television to more households via cable and satellites will only augment the opportunities for individuals to watch television. An appliance owner who had difficulty selling television sets in rural areas because of poor reception invented cable television, originally christened Community Antenna Television or CATV. To solve the problem of limited signals, John Watson placed an antenna atop a large utility pole and installed it on top of a nearby Pennsylvania mountain. As television signals were received and transported to his store, Watson sold more sets. [http://www.telecom.ksu.edu/cable/history.html.]

By 1992, cable served 60% of American households. [Turner v. FCC, 520 U.S. 180, 117 S.Ct. 1174 (1997).] Cable television has since grown into a successful fee-paid business with 60 million subscribers in the United States and millions more around the globe.

Digital and satellite transmission became more popular in the 1990s as it offered varied channels and promised clear picture by up-linking signals to satellites orbiting in space and beaming those signals to dishes. [Satellite Broadcasting and Communications Ass'n v. F.C.C., 275 F.3d 337 (4th Cir. 2001).]

By 2001, only 20% of American households relied exclusively on the major broadcast networks for their television programming. Cable and satellite companies served around 80% of the television households, with cable accounting for 67% and satellite carriers responsible for 13%. While broadcast networks rely on advertising as their primary source of revenues, cable and satellite companies depend on subscription fees. One difference between cable and satellite TV is that cable uses local wire networks to deliver signals, whereas satellite TV is a national service that transmits a single signal covering the entire continental U.S. and delivering between 450 and 500 channels. [*Id.*]

The Federal Communications Commission regulates all television, including network, cable, and satellite transmissions. In the 1960s, it expressly preempted any state and local regulation of cable television. [Capital Cities Cable, Inc. v. Crisp, 467 U.S. 691 (1984)] In 1965, the FCC promulgated rules requiring cable systems to carry the signals of all local stations in their areas. Oklahoma, which had deemed it unlawful to sell and consume alcoholic beverages within the state, passed legislation requiring these same cable television operators to delete all advertising for alcoholic beverages contained in the out-of-state signals that retransmit into Oklahoma. The Supreme Court concluded that because the FCC preempted cable regulation, Oklahoma lacked the power to regulate cable broadcasters. [*Id.*]

Cable companies have also challenged Congressional mandates regulating cable television, particularly the "must carry" provisions that require them to offer local programming. In *Turner v. FCC*, 520 U.S. 180 (1997), the Supreme Court found "a substantial basis to support Congress's conclusion that a real threat justified enactment of the must-carry provisions." The threat that concerned Congress was that cable companies possessed a local monopoly over cable households, with only one percent of communities being served by more than one cable system. As such, the Court noted they could "silence the voice of competing speakers with a mere flick of the switch." [*Id*. at 197.]

Before passing the Cable Television Consumer Protection and Competition Act of 1992, Congress reviewed evidence that because of the competition between network and cable television for the same advertisers, cable television has substantial incentives to drop broadcast stations. One cable-industry executive said in *Turner v. FCC*, 520 U.S. at 201, "[O]ur job is to promote cable television, not broadcast television." The Supreme Court observed, "By the time the Cable Act was passed, 1,261 broadcast stations had been dropped for at least one year, in a total of 7,945 incidents." [*Id*. at 205.] The Court concluded that must-carry provisions serve the Government's interest by ensuring "that a number of local broadcasters retain cable carriage, with the concomitant audience access and advertising reve-

nues needed to support a multiplicity of stations."
[*Id*. at 213.]

Initially, direct broadcast satellite companies re-
sisted carrying broadcast networks. To counter this
resistance, Congress passed the Satellite Home
Viewer Improvement Act (SHVIA) in 1999 to require satellite carriers to provide secondary transmissions to subscribers of all local channels. The
SHVIA Act included a "carry one, carry all rule,"
mandating satellite carriers who chose to carry one
broadcast station in a local market "to carry all requesting stations within that market." [Satellite
Broadcasting and Communications Ass'n., 275 F.3d
337 (4th Cir. 2001)] To provide an incentive for satellite carriers, Congress created a statutory copyright
license that allows them to carry the signals of local
broadcast television stations without obtaining authorization from the holders of copyrights in the individual programs aired by the stations. [*Id*.]

When the "carry one, carry all" rule was challenged by satellite carriers, the Fourth Circuit Court
of Appeals held that the rule does not violate the
Constitution. It observed that the rule was a "narrowly tailored means of promoting the government's
important ends of preserving a vibrant mix of local
broadcast outlets for over-the-air viewers and min-
imizing the unintended side effects of SHVIA's statutory copyright license on local broadcast advertising markets." [*Id*. at 365.] As such, the Fourth Circuit concluded, "The carry one, carry all rule is

therefore consistent with the First Amendment."
[*Id.*]

Subsequently, the FCC created controversy with
its proposal to relax the federal rules on media ownership that restrict conglomerates from owning
more than one television station in the same city, or
both a newspaper and TV or radio station in the
same city. In *Prometheus Radio Project v. F.C.C.*,
373 F.3d 372 (3rd Cir. 2004), the Third Circuit Court
of Appeals blocked the new rules, which lifted a
1975 ban on such consolidation of ownership from
taking effect. The Third Circuit remanded the FCC's
order for additional justification on its chosen nu-
merical limits for local television ownership, local
radio ownership and cross-ownership of media within local markets. [*Id.*]

The new rules turned out to be controversial in
unexpected circles. Ted Turner, who built CNN into
a major player and then sold it to Time Warner, op-
posed the rules. In an op-ed piece, he postulated
that the proposed change would "stifle debate, inhibit new ideas and shut out smaller businesses trying to compete. If these rules had been in place in
1970, it would have been virtually impossible for me
to start Turner Broadcasting or, 10 years later, to
launch CNN." [Turner, *Monopoly or Democracy*.]

In another op-ed piece, Bob Hebert argued that
the FCC had become cozy with the very telecommunications and broadcasting industries they regulate.

Hebert cited a Center for Public Integrity study that examined the travel records of FCC employees and found that "over the last eight years, commissioners and staff members have taken 2,500 trips costing $42.8 million that were 'primarily' paid for by members of the telecommunications and broadcast industries." [Hebert, *Cozy with the F.C.C.*.] Hebert reported that the top destination for these FCC trips was Las Vegas (330 trips), followed by New Orleans (173 trips) and New York (102 trips). International destinations included London, Buenos Aires, and Beijing.

The consequences of FCC plans to deregulate the industry can already be seen in the decline of independently produced television shows. According to another study, for the fall 2003 prime time schedule, the four networks had a stake in 67% of the programs they aired, compared to 32% in the fall of 1992. Only 2% of the fall 2003 lineup came from independent producers compared with 30% in 1992. [Carter and Rutenberg, *Deregulating the Media*.]

D. INTERNET VIEWING

Television further pervades individuals' lives through the Internet. The four major networks-- ABC, CBS, FOX, and NBC--offer free, advertising-supported shows online. [Gentile, *NBC Offers Free TV Online*.] Indeed, they advertise immediately after an episode has aired that it is available for viewing on the Internet. CBS experimented for eight months with charging 99 cents to download episodes of its prime time shows, but scrapped the experiment after finding that viewers didn't want to pay for television. [James, *Viewers Snub 99-Cent TV.*]

The Internet also permits sports fans to observe matches and games that a network may choose not to broadcast. Spectators can observe tennis matches live on the U.S. Open and Wimbledon tennis tournaments that are not being covered on network or cable television.

Because of the Internet, individuals can receive podcasts of meetings and forums that might not otherwise be picked up on CSPAN or other educational channels. The American Booksellers Association, for example, podcasts its annual convention seminars on its website. Individuals unable to attend the convention could thus observe and learn from its famous lecturers by downloading the seminars to their computer, handheld Blackberry, or iPad.

On the website www.youtube.com, people can broadcast homemade videos that might not find another distribution outlet on the Internet, thereby creating a form of people's television. In 2006, Google Inc. purchased YouTube for $1.65 billion. The Associated Press reported that Google perceived the website as a lucrative marketing hub "as more viewers and advertisers migrate from television to the Internet." [Liedtke, *Google Buying YouTube for $1.65B.*]

The next chapter explores business and legal issues peculiar to the music industry.

CHAPTER 3

THE MUSIC INDUSTRY

The music business encompasses a lucrative, although ever-changing, component of the entertainment industry. According to the Recording Industry Association of America (RIAA), manufacturers shipped 255,700,000 units of music in 2011 worth $3,381,100,000, down 4.5% from 267,700,000 units in 2010, worth $3,663,900,000. By contrast, the industry shipped 305.72 million units during just the first half of 2004. [Gallo, Music Sales Sing.]

While sales of physical music have declined drastically over the years, digital sales continue to skyrocket. For example, the value of digital downloads and musical videos rose 17.3% from $2,232,900,000 in 2010 to $2,619,700,000 in 2011. When digital, physical and performance and synchronization royalties were added together, the industry gained 0.2% in value from $6,995,000,000 in 2010 to $7,007,700,000 in 2011.

Music's popularity stems from its intimate connection to and reflection of society. Groups produce different types of sounds to reflect their immediate cultural experiences. Music that is popular with one generation easily becomes passé or old school with the next. Classical music is an art form that originated in Europe with composers ranging from Mozart and Haydn to Beethoven and Ravel contributing to its popularity. While classical music is still played by symphony orchestras around the world, it struggles to modernize and become relevant to a current age when youth prefer heavy metal bands like Metallica or rap artists like Dr. Dre and 50 Cent.

African-Americans created spiritual music during their enslavement. Songs such as "Go Down Moses" and "Swing Lo, Sweet Chariot" reflected their loss of freedom and hopes for better lives. The blues evolved during the Jim Crow decades that followed emancipation when Blacks were physically free, but had yet to achieve political and economic liberation.

Rock and roll became a popular upbeat music form during the 1950s and 1960s, accompanied by and derived from rhythm and blues and soul music. In the 1990s and the decade of 2000, hip-hop and rap music became the battle cry for a generation that felt trapped in urban areas, held back from the American dream, and at war with the police. While all music written for voice can be termed poetry set to instrumental music, rap music takes this to the extreme as the words are spoken in a beat to limited accompaniment.

Music regularly crosses ethnic and racial boundaries, leading to a shaping and sharing of cultural values. Like Picasso who was inspired by visits to Africa to create his cubist work, Elvis Presley frequented blues and jazz bars in Memphis prior to fashioning his unique form of rock and roll. Contralto Marian Anderson was the first Black to sing at the Metropolitan Opera House in New York City, making her debut in 1955 as Ulrica in Verdi's *Un Ballo in Maschera* (A Masked Ball). In 2004, Caucasian artist Eminem won the Grammy Award for Best Male Rap Solo Performance.

This chapter begins by discussing the music process and the major players in the business. For centuries, musicians have made money from three primary sources: publishing, performing, and touring. Secondary sources for some, although primary to others, are teaching, album sales, and merchandizing their likenesses. This chapter discusses the three primary sources, as well as indebtedness, a legal issue confronting musicians at a higher rate than other entertainers. As a consequence, musicians often become ensnared in bankruptcy and tax pitfalls that jeopardize their financial well-being.

A. THE MUSIC PROCESS

As music has evolved over the centuries, so have the methods of capturing it for posterity. Mozart and his cohorts published sheet music and performed it before royalty and nobility in private musicales and elaborate concert halls. Composers like Elton John continue to produce sheet music available for purchase at music stores. Modern musicians are, nevertheless, more likely to perform at public venues for several hundred or several thousand music-loving souls. Superstar musicians may play in stadiums containing 100,000 seats.

Contemporary musicians also have an advantage over musicians of the 1600s and 1700s in that the former can record their songs in a studio on machines and later release them for public consumption. In the month or so before he was killed, Tupac Shakur practically lived in a studio with his group, creating numerous songs that have been released as CDs after his untimely demise. Indeed, his record company released more of Shakur's CDs after his death than were released during his abbreviated life. The mechanical recording of music provides another means of achieving immortality for creators whose works resonate with the public.

Interviews with musicians and bands of various genres reveal there is no one true path to becoming a successful musician. One truism often repeated in the music business is that an artist gets his whole life to produce his first CD and only six months to produce the next one if the first is a hit.

Keali'i Reichel, a professor of Hawaiian language and culture at Maui Community College, often crooned in the shower and around his home until friends began begging him to record his voice. [Author Interview with Reichel.] In 1994, Reichel independently produced and released a collection of Hawaiian traditional and contemporary music called *Kawaipunahele* to considerable accolades. His debut album received five 1995 Na Hoku Hanohano Awards, the Hawaiian equivalent of the Grammys. He won Popular Hawaiian Album of the Year, Male Vocalist of the Year, Album of the Year, Entertainer of the Year (by public vote), and Most Promising New Artist. His success meant he had only a few months to produce his next album *Lei Hali'a*, which also won five Hoku awards. In the decade following his debut album, Reichel played in venues as diverse as the Hollywood Bowl and Carnegie Hall, and opened for LeAnn Rimes, Ccline Dion, and Sting.

Bob Guiney started singing soft rock music as part of a group calling itself Fat Amy in 1992. At the time, he and his band members were college students at Michigan State University. Fellow band member Matt Jackson says, "We began as a bar band, playing whatever gigs we could get." Early on, Guiney and Jackson served as the band's managers and booking agents. They shopped their demo tapes around town to line up gigs. [Author Interviews with Guiney and Jackson.]

Fat Amy changed its name to The Bob Guiney Band after Guiney was cast on the reality television shows *The Bachelorette* and *The Bachelor*. When he became the popular "Bachelor Bob," Wind-up Records pursued him and offered his band publishing and recording contracts. Wind-up Records also underwrote a radio tour to get radio stations to play his band's music.

Matt Jackson explains the necessity of bands traveling the country to perform at venues sponsored by radio stations. "It used to be the stations played 60 or 70 records throughout the day," he says. "Now they play 17-19 records all day long. We're trying to get in that mix so that people are hearing our songs and wanting to buy our CDs." [Author Interview with Jackson.]

After Wind-up Records decided to promote the Bob Guiney Band, they acquired a team of agents, managers and lawyers to assist them. "When you get to this level," says Jackson, "You can no longer do it all." [*Id*.]

Other musicians have been discovered singing at karaoke bars or in their churches. Tina Turner sang gospel music in church choirs before being discovered by Ike Turner. After marrying her, he changed her name from Anna Mae Bullock to her stage moniker.

Since there is no one path into the music business, the challenge for musicians is to produce their best work at all times. They never know who will drop by a bar, watch them perform on a reality TV show, or even listen to them sing in the shower. Once they enter the business, they become one of the players in the industry.

B. THE PLAYERS

The technology revolution enables musicians like Reichel to produce albums at low cost, either by establishing sound booths in their own homes or by renting space at less expensive fees than before. Some of the music industry's major players are (1) composers, performers, producers; (2) music publishers; (3) performance rights societies; (4) recording companies; and (5) tour promoters. This section examines their contributions to the music process.

1. COMPOSERS, PERFORMERS, PRODUCERS

As with films where the blueprint is the script, making the writer a key player in movie-making, crafting songs launches the music process. Some composers write both the lyrics and music. Richard Rodgers and Oscar Hammerstein, for example, collaborated with one contributing the lyrics and the other producing music. Their partnership created legendary musicals, like *Oklahoma!*, *South Pacific*, and *The Sound of Music,* that are still performed in theaters today and have been turned into film musicals.

Performers supply their unique voices or instrumental skills to the songwriters' material. While Charles Fox wrote "Killing Me Softly With His Song," Roberta Flack gave it a soulful rendition.

Performers can pick and choose from a wealth of material, some of which is in the public domain, available for anyone to use. For centuries, classical music artists made a living performing the works of composers who left behind an enormous body of work that is now free. More recent creations may be protected by copyright laws, which require performers to pay royalties to the owner(s) of songs. Performers who write their own music have a safer shot at immortality, as others may play their music into eternity. During his lifetime, Mozart performed, conducted, taught, and composed. He is most remembered for his compositions because orchestras and classical musicians continue to perform and record them more than 250 years after his birth.

Once performers decide to record their music in a mechanical form so that it can be sold to the public as a CD, LP, DVD, or in mp3 file formats for downloading, they often seek producers to assist them. As in the film industry, producers help bring the final product together. They can find the perfect material for a particular artist's voice and then choose the sound engineer who puts it all into an appropriate form.

Gifted producers often possess exceptional ears and can tell immediately when a note sounds sharp or falls flat. As demonstrated in the film *Laurel Canyon*, producers spend a great deal of time helping performers mold the right sounds into an album they can sell.

Producers receive upfront fees and a share of the royalties. Often they are paid before the artist receives his or her share. They can earn more than performers.

2. MUSIC PUBLISHERS

A principal source of income for Mozart was the concerts he gave of his own work. Another source was publishing his music.

Music publishing houses assist artists by reproducing, selling, and licensing their work. Charles Fox's songs, along with those of hundreds of thousands of composers, can be purchased either individually or in a compilation in stores that sell sheet music. The music publishing company authorizes these sales and receives revenue in return, which it shares with the composer.

Publishers also license other uses of their artists' works. Under the copyright laws, which will be discussed in more detail in Chapter 6, any performer can make an exact cut of a song and pay royalties set by statute to the music publisher. The publisher then splits the royalties with the copyright claimants.

If movie or television producers want to synchronize a song to a film or show, they must obtain a synchronization license from the music publisher. If producers are interested in a particular rendition of the song, they must also obtain a mechanical license from the recording company. This license is necessary when film producers seek to incorporate a sound recording into the soundtrack of a taped commercial television production. [Agee v. Paramount Communications, 59 F.3d 317 (2nd Cir. 1995)]

Further, if the recording company grants a right to synchronize a master recording to a film that includes the right to exploit, distribute, market, and perform the picture "by any means or methods now or hereafter known," that grant includes distribution on videocassettes [Platinum Record Co., Inc. v. Lucasfilm, Ltd., 566 F.Supp. 226 (D.N.J. 1983)], DVDs, or Blu-ray disks.

Some of these licenses can be acquired from performance rights societies.

3. PERFORMANCE RIGHTS SOCIETIES

Composers, songwriters, lyricists, and music publishers join performance rights societies like ASCAP (American Society of Composers, Authors, and Publishers) and BMI (Broadcast Music Industry) because they keep track of wide-ranging uses of songs. Membership in performance rights societies is generally open to musicians of all genres of music.

Performance rights societies license and distribute royalties for public performance of copyrighted works. They collect fees from radio stations, broadcast and cable television networks, Internet users, and live and recorded performances. Even when a company plays music on their telephones or in their elevators, they may owe royalties to performance rights societies. These societies redistribute their collections to their members based on statistical sampling of the songs in their catalogue. The higher the percentage play of a particular song, the more revenue the owner receives. BMI and ASCAP sell single use, single fee licenses, and blanket licenses. The latter's fees are based on the company's revenue, and give the licensee the right to exploit any song in the catalogue.

Established in 1927, the New York-based Harry Fox Agency also issues blanket licenses, although it concentrates on mechanical licenses. Harry Fox licenses the use of copyrighted musical compositions for use on CDs, records, tapes, and certain digital configurations such as DVDs or downloads. During the early days of rap music, when sampling other artists' work was common, the musicians were unaware that they needed a mechanical license to make use of another person's song. Harry Fox notes on its website, www.harryfox.com, that its mechanical license does not include the right to display or reprint lyrics or the right to print sheet music, nor does it cover the use of songs on karaoke machines. It advises readers to contact the music publisher(s) directly for those rights. [Id.]

SESAC, the Society of European Stage Authors and Composers, is a privately held corporation with offices in London, Los Angeles, Nashville, and New

York. Initially, SESAC's repertory was limited to European and gospel music, but it has diversified to include dance hits, rock classics, Latin music, jazz, country, and contemporary music, according to its website, www.sesac.com.

JASRAC, the Japanese Society for Rights of Authors, Composers and Publishers, was founded in 1939 to assist Japanese musicians and publishers. It initially set fees for concerts, dramatic representation, radio broadcasting, talkies, and publications. [JASRAC, *The Organization and Operations of JASRAC*, at 4-8] In an interview at their corporate offices in 1993, several JASRAC officers said that they actively pursue karaoke bars and machines to sell them licenses.

There are a host of performance rights societies throughout the world. Countries that have a music industry often have a performance rights society to monitor the uses of the music.

4. RECORDING COMPANIES

The music industry contains companies that record and distribute songs for musicians. Musicians seek record contracts, but often find that recording companies will not risk enormous sums to advance their careers until they see the band perform. Yet, it may be difficult for musicians to obtain engagements until they have a CD that demonstrates their abilities. Many bands resolve this Catch-22 by spending their own resources to record an initial demo tape.

Because of the enormous risk associated with bringing out new artists, recording companies try to lower their exposure by sending out scouts, called A and R (artist and repertoire) people to clubs to find fresh, new talent. Recording companies are then known to sign artists to draconian contracts and advance them money against their future revenue stream. This sinks many artists into financial holes from which some never emerge.

Attorney Peter Thall says that many of his clients believe that the more money they owe their recording company, the more likely the company is to promote them. Thall finds the contrary to be true. He says that companies prefer "to write off the expense as a bad debt than to throw good money after bad." [Thall, *What They'll Never Tell You About the Music Business*, at 28.]

Mariah Carey's situation proves Thall's point. In January 2002, Virgin Records terminated its contract with Carey after her "Glitter" album sold only 500,000 copies in the United States. Virgin Records paid Carey $28 million to cancel their agreement, and allowed her to retain the $21 million she received when initially signing with them. The company essentially paid Carey $98 for every album it sold, this after having cut the cost of the single "Loverboy" to 49 cents to help it climb the charts.

Virgin Records' risk, valued at $80 million for four albums, was based on Carey having sold more than 150 million singles and albums worldwide since her debut in 1990. However, Carey developed personal problems and was hospitalized during summer of 2001 just prior to the release of the "Glitter" album and *Glitter* film. Virgin Records decided to write-off the deal after one album and not take further chances with the remaining ones. Carey subsequently produced 2005's best-selling CD, "The Emancipation of Mimi," with Island Records.

The earlier Mariah Carey events, nevertheless, illustrate why record companies will fight to protect their interest if artists produce hits while under contract. In *Isley v. Motown Record Corp.*, 69 F.R.D. 12 (S.D.N.Y. 1975), the recording company sought a declaration that the Isley Brothers were under contract when they recorded "It's Your Thing," which sold 1,750,000 copies. At issue was whether the Isley Brothers recorded "It's Your Thing" in November 1968 while under contract with Motown or in January 1969 after they had been released from their agreement. Their deal required Motown to advance money for recording sessions and, in return, Motown would own all copyrights to the Isley's compositions and all master recordings.

A jury determined the song had been recorded after January 1969 and belonged exclusively to the Isley Brothers. The district judge, however, set aside the jury's verdict, finding it based on contradictory and self-serving testimony from the Isley Brothers. At trial, the Isleys repudiated their own earlier sworn testimony by characterizing it variously as a lie and false. The judge found their first testimony supported the contrary conclusion that the music was created in November 1968.

In their 1969-70 depositions, the Isleys testified that after finding the back-up band, they asked Motown to advance them money for a recording session in which they planned to record music of their own. The tape of the 6 November 1968 session disappeared. At trial, the Isleys said they asked Motown for the recording session money because they were broke and needed to buy Christmas presents and pay household expenses. They later said their mother threw out the tape of the 6 November 1968, session while cleaning house.

The court queried whether the mother of successful recording artists would throw out any tape, let alone one a month old. The court also questioned why the Isleys had not sent the tape immediately to Motown as they had agreed to do in their 1 November letter requesting the funds. Based upon Motown's proof of contemporaneous writings and the testimony of musicians who played at the 6 November session, the court concluded that the Isleys' trial testimony constituted false evidence. After determining that the jury's verdict resulted "in a miscarriage of justice" based on untrue statements, the court ordered a new trial.

The Isley Brothers' lives would continue to be marked by professional successes and encounters with legal matters. In 1992, the group was inducted into the Rock and Roll Hall of Fame. Nevertheless, in 2006, Ronald Isley was convicted of tax evasion. He was sentenced to serve three years in federal prison and ordered to pay $3.1 million to the Internal Revenue Service.

Many musicians feel that recording companies do not offer fair deals. However, courts rarely set aside contracts as unconscionable on that basis alone. While musicians in the early stages of their careers may have limited negotiating power, they should have attorneys explain their contracts so they at least understand the bargain they are making and do not overspend while expecting to receive royalties that never materialize.

The assignment clause in contracts, for example, can lead to bands ending with a different recording company if a merger takes place. With the consolidation of the entertainment industry, executives who nurtured a particular band's career may depart, abandoning them to the mercy of new personnel who may lack interest in their success and want to develop their own discoveries.

California law considers recording agreements as contracts for personal services. California Civil Code § 3423 mandates that these agreements guarantee the artists will make a minimum of $9,000 the first year of the contract, $12,000 the second year, and $15,000 in years three through seven. [Cal. Civ. Code § 3423 (A)(i).] Further, section 2855(a) of the California Labor Code limits the enforcement of personal service contracts to seven years. Section 2855 (b) provides record companies the opportunity to sue to collect damages should an artists fail to provide the number of records they committed to in their contracts.

5. TOUR PROMOTERS

For centuries, musicians supported themselves, at least in part, through touring. In the 1700s, Mozart toured often as a child; at one point, he and his father, an accomplished violinist, author, and teacher, traveled Europe for two years. He performed his own concertos in concert halls and in the salons of wealthy and royal Europeans. This touring provided reliable sources of income, along with teaching, an activity that he rarely enjoyed. [Gay, *Mozart*.]

Bands tour for the same reasons that authors conduct book signings. By placing their names in the public eye, they spawn more interest in their creative products. Musicians expand their fan base through touring. They also generate additional sales for their records and concert related material.

Nevertheless, tours can be expensive, and bands have to be careful not to spend more on the tour than they generate in revenue. Unbeknownst to some bands, when recording companies advance revenue to support the transportation, living, and other expenses associated with a tour, they recoup those costs from the band's royalties.

Bands sign agreements with tour promoters or their companies or both. Tour promoters contract to bring bands to particular locales and make all the local arrangements. The promoters expect bands to perform in a professional manner and give a great concert.

Tom Moffatt began bringing musicians to Hawaii in the 1950s. [Author Interview with Moffatt.] He worked with Colonel Parker to set up Elvis Presley concerts in 1957, in 1960 right after Presley got out of the army, and in 1973 while he was in the islands to film *Blue Hawaii*. Over the decades, Moffatt has dealt with a range of issues in staging an elaborate concert. He says the biggest and most unusual show occurred when Michael Jackson hired two Russian cargo planes to fly in an army tank that was part of his act. This did not surprise Moffatt because he knows of pianists who ship their personal Yamaha piano to Japan. He says musicians become attached to and prefer using particular instruments.

Depending on the size of the show, Moffatt may have to hire local technicians to help with the set-up, although each band usually brings in a specialist to supervise the work. The size of the show's equipment and the accompanying entourage affect the cost of the show and the associated ticket prices.

When setting up a concert, promoters enter into agreements laying out the parameters of the tours. These negotiations may take place in person, on the phone, by fax, through e-mail, or any other available means of communication. Moffatt says that after he realized the 1997 Michael Jackson show would sell out in a few hours, he called Jackson's people to ask if he could add another show to accompany the Friday one. Jackson's agents agreed, but wouldn't confirm a date. They couldn't say if it would be on a Saturday or Sunday because Jackson normally did not do two shows in a row. Moffatt then announced a second engagement without a firm date. He simply had the tickets stamped TBA. Both shows sold out in one day.

Because of their sometimes frantic and unpredictable nature, setting up a tour can lead to misunderstandings if the two parties aren't determined to make the event happen. In April 1996, pop singer Michael Bolton and Australian corporation Michael Coppel Promotions (MCP) exchanged telefaxes and telephone calls to set up an eight-concert Australian tour from May 14 to 28, 1996. In return for performing in various Australian cities, Bolton was to be paid "the greater of $1,200,000 or 85% of the net door receipts of ticket sales." With the consent of Bolton's booking agent, MCP commenced ticket sales for six of the eight tour dates.

After problems developed with the Korean leg of Bolton's tour, his representative canceled the Australian tour, citing problems with ticket sales. MCP sued Bolton, who insisted that no oral or written agreement had been reached because many items remained to be worked out. For example, there was conflict over the entourage's accommodations. For Bolton's previous Australian tour, MCP furnished lodging for 29 people. For the 1996 tour, Bolton requested that MCP provide breakfast and hotel rooms for 42 individuals.

The District Court determined in *Michael Coppel Promotions v. Bolton*, 982 F.Supp. 950 (S.D.N.Y. 1997), that although some details remained to be ironed out, the parties had manifested intent to enter into a contract. The court noted that MCP had partially performed the contract based on the oral agreement by selling tickets. The court concluded that a contract has been formed if an initial meeting of the minds has occurred to the contract's material terms.

The *Bolton* case illustrates that once an agreement has been reached and the other party proceeds to act on it, the performer is expected to show up. European concert promoter Marcel Abram sued Michael Jackson for canceling two New Year's Eve 1999 concerts. To celebrate the millennium, Jackson was to perform in Sydney, Australia, and then board a jet to carry out a second engagement in Hawaii on the same day. The jury awarded Abram $5.3 million in damages against Jackson. [http://www.cnn.com/2003/LAW/03/13/jackson.lawsuit/]

Promoters must also deal with the expectations of fans. When one well-known R and B artist walked onto a concert stage, sniffed around, declared "I don't like the audience," and then left, the promoter refunded the ticket costs to the audience.

Refunds become a thorny issue when the artist does actually play, but gives an unsatisfactory performance. In *Kass v. Young*, 67 Cal.App.3d 100, 136 Cal.Rptr. 469 (Cal.App. 1 Dist. 1977), one of the 14,000 patrons at a rock concert sued Neil Young because he terminated the concert by abruptly walking off the stage. Kass sought to certify a class of all 14,000 present and retrieve their money.

The District Court certified the class and awarded damages of $91,000, which represented the cost of tickets purchased and a 40% attorney's fee. On appeal, the court vacated the judgment. It questioned whether all 14,000 patrons were equally damaged. The court postulated that "many of the patrons or 'fans' of the performer who had entertained them for an hour did not regard themselves cheated or that some may have sympathized with his antagonism toward a number of the security guards." [*Id.* at 106-107.] The court ruled that Kass' individual case could proceed following final determination of the class action.

Sometimes the misbehavior of musicians, their representatives, or even their fans places promoters in uncomfortable positions. Electric Factory Concerts (EFC), the local promoter of The Who concert at the Cincinnati Riverfront Coliseum on 3 December 1979 was among the many defendants sued for wrongful death. A delay in opening the concert doors led fans to rush in and trample several individuals to death. The appeals court found that EFC had received a permit to use and occupy the arena from 8:00 p.m. to 11:00 p.m. on 3 December 1979. [Bowes v. Cincinnati Riverfront Coliseum, 12 Ohio App. 3d 12, 465 N.E.2d 904 (Ohio App. 1 Dist. 1983).]

According to the permit, EFC was required to have a prescribed number of security and safety personnel in attendance. The court also found that the general manger and office manager for EFC was present on December 3rd and was a key person in determining when the doors would open. The court then reversed the trial court's order dismissing punitive damage claims against EFC. [*Id*. at 23.]

Because tragic incidents have taken place at several concerts, promoters have increased security. At one Snoop Dogg concert, fans entered through doors pasted with signs reading "No Weapons Allowed" and "No Gang Activity Permitted Inside." They then encountered metal detectors and were subjected to security pat-downs. While guards removed weapons, they did not confiscate drugs. After the leader of the warm-up band mounted the stage, he asked the crowd, "Where's the dope? Who's got the dope?" [Burr, *Snoop Dogg, Schwartz Bob*.]

"Over here, over here," the crowd responded as hundreds of hands shot up.

Whether it was the cloud of marijuana smoke or the deafening sounds, one patron fainted and had to be evacuated on a gurney. [*Id.*] No lawsuits were later announced as a result of this concert. Some fans apparently have decided that they pay their money and take their chances with these kinds of events, a fortunate result for the local promoter.

C. MUSICIANS AND INDEBTEDNESS

For centuries, prominent musicians ranging from Mozart to Michael Jackson have experienced money troubles. Sometimes the musician's indebtedness arises from poor management of substantial resources. At other times, the musicians overestimate their anticipated revenues from their recording, tour, and music publishing contracts. The result is that musicians, more than other entertainers, seem more likely to have confrontations with creditors and the IRS. Attorneys and law students who seek to create a music law practice should study bankruptcy and tax law.

Mozart earned more than double what he estimated it would cost a reputable family to survive in Vienna in the late 1700s, yet he routinely sent out begging letters to supplement his income. [Gay, *Mozart.*] In seeking a path to the esteem of the nobility, Mozart wanted to appear as a cultivated artist and an equal, rather than as a hired hand. He spent considerable amounts on luxurious living quarters, paying in Vienna more than triple the amount he shelled out for a modest Salzburg apartment or what his family paid to live in his Salzburg birth house. Biographer Peter Gay wrote about Mozart, "What he craved he bought." Among other things, he purchased a specially built piano, acquired a billiard table, and performed on tour with expensive hand-made shoes and fashionable clothes. For his comfort, he kept a horse and deemed a carriage a necessity.

To cover the additional cost associated with his extravagant lifestyle, Mozart wrote his friends and supporters. To one he said, "I beg you to help me with only a little money." He even requested that one associate lend him a substantial amount of money at an appropriate rate of interest so that he could secure a "sense of safety." He wrote, "It is nasty, indeed impossible, to live when one has to wait earnings to earnings." Mozart felt he needed "a certain serenity to do his composing." [Id.]

Some contemporary musicians could easily sympathize with Mozart's plight because they live from royalty check to royalty check. Part of the current problem is that musicians do not understand their recording contracts before signing them and, therefore, misperceive their potential earnings. Once their album or single sells at the gold, platinum, or diamond levels, which are 500,000, 1,000,000, 10,000,000 units respectively, musicians expect the funds to pour in. In anticipation, they buy on credit a Cadillac SUV or full-size Mercedes, the equivalent of Mozart's carriage and horse.

Michael Jackson allegedly became so mired in debt in early 2003 that he was unable to pay his bills. Financial expert John Duros O'Bryan, who acknowledged that he was working from partial records, estimated that Jackson was spending $20 million to $30 million more than he was earning in income. [Broder, *Witness Says Jackson Had 'Cash Flow Crisis'*.] Based on prosecution documents submitted in Jackson's 2005 molestation trial, O'Bryan testified that Jackson annually spends $5 million on lawyers and professional services, $5 million on security and maintenance for his Neverland Valley ranch, $7.5 million on personal expenses, and $2.5 million on other costs, largely insurance. [*Id.*] During the year following Michael Jackson's final curtain call, his estate brought in over a billion dollars, mostly due to "This is It," the most successful concert film of all times, and a record deal with Sony Music. [http://www.thewrap.com/movies/article/jackson-estate-earnings-cross-1b-mark-18578]

It was the building of an elaborate home that precipitated rap-star MC Hammer filing for bankruptcy in the mid-1990s. Acknowledging that he had his priorities out of order, Hammer later became a minister. He was among the many musicians to find their coffers empty despite tremendous success.

When Mozart's creditors demanded payment, he begged for funds from others to pay them, constantly juggling his debt. [Gay, *Mozart*.] Modern musicians accomplish the same outcome by using one credit card to pay another. After Motown sued them, the Isley Brothers mentioned at their trial that they were having trouble making ends meet and initially planned to use the money Motown advanced them to pay bills and buy Christmas presents. While the jury believed them, the judge did not and ruled for Motown. [Isley v. Motown Record Corp., 67 F.R.D. 12 (S.D.N.Y. 1975)]

Presently, musicians seek relief from their debts and contracts in bankruptcy court. Recording companies challenge the Chapter 11 filings by musicians, charging that they seek to be released from their agreements in bad faith. The bankruptcy court then examines the situation to determine if there is genuine financial distress.

James Taylor, the former lead singer of Kool and the Gang, was able to reject his executory contracts with PolyGram Records and two other publishing companies after filing for bankruptcy. [Matter of Taylor, 103 B.R. 511 (Bankr. D.N.J. 1989)] The group arranged its recording, publishing, and tour-related contracts and legal relationships through at least three furnishing companies. By October 1986, Kool and the Gang had accumulated debts exceeding $1,719,000. By December 1987, the group had outstanding loans and accounts totaling $3,352,109, which did not include another $950,000 advanced by PolyGram. Taylor, who petitioned for Chapter 11 bankruptcy relief on May 24, 1988, had personally guaranteed over $1.2 million of these loans. He also filed a motion for authority to reject certain executory agreements.

The recording and publishing companies filed a cross-motion seeking dismissal of Taylor's Chapter 11 petition for having been filed in bad faith. The court disagreed with the recording companies' claim. The court examined Taylor's financial situation and noted that his liabilities of $4,518,701.50 far exceeded his assets of $734,215.00. [*Id.* at 521.] In affirming the decision of the Bankruptcy Court, the court observed that three contingent liabilities totaling over $1.2 million alone were sufficient to justify bankruptcy. [*Id.*] As a consequence, Taylor was able to reject his contracts and receive a "fresh start." [*Id.* at 517.] The Third Circuit affirmed that a debtor could, with court approval, reject an executory contract for personal services. [*Matter of Taylor*, 913 F.2d 102, 108 (3rd Cir. 1990)]

The singing group TLC, which posted four No. 1 singles on Billboard's Hot 100 chart and sold 21 million albums in the United States alone, used a Chapter 11 bankruptcy filing to reject their existing management agreements. When the creditors charged bad faith, the court found that they too were financially distressed. The three women who comprised TLC had borrowed substantial sums totaling $349,922.26 from LaFace Records in March 1995. Their indebtedness was evidenced by demand promissory notes, which were to be payable from royalties. [In re Watkins, 210 B.R. 394, 395 (Bkrtcy. N.D.Ga. 1997)]

TLC used their LaFace loans to catch up on delinquent bills. Each woman testified that her financial problems had begun as early as 1994. All of them had difficulties meeting monthly payments and were constantly behind in paying their debts. Sometimes they were more than three months in arrears. Their December 31, 1994 royalty statement, which was received prior to their filing for bankruptcy, reflected a negative balance of $576,828.98.

One woman had credit card companies demanding payment, and couldn't pay her bills from month-to-month. When asked how the three came to the decision to file for relief, band member Rozonda Thomas stated that "[we pulled] out our pockets with nothing in them. That is exactly how we decided. None of us could pay our bills." [*Id.* at 398-399.]

Lisa Lopes, who would later die in a car wreck in Honduras at the age of 30, testified that she faced foreclosure on her Diamond Circle property, and two other creditors had sued her. [*Id.* at 399.] The court considered TLC's financial situation sufficiently dire to justify bankruptcy relief. [*Id.* at 403.] After their bankruptcy filing, TLC went on a five-year hiatus before releasing "Fanmail," their hit that sold more than 6 million copies.

Concerned about the increasing number of musicians filing for bankruptcy, the Recording Industry Association of America [www.riaa.com/] lobbied for an addition to the 1998 bankruptcy bill. The RIAA sought to make it harder for musicians to declare legal insolvency and escape their contracts. Their efforts fizzled out. Filing for bankruptcy remains an option for musicians seeking to escape their debts and oppressive contracts.

Even when musicians have sufficient funds coming in, some of them forget to pay their taxes. When the IRS sued country music singer and songwriter Willie Nelson and his wife Connie for failure to pay $1,514,752 in income taxes for the years 1975-1978, he petitioned to seal his records so his tax problems would not leak to the media and the general public. [Willie Nelson Music Co. v. C.I.R., 85 T.C. 914 (Tax Ct. 1985)]

The Nelsons claimed that sensationalism of their tax problems was causing them "undue embarrassment and considerable emotional distress." [*Id.* at 916.] They also claimed they had been "unable to negotiate large up front payments in long term endorsement contracts." [*Id.*]

The court examined 37 newspaper articles and concluded that none of them suggested that the Nelsons were subject to criminal prosecution. Rather, the newspapers gave a factual report on the Nelsons' tax situation, and none said that part of the underpayment was due to fraud. [*Id.* at 925-926.]

The court concluded that the Nelsons had not demonstrated sufficient good cause to seal the records and denied their motions. Historically, courts have sealed records where patents, trade secrets, or confidential information is involved. [*Id.* at 921.] This court said that showing the information "would harm a party's reputation is generally not sufficient to overcome the strong common law presumption in favor of access to court records." [*Id.*]

Nearly 20 years later, Nelson himself reminded the public of his tax problems by plugging H&R Block in television commercials during tax season. In 2006, the Associated Press reported that Nelson, who hails from Spicewood, Texas, and four of his band members were cited for possession of narcotic mushrooms and marijuana after a traffic stop on a Louisiana highway. [The Associated Press, *On the Road Again, Nelson Is Busted*.] Nelson also published his third book in 2006. In *The Tao of Willie: A Guide to the Happiness in Your Heart* (Gotham Press), Nelson offers lessons from his music career, such as "Do not corner something you know is meaner than you," "keep skunks of all kinds at a distance," and "if you forgive your enemies, it messes up their heads." [Bertsche, *Three Home Truths from Willie Nelson*.]

In conclusion, lawyers should encourage their musician clients to obey all laws, pay their taxes, and refrain from buying a SUV, the modern equivalent of Mozart's carriage and horse, until they have the royalty check in hand.

CHAPTER 4

THE VIDEO GAME INDUSTRY

Video games are the newest form of entertainment to become a multi-billion dollar industry. Indeed, video game sales have become so popular that they sometimes exceed film sales. As mentioned in Chapter 1, the 2011 *Call of Duty: Modern Warfare 3*, made its first billion in sales in 16 days, which bested the record set by the 2009 film *Avatar*.

According to data compiled by the NPD Group, a global market research firm, and released by the Entertainment Software Association (ESA), the computer and gaming industry sold 273 million units between 2005 and 2009 leading to an "astonishing $10.5 billion in revenue." [http://www.esrb.org/about/images/vidGames04.png] The ESA describes entertainment software as one of the fastest growing industries in the U.S. economy. [www.theesa.com/facts/econdata.asp] According to the ESA, from 2005 to 2009, the entertainment software industry's annual growth rate exceeded 10%, compared with less than 2% for the entire U.S. economy. Computer and video game companies directly or indirectly employ more than 120,000 people in 34 states, with an average salary for direct employees of $90,000. More than 22,000 workers are employed in the five states of California, Texas, Washington, New York, and Massachusetts. [*Id.*]

The ESA reports that consumers spent $24.75 billion on video games, hardware and accessories in 2011, and that purchase of digital content accounted for 31% of games sales. [*Id.*] By July 2012, there had been a retrenchment with major video game companies reporting a decline in revenue. On 12 July 2012, for example, NPD Group reported that U.S. retail sales of video game hardware, software and accessories fell 29% in June to $700 million, and this represented the seventh consecutive month of decline.   [http://abcnews.go.com/Technology/wire Story/video-games-industry-faring-16861128]

According to the ESA's research, the average U.S. household, according to the ESA, owns at least one dedicated game console, PC or smart phone. Further, the average gamer is 30 years old and has been playing games for 12 years, yet the average age of the most frequent game purchaser is 35 years old.   [www.theesa.com/facts/econdata.asp]   Women account for 47% of all game players. Indeed, the ESA reports that "women over the age of 18 represent a significantly greater portion of the game-playing population (30 percent) than boys 17 and younger (18 percent)." The ESA's research also reveals that parents "are present when games are purchased or rented 90% of the time." [*Id.*]

Games have transitioned from the advent of coin-operated arcades in the 1970s that featured popular two-dimensional games like Pac-Man and Mario Brothers. As a medium, video games have benefitted from the development of the personal computer and entertainment technology such as the iPhone and iPad.

Apple co-founder Steve Jobs, who ascended to the computer heavens in 2011, is regarded as a video game pioneer for making it easier for game publishers to get their product to market. In a Forbes Magazine article, John Gaudiosi wrote that "Before the iPhone, game publishers literally had to create over 700 versions of a mobile game for the various phones that consumers used around the world. Apple streamlined that process into one version which allowed game developers to get more creative with the titles they released." [Gaudiosi, Why Steve Jobs] Gaudiosi cites the game *Angry Birds* as a success story. Steve Jobs began his career in the computer industry as a technician for Atari, an early video arcade and software game company.

According to the ESA, excluding small handheld devices, the three main game systems are the XBox360, Wii and PS3, or Sony's Play Station 3. In 2009, 273 million units (video games) were sold by the video game industry, which brought in a total of $9.9 billion in sales revenue. This data was by the NPD Group, a global market research company. [http://www.esrb.org/about/video-game-industry-statistics.jsp]

This chapter explores video game types, production processes, and legal issues.

A. VIDEO GAME TYPES

Similar to film, television, and music, there are many genres of video games. From educational games designed to teach elementary students literacy, to single-shooter games simulating the experience of war, to fantasy role playing and sports games, there are sufficient video games to appeal to all audiences for varied reasons.

Table 4-1 depicts the top-selling video games in units and their genres in 2012. Three of the top leading games in 2012 were sports and racing games. Three were platform games.

Table 4-1: 2012 VIDEO GAME SALES			
GAME	YEAR	GENRE	UNITS (millions)
Wii Sports	2006	Sports	79.15
Super Mario Bros.	1985	Platform	40.24
Mario Kart Wii	2008	Racing	32.22
Pokémon Red/Green/ Blue Versions	1996	Role-playing	31.37
Tetris	1989	Puzzle	30.26
Wii Sports Resort	2006	Sports	29.78
Wii Play	2006	Misc.	28.58
New Super Mario Bros.	2006	Platform	28.38
Duck Hunt	1984	Shooter	28.31
New Super Mario Bros. Wii	2009	Platform	25.64

Wikipedia defines platform games as "a video game characterized by requiring the player to jump to and from suspended platforms or over obstacles (jumping puzzles). ... The most common unifying element to games in this video game genre is a jump button." [http://en.wikipedia.org/wiki/Platform_game]

The various versions of *Pokémon* involve role-playing, and the Tetris game is a puzzle. Three-dimensional video games because of their graphic superiority permit players an advanced level of participation. These games can be played by individual or multiple players. The latter games allow virtual strangers, separated by geography, to compete against each other in real time via the Internet.

Table 4-2 depicts *Call of Duty: Black Ops* as the number one bestselling video game title in 2010 around the globe in terms of earnings and units.

Table 4-2: 2010 VIDEO GAME SALES			
Title	*Producer*	*Formats*	*Earnings/ units*
Call of Duty: Black Ops	Activision Blizzard	Xbox 360 PS3, Wii, PC, DS	$719.9M/ 12.2 M units
Madden NFL 11	Electronic Arts	Xbox 360, PS3, Wii, PS2, PSP	$254.1M/ 4.7M units
Halo: Reach	Microsoft	Xbox 360	$276.4M/ 4.4 M units

[http://www.joystickdivision.com/2011/01/the_best-selling_video_games_o.php]. Call of Duty: Black Ops is part of a franchise of games based on U.S. military involvement in Iraq.

In addition to genre, video games differentiate based on player interface. The most popular types of interfaces include "first-person shooters" or "FPS", in which the player experiences the game as though inhabiting the game environment, and "third-person shooters" or "third-person role play", in which the player assumes the role of an animated character within the game. Popular titles of "first person shooter" games include the *Call of Duty*, *Assassin's Creed* and *Saints Row* series of games. *World of Warcraft* is a popular third-person multiple player game that allows numerous players to remotely engage in a role playing fantasy game in real time.

Casual games, such as those by Zynga, are less dependent on narrative than first-person shooter games. *Zynga Poker*, *FarmVille*, *CityVille* and *Mafia Wars*, for example, are less graphically sophisticated games that are played on Facebook, which reports how many people are currently playing the game when you sign on.

FarmVille, for example, lets players cultivate farms by plowing, planting and harvesting crops and trees. They also care for farm animals, by milking cows and collecting eggs from chickens. Players accumulate virtual "farm coins" by harvesting virtual crops and tending to virtual livestock. Players can interact with Facebook friends in real time while playing the game.

The New York Times reported in 2012 that the company was experiencing financial challenges. Because most Zynga games are free, the company "makes money from a small core of dedicated users who buy virtual goods like tractors in *FarmVille*," according to The Times. Between 2011 and 2012, however, "the average daily amount of money Zynga took in from these core users dropped 10 percent even as the overall number of users expanded." One commentator, Michael Gartenberg of Gartner, told The Times, "Increasing the number of players doesn't mean you're making money off them." He added, "At the end of the day, though, virtual goods might not be a viable business strategy. People eventually stop spending money in virtual goods and want to spend that money on real goods." [Steitfeld, The News Isn't Good.]

In terms of games for mobile devices, *Angry Birds*, in which a single player earns points and advances levels by knocking over green pigs in castles with small bird projectiles, is the top-selling game. The Sun newspaper in the United Kingdom estimated that it cost the Rovio firm in Finland £80,000 (approximately U.S. $126,000) to develop *Angry Birds* in 2009. Its popularity has resulted in Rovio being valued at £750 million (approximately U.S. $1.2 billion). [Price, A*ngry Management*] Since its inception, the original game and its successors have now been downloaded more than 700,000,000 times, making it the most successful app of all times.

Angry Birds has also been adapted into a television show, and theme park, which opened in Tampere, Finland. Rovio creative director Peter Vesterbacka said, "*Angry Birds* was our 52nd game." He said the company knew *Angry Birds* was going to be special when it was shown to the mother of one of the creators, she started playing the game and didn't return the phone. According to The Sun, Peter Vesterbacka has been dubbed the Steve Jobs of the app world for his "lofty ambitions for the brand's theme park expansion." He envisions having Angry Bird activity parks in cities all over the planet. [*Id.*]

As Rovio's experience indicates, producing games can take a great deal of effort with no guarantee of success. But when triumph does come, it can be huge.

B. VIDEO GAME PRODUCTION PROCESS

Similar to film and television, producing video games is a collaborative enterprise, requiring the aid of many individuals and groups to bring a final product to completion and find an audience. The process of creating a video game also consists of pre-production, production, and post-production periods.

1. VIDEO GAME PRE-PRODUCTION

According to the PBS documentary "The Video Game Revolution," creating a video game can be as complex as producing a Hollywood blockbuster, almost as expensive, and requires the skills and talents of a variety of professionals. [See http://www.pbs.org/kcts/videogamerevolution/inside/how/index.html] As is true with film, making a video game is a multi-media production that involves script writing, character development, casting voice talent, programming and commissioning music scores.

Sophisticated games begin with the pitching of a concept. Ideas for video games often come from other forms of entertainment, such as popular movies, sequels to existing games, or are drawn from current events. For example, as mentioned above, several "single-shooter" video games are based on the U.S. military's war in Iraq. Once developed, these video games are sometimes used in U.S. military training for simulated combat.

Once the basic game concept is decided, according to *The Video Game Revolution*, writers and artists create a storyboard, or visual representation of the narrative that serves as a reference for character designers and animators. [*Id.*] As the storyboard is being made, designers begin creating the characters—starting with an initial sketch that will be eventually scanned into a computer. A graphical overlay is applied to the figure, which defines the character's shape and gives the programmer control points with which to animate the figure. [*Id.*].

2. VIDEO GAME PRODUCTION

Once the characters are digitally animated, the environment must be created. This is done by programmers in a process called "texture mapping", which creates a three-dimensional environment that the characters inhabit. The essential structure, within which all of the game elements function but which is invisible to the player, is the code or computer programming language. Code controls every part of the game, and programmers usually use a custom developed code based on the C programming language. [*Id.*]

3. VIDEO GAME POST-PRODUCTION

Once produced, the post-production work begins: bug testing, reviewing, marketing, and finally, distribution. Testing normally includes at least two levels, "alpha" testing, in which the game is distributed in-house to identify major flaws, and then a second "beta test" round, which might include the public. [*Id.*]

During the later testing phase, a copy of the game is sent to the Entertainment Software Rating Board (ESRB), which assigns one of six ratings as depicted in Table 4-3: Video Game Ratings. The ESRB describes the content of these ratings on its website, http://www.esrb.org/ratings/index.jsp. Video games receiving the EC=Early Childhood rating contains material no parent would find inappropriate.

TABLE 4-3: VIDEO GAME RATINGS	
Rating	*Applicable Ages*
eC: early childhood	3 and older
E: everyone	6 and older
T: teen	13 and older
M: mature	17 and older
Ao: adults only	18/21 and older
RP	Rating pending

Those games rated E=Everyone may contain minimal violence, comic mischief, and/or mild language. *Angry Birds* is rated E for everyone. A rating of T=Teen may contain violent content, mild or strong language, and/or suggestive themes, whereas a M=Mature rating signals that the game includes mature sexual themes, more intense violence and/or strong language. *Assassins Creed*, *Call of Duty 4: Modern Warfare* and *Saints Creed*, for example are all rated M for the mature audience.

The platform can make a difference in the rating. Grand Theft Auto for the palm pilot is rated T with a content descriptor of "mild violence." Grand Theft Auto for a personal computer or play station is rated M with the content described as including animated blood and strong language.

Those games designated as AO=Adults Only include graphic depictions of sex and/or violence. The

RP=Rating Pending designation is placed on titles that have been submitted to the Entertainment Software Rating Board but are awaiting a final rating.

Once a video game is tested and rated, it must find an audience. According to the Entertainment Software Association, a 'blockbuster' video game, such as *Grandtheft Auto: Vice City* can cost between $3 to $5 million to produce, and an additional $10 million to promote and market. [*Id.*] Video games are promoted online, through the release of trailers, similar to those for film, and the release of demonstration versions or "demos". Demos are abbreviated versions of the game, free to download, which allow players to experience a sneak peak before deciding to spend $15 to $60 for the full game. [*Id.*]

C. VIDEO GAME LEGAL ISSUES

Once out in the market, video games encounter the same challenges as other entertainment media. They can be censored, have their copyrights infringed, their brand names used inappropriately, and their contracts broken. Indeed, infringing video game activities can be expensive. A federal judge awarded Blizzard Entertainment $3,052,339 in disgorged profits, $85,478,600 in statutory damages, and $63,600 in attorneys' fees after evidence established that 427,393 users downloaded *World of Warcraft* from the Scapegaming website. [Blizzard Entertainment, Inc. v. Reeves, 2010 WL 4054095

(C.D.Cal.,2010)]. Several legal issues are discussed in the following chapters.

CHAPTER 5

CENSORSHIP

Censorship in the entertainment industry takes many forms as individuals and governments seek to prohibit public exposure to material deemed politically, sexually, or violently offensive. Governments have blacklisted entertainers accused of supporting Communism and enacted mandatory and voluntary ratings codes. Throughout history, individuals and groups have banned and burned books, boycotted films and television programs, and labeled music as containing offensive, brutal lyrics. More recently, groups have targeted interactive games and the Internet for containing distasteful material. For their pains to eliminate the repulsive from public view, censoring groups have often just brought the items and their creators more attention or revenue, or both.

Consider the following three examples.

Before its scheduled release date on February 25, 2004, Mel Gibson's *The Passion of The Christ* became the subject of boycott calls from individuals who thought the film anti-Semitic and harsh toward Jews. *The Passion of The Christ*, which cost $25 million to make, earned $23.6 million on its opening day and $295.3 million during its first 26 days at the box office, making it the highest grossing R-rated film in history. Within 145 days, *The Passion*

of The Christ grossed $370,257,518 in the United
States and over $600 million worldwide.

Similarly, African-American leaders called for a
boycott of *Barbershop* because of one character's ir-
reverent comments toward famed civil rights leaders Rosa Parks, Dr. Martin Luther King Jr., and the
Reverend Jesse Jackson. After *Barbershop* grossed
$75.8 million in 2002, the producers released *Bar-
bershop 2: Back in Business* in 2004. With no boycott urged, the second one took in less revenue
($65,111,277) than the first.

In May 2004, The Walt Disney Corporation
blocked its subsidiary Miramax from distributing
the Michael Moore documentary *Fahrenheit 9/11*
because it harshly criticized President Bush during
an election year. *Fahrenheit 9/11* linked President
Bush to prominent Saudi Arabians, including the
family of Osama bin Laden. It criticized the President's actions before and after the 11 September
2001 terrorist attacks. Although Disney and
Miramax had a contractual agreement that allowed
Disney to prevent Miramax from distributing films
under certain circumstances, such as an excessive
budget or an NC-17 rating, Miramax claimed that
neither applied to *Fahrenheit 9/11*.

Disney acknowledged that it was apprehensive
that the film might endanger tax breaks for its
theme parks, hotels and other ventures in Florida,
where President Bush's brother, Jeb, served as gov-

ernor at the time. Miramax bought back Disney's share and contracted with Lion's Gate and IFC to distribute the film. Released on 25 June 2004, *Fahrenheit 9/11* became the weekend's #1 film, earning $93,984,261 during its first 26 days and becoming the first documentary to gross over $100 million domestically and $250 million worldwide. With no boycott, Moore's *Capitalism: A Love Story* took in only $14 million during its box office run.

Disney and the Weinstein brothers, the founders of Miramax, subsequently parted company. Disney kept the Miramax name and film library. The Weinstein brothers established the Weinstein Company to continue making movies.

These three film examples are merely the tip of the censorship iceberg. This chapter first discusses the obscenity tests that common law courts have developed over the last two centuries and then the specific efforts to ban books, films, music, and television programs from public view or rate their content.

A. OBSCENITY TESTS

In case of *Regina v. Hicklin,* (1867-68) L.R. 3 Q.B. 360 (April 29, 1868), a British court declared a pamphlet called "The Confessional Unmasked, shewing the depravity of the Romish priesthood, the iniquity of the Confessional, and the questions put to females in confession" to be obscene, an offence against the law of the land. The *Hicklin* court asked, "whether the tendency of the matter charged as obscenity is to deprave and corrupt those whose minds are open to such immoral influences, and into whose hands a publication of this sort may fall?"

In applying its test to the "The Confessional Unmasked," the *Hicklin* court declared that it would suggest to the young and old "thoughts of a most impure and libidinous character[,] ... thoughts and desires which otherwise would have not occurred to their minds."

In 1957, the United States Supreme Court rejected the *Hicklin* test as too restrictive of the freedoms of speech and press. In *Roth v. United States*, 354 U.S. 476 (1957), the Supreme Court declared that obscenity should not be judged by "the effect of isolated passages upon the most susceptible persons" because this "might well encompass material legitimately treating with sex."

Samuel Roth was convicted under a federal obscenity statute for mailing obscene circulars, advertising, and a book. The Supreme Court upheld Roth's conviction under the federal obscenity statute, which declared, "Every obscene, lewd, lascivious, or filthy book, pamphlet, picture, paper, letter, writing, print, or other publication of an indecent character ... [i]s declared to be nonmailable matter and shall not be conveyed in the mails or delivered from any post office or by any letter carrier."

Sixteen years later, the Supreme Court affirmed Roth's holding that "obscene material is not protected by the First Amendment, and pronounced a comprehensive obscenity test in *Miller v. California*, 413 U.S. 15 (1973). The *Miller* Court requires a trier of fact to consider:

(a) whether 'the average person, applying contemporary community standards' would find the work, taken as a whole, appeals to the prurient interest;

(b) whether the work depicts or describes, in a patently offensive way, sexual conduct specifically defined by the applicable state law; and

(c) whether the work, taken as a whole, lacks serious literary, artistic, political, or scientific value.

Marvin Miller was convicted under a California obscenity statute after mailing brochures advertising "four books entitled 'Intercourse,' 'Man-Woman,' 'Sex Orgies Illustrated,' and 'An Illustrated History of Pornography', and a film entitled 'Marital Intercourse'" to a California restaurant. The manager of the restaurant and his mother opened the envelope.

The Supreme Court declared that "[s]ex and nudity may not be exploited without limit by films or pictures exhibited or sold in places of public accommodation any more than live sex and nudity can be exhibited or sold without limit in such public places." It noted, nevertheless, that medical books may contain graphic illustrations and descriptions of human anatomy, but would not be deemed obscene. Miller's conviction was vacated and remanded for further proceedings consistent with the new test.

In *Pope v. Illinois*, 481 U.S. 497 (1987), the Supreme Court addressed the third prong of the *Miller* test and said, "The proper inquiry is not whether an ordinary member of any given community would find serious literary, artistic, political, or scientific value in allegedly obscene material, but whether a reasonable person would find such value in the material taken as a whole."

These obscenity tests have been applied to numerous entertainment materials as individuals or groups have sought to ban books, films, music, video games, and television programs as obscene. The film, music, television, Internet, and video game industries have responded with self-regulation. They have all enacted voluntary ratings that alert potential purchasers or viewers that the certain material may give offense.

B. FILM CENSORSHIP

The film industry has been faced with efforts to censor movies for their political, sexual, and violent content. After World War II, filmmakers became subjected to political censorship. During the 1960s, states sought to censor certain films by imposing ratings codes. Beginning in the 1970s and continuing today, the Motion Picture Association of America, in an attempt to self-regulate, adopted rating categories (X, R, PG, and G) to give viewers an indication of what to expect in terms of content. Each of these periods will be discussed herein, as well as more modern efforts to hold the media accountable when individuals emulate violent or tortious behavior that leads to the death of, or causes harm to, other innocent civilians.

1. THE MCCARTHY ERA

In 1938, the House of Representatives established its Committee on Un-American Activities. With the rise of the Cold War following World War II, this Committee announced a wide-ranging program to investigate Communist influences in Hollywood in 1947.

Congressional leaders, led by Wisconsin Senator Joseph McCarthy, became concerned that Communists had infiltrated the Hollywood film industry. As a result, a multitude of screenwriters, directors, and actors were blacklisted as suspected members of the Communist Party, and had their careers nearly destroyed or ruined. Screenwriter Lillian Hellman, for example, wrote four films before being blacklisted in 1952. Subsequently, she penned only one film, *The Chase*, which starred Marlon Brando, Robert Redford, and Jane Fonda. It premiered in 1966.

When screenwriters John Howard Lawson and Dalton Trumbo appeared before the House Committee on Un-American Activities, they refused, as did several other filmmakers, to answer whether they had been or were members of the Screen Actors Guild and of the Communist Party. They were subsequently convicted under 2 U.S.C.A. § 192, which makes it a misdemeanor to refuse to answer the questions of a Congressional Committee. They argued on appeal in *Lawson v. United States*, 176 F.2d 49 (D.C. Cir. 1949), that the Bill of Rights protects citizens from being compelled to disclose their private beliefs and associations.

The District of Columbia Court of Appeals, however, disagreed with Lawson's and Trumbo's assertions and affirmed their convictions. The court expressly held "that the House Committee on Un-American Activities, or a properly appointed subcommittee thereof, has the power to inquire whether a witness subpoenaed by it is or is not a member of the Communist Party or a believer in communism and that this power carries with it necessarily the power to effect criminal punishment for failure or refusal to answer that question under 2 U.S.C.A. § 192." The court held that the committee's power also included the right to inquire into membership in the Screen Actors Guild.

In 1962, eight screenwriters and four screen actors, all blacklisted, claimed that the Sherman Antitrust laws prohibited seven motion picture producing and distributing companies and two motion picture trade associations from inquiring into their political associations and beliefs. In *Young v. Motion*

Picture Association of America, 28 F.R.D. 2 (D.D.C. 1961), the filmmakers charged that the MPAA had circulated and published throughout the motion picture industry a "blacklist" containing the names of persons, including the plaintiffs, who were accused of Communist Party membership or affiliation.

Once the plaintiffs' names appeared on the blacklist, they claimed that defendants refused to distribute motion pictures utilizing their services, or refused to utilize their services except on a black market at greatly reduced prices. The plaintiffs also accused the defendants of maintaining an industry-wide clearance program that permitted the use of only those individuals whose names had been cleared.

Judge Walsh refused to declare that the activities of the defendants were *per se* unlawful under the Sherman Act. Walsh found that the defendants might have legitimate business interest in "(1) controlling the possible subversive Communist propaganda that the hiring of Communist Party members might introduce to the movie-going public, and (2) protecting their investment in the motion picture business from poor attendance or boycotting by the theatergoing public because of the employment therein of suspected members of the Communist Party." The case was affirmed in *Young v. Motion Picture Association of America,* 299 F.2d 119 (D.C.Cir. 1962).

Congress formally abolished the House Committee on Un-American Activities in 1974.

2. STATE CENSORSHIP ORDNANCES

During the 1960s, states began enacting ordinances requiring the film industry to apply for permits, submit all motion pictures for examination prior to their public exhibition, and pay license fees. When Time Film Corp., which owned the exclusive right to publicly exhibit *Don Juan* in Chicago, applied for its permit, it paid the license fee but refused to submit the film for examination. After the permit request was denied, TFC sued, claiming that the Chicago ordinance violated its First Amendment rights to free speech. The U.S. District Court dismissed the suit and the Court of Appeals affirmed.

In *Time Film Corp. v. City of Chicago*, 365 U.S. 43 (1961), the U.S. Supreme Court held that states and cities could require producers to submit their films in advance for a prior determination of whether they contained obscene material. The Supreme Court cited its holding in *Roth v. United States* that "obscenity is not within the area of constitutionally protected speech." The Supreme Court noted, however, that city officials do not have "the power to prevent the showing of any motion picture they deem unworthy of a license."

Nevertheless, when Ronald Freedman was convicted of exhibiting a film before submitting it to the board of censors, the Supreme Court overturned his conviction in *Freedman v. State of Maryland*, 380 U.S. 51 (1965), finding the Maryland statute too burdensome. When the case was argued in November 1964, only four states (Maryland, New York, Virginia, and Kansas) and four cities (Chicago, Detroit, Fort Worth, and Providence) had active censorship laws. Twenty-eight municipalities had inactive ordinances.

In his concurrence in the *Freedman* case, 380 U.S. at 62, Justice Douglas indicated the Supreme Court required movie censorship systems to contain at least three procedural safeguards if they are not to run afoul of the First Amendment: (1) the censor must have the burden of instituting judicial proceedings; (2) any restraint prior to judicial review can be imposed only briefly in order to preserve the status quo; and (3) a prompt judicial determination of obscenity must be assured. Justice Douglas also stated that the Chicago censorship ordinance, upheld in *Times Film Corp.*, would not survive these standards.

3. MPAA RATINGS CODES

The state censorship ordinances gave way to more stringent industry self-regulation in the late 1960s. The Motion Picture Association of America (or MPAA), a New York not-for-profit corporation, is composed of producers and distributors of motion pictures and television programs. According to Edward Jay Epstein, the trade organization is financed by Warner Bros., Fox, Universal, Disney, Sony, and

Paramount, with each studio providing about $10 million per year. [www.thehollywoodeconomist.blog spot.com.

Right after Jack Valenti, a former aide to President Lyndon Johnson, became the MPAA president in 1966, controversy arose around the use of the word "screw" and the phrase "hump the hostess," along with the display of nudity, in the film *Who's Afraid of Virginia Woolf?* To resolve this controversy, the MPAA banded together with other industry groups to create four ratings codes that would give parents advance cautionary warnings so they could make informed decisions about the movies their young children see. In 1968, the initial four categories were "G for General Audiences;" "M for mature audiences;" "R for restricted to Parents who must accompany children;" and "X for no one under 17 admitted." The "M" rating was later changed to "PG: Parental Guidance Suggested" because some parents regarded "M" as sterner than "R." Subsequently, the MPAA split the PG category into PG and PG-13 in 1984, and changed the X to NC-17 in 1990.

The MPAA website, www.mpaa.org, states that its Rating Board, composed of 8 to 13 members located in Los Angeles, applies the ratings in one of the following categories as depicted in Table 5-1. It does not rate movies on their quality or lack of quality, according to the website. Rather, the "basic mission of the ratings system is a simple one: to offer to parents some advance information about movies so that parents can decide what movies they want their children to see or not to see." [*Id.*]

TABLE 5-1: MPAA FILM RATINGS	
RATING	*APPLICABLE AUDIENCE*
G—General Audiences	All ages admitted.
PG—Parental Guidance Suggested	Some material may not be suitable for children.
PG-13—Parents Strongly Cautioned	Some material may be inappropriate for children under 13.
R—Restricted	Under 17 requires accompanying parent or adult guardian.
NC-17	No one under 17 admitted

The MPAA also rates movie trailers, which advertise coming attractions, as either approved for "all audiences" or "restricted audiences." If the trailer receives the latter tag, then it can only be advertised with feature films rated R or NC-17. According to director John Carlos Frey (*The Gatekeeper*), this makes a huge difference in efforts to advertise movies. Frey re-cut his trailer to eliminate a scene where guns are raised toward the audience after it received a "restricted audience" rating. [Author Interview with Frey.]

Producers, studios, and distributors must elect to submit their films to the Rating Board. If they chose to forgo a rating, they may market their films as not rated or in any way they prefer so long as "it is not confusing similar to the G, PG, PG-13, R, and NC-17. These ratings symbols are federally–registered certification marks of the MPAA and may not be self applied." [*Id.*]

Those producers, studios, and distributors who opt to submit their films for ratings and become unhappy with the results may appeal the ratings to the Rating Appeals Board, comprised of 14 to 18 men and women from industry organizations that govern the ratings systems. By a two-thirds vote, the Rating Appeals Board can overturn a Rating Board decision.

If the submitting individual or company remains unhappy with this result, they may protest to the public or appeal to the court system. When the Rating Appeals Board upheld the R rating given to *Fahrenheit 9/11*, Michael Moore encouraged "all teenagers to come see my movie, by any means necessary." He added, "If you need me to sneak you in, let me know." [Snyder, *MPAA going 'R' way on '9/11' rating.*]

Miramax Films Corp. challenged the X rating given to director Pedro Almodovar's *Tie Me Up! Tie Me Down!* in court, claiming the granting of the X rating was arbitrary and capricious conduct while requesting a judicially imposed R rating. The Rating Board unanimously accorded an X rating to the film because of two sexually explicit scenes and the visual depiction of sex acts. While Miramax and Almodovar were accorded an opportunity to delete or edit the objectionable scenes, they declined. They petitioned the Rating Appeal Board for a review, but it upheld the X rating.

In *Miramax Films Corp v. MPAA*, 560 N.Y.S. 2d 730 (1990), the New York Supreme Court declared that the rating system was "censorship from within the industry rather than imposed from without, but censorship nonetheless." It admonished that "the rating system's categories have been fashioned by the motion picture industry to create an illusion of concern for children, imposing censorship, yet all the while facilitating the marketing of exploitive and violent films with an industry seal of approval." The court, however, dismissed the petition and denied the requested relief to change the rating to an R because the court was not the appropriate vehicle to afford such relief.

In *Maljack Productions v. MPAA*, 52 F.3d 373 (D.C. Cir. 1995), an independent movie and video production company sued the MPAA because of the X rating given to *Henry: Portrait of a Serial Killer* for its violent content. Maljack, which elected to distribute the film as unrated, claimed that the picture was not as successful as it would have been had it received an R rating. Maljack alleged in its complaint that the MPAA discriminated against it and gave the *Henry* film an X rating because Maljack was not a MPAA member.

The District Court dismissed the complaint for failure to state a claim, but the Court of Appeals for the District of Columbia Circuit overturned the dismissal and remanded. The court said that if the MPAA had indeed given *Henry* an X rating because Maljack was not a member, then it breached its implied covenant of good faith and fair dealing.

While the X rating generated controversy, the R rating also led to lawsuits. In *Borger by Borger v. Bisciglia*, 888 F. Supp. 97 (E.D. Wis. 1995), a 16-year-old sued the Kenosha School District and its superintendent for refusing to allow *Schindler's List*, an R rated film, to be shown as part of his high school curriculum. The superintendent rejected several history teachers' requests to take their students to a local theatre to see *Schindler's List* because it was R rated. The school board's policy dictated that "no films having a rating of R, NC-17, or X shall be shown to students at any school."

The court in *Borger* noted that while "[s]tudents do not lose their First Amendment rights when they walk through the schoolhouse door," the School Board can use "the ratings system as a filter of films." In dismissing Borger's motions for summary judgment, the court further stated that the School Board established that the MPAA ratings are "a reasonable way of determining which movies are more likely to contain harsh language, nudity, and inappropriate material for high school students."

4. FILM VIOLENCE

Critics have often charged, as in the cases above, that the MPAA is more likely to censor for explicit sex than violence. The violent content of films has become even more of a concern as individuals have imitated certain films' dangerous acts. The have sometimes caused great bodily harm or even death to others, such as when such as when James E. Holmes shot up a Century 16 complex in Aurora, Colorado, as audience members watched the midnight premier of *The Dark Knight Rises* in 2012.

Holmes' bullets collided with 70 individuals, initially killing 12 of them. When he appeared for his arraignment, Holmes' hair was colored orange-red in the style of the Joker as depicted by actor Heath Ledger in *The Dark Knight* in 2008. After the tragic shooting, Warner Bros. Animation ordered a review of "Beware the Batman" to minimize the amount of weapon imagery deemed too realistic before its release on the Cartoon Network. [Wallenstein, Warner Bros. tones down 'Batman'] According to Variety, Warner Bros. also postponed the release of its film "Gangster Squad" for reshoots because of a scene depicting a shooting at a movie theater. [*Id.*]

In *Yakubowicz v. Paramount Pictures*, 536 N.E.2d. 1067 (Mass. S. Jud. Ct. 1989), William Yakubowicz sued Paramount Pictures and the Saxon Theatre Corporation, charging that they were responsible for the knifing death of their son. A Saxon Theater patron, Michael Barrett, watched

Paramount's film *The Warriors*, which depicts juvenile gang-related violence, before killing Martin Yakubowicz.

William Yakubowicz claimed that Paramount and Saxon Theater should be held liable for his son Martin's death on both negligence and First Amendment grounds. The court found that the defendants did not violate their duty of reasonable care and that the film was protected on First Amendment grounds. Yakubowicz raised the "incitement" exception, which applies to "speech which advocates the use of force or of law violation . . . where such advocacy is directed to inciting or producing imminent lawless action and is likely to incite or produce such action." [*Id.* at 631.] However, the court noted that speech does not lose its First Amendment protection merely because it has "a tendency to lead to violence." [*Id.*]

The Yakubowicz court found that the fictional film does not "at any point exhort, urge, entreat, solicit, or overtly advocate or encourage unlawful or violent activity on the part of viewers." [*Id.*] The court held that Paramount did not act unreasonably in producing, distributing and exhibiting the film, nor did Saxon Theater act unreasonably in exhibiting it. Since the killing took place several miles from the theater, Paramount did not fail to take reasonable steps to warn patrons and Saxon did not fail to exercise proper supervision. The court placed Barrett's killing of Yakubowicz squarely on Barrett's shoulders.

A film that generated even more concern for its violent content was *Natural Born Killers*. Sarah Edmondson and her boyfriend Benjamin Darrus watched *Natural Born Killers* over and over again the night before they went on a shooting spree, during which they shot Patsy Byers, rendering her a paraplegic, and murdered William Savage. In *Byers v. Edmondson*, 826 So. 2d 551 (La. Ct. App. 2002), Patsy Byers sued Edmondson along with Time Warner and Oliver Stone, the director of *Natural Born Killers*, for damages related to her injuries. The court granted the motion to dismiss the actions against Stone and Warner because it found *Natural Born Killers* to be protected speech.

Byers alleged that the film was not entitled to First Amendment protection because it was either inciteful or obscene, but the court disagreed. While the court acknowledged that *Natural Born Killers* was permeated with violent imagery, the violence was fictionalized and did not "order or command anyone to perform any concrete action immediately or at any specific time." The court also noted that Byers failed to allege that *Natural Born Killers* met the three *Miller* test criteria to be judged obscene. In *State v. Johnson*, 343 So.2d 705, 709-10 (La. 1977), the Louisiana Supreme Court noted that "The First Amendment does not permit a violence-based notion of obscenity."

C. TELEVISION CENSORSHIP

Should television networks be mandated to portray only those shows that do not offend the sensitivities of the American populace? Most people would say no, although many think there should be a warning system. Because of this concern, private and public institutions have adopted ratings to alert Americans as to the programming content appearing on their small screens.

For the most part, the broadcast industry self-regulates to keep indecent programming from appearing on the airwaves at inappropriate times. In 1996, Congress asked the industry to establish a voluntary ratings system for TV programs to alert parents about the material their children watch. The National Association of Broadcasters, the National Cable Television Association, and the Motion Picture Association of America collaborated to establish these six ratings codes, which appear on the screen during the first 15 seconds of each television program.

These ratings are depicted graphically in Table 2-1. The first three ratings are directed solely towards children. The TV-Y (All Children) designation means that the show is appropriate for all children. It is found only on children's shows. The TV-7 (Directed to Older Children) label is also only attached to children's shows. TV-7 indicates the show is most appropriate for children ages 7 and older. TV-G

(General Audience) marks the program as suitable to all ages, although it may not be a children's show.

TABLE 5-2: TELEVISION RATINGS	
TV RATING	*APPLICABLE AUDIENCE*
TV-Y	All Children
TV-7	Directed to Older Children
TV-G	General Audience
TV-PG	Parental Guidance Suggested
TV-14	Parents Strongly Cautioned
TV-MA	Mature Audience Only

The TV-PG (Parental Guidance Suggested) tag is similar to its film equivalent, PG. It recommends parents decide whether the material is suitable for younger children. TV-PG may also be accompanied by a V for violence, an S for sexual situations, an L for language, or a D for suggestive dialogue.

The final two ratings are TV-14 (Parents Strongly Cautioned) and TV-MA (Mature Audience Only). The first rating indicates a show that may be unsuitable for children under 14. The V, S, L, and D labels associated with TV-PG may also accompany TV-14. The rating TV-MA suggests a show is unsuitable for children under 17 because the program may contain explicit sexual content. A complete description of this ratings system is available through the Federal Communications Commission website, which is accessible at www.fcc.gov.

The TV Parental Guidelines Monitoring Board is composed of 24 members from the broadcast and cable television industries, the program production community, and the advocacy community. It scrutinizes the application of these ratings to make sure they are being applied accurately and consistently. Any parent or other member of the general public can protest a rating they believe to be misapplied.

To aid parents in applying these ratings codes within their homes, the Federal Communications Commission requires all television sets 13 inches or larger contain V-chip technology if manufactured after January 1, 2000. The V-chip allows parents to block their children from watching certain programming. Since the V-chip reads the ratings, parents can use a remote control to keep certain programs from appearing on their screens.

1. FCC INDECENCY REGULATIONS

The Federal Communications Commission's oversight of television extends to enforcing the federal law that forbids the broadcast of obscene material and limits the showing of indecent and profane programs. The FCC follows the *Miller* three-part definition of obscenity that is prohibited by the First Amendment. The FCC defines indecency as

> language or material that, in context, depicts or describes, in terms patently offensive as measured by contemporary community broadcast

standards for the broadcast medium, sexual or excretory organs or activities.

[http://www.fcc.gov/guides/obscenity-indecency-profanity-faq]
On this website, the FCC also defines profanity as language that:

> denote[s] certain of those personally reviling epithets naturally tending to provoke violent resentment or denoting language so grossly offensive to members of the public who actually hear it as to amount to a nuisance."

The First Amendment protects profane speech and indecent programming because they do not rise to the level of obscenity. Rather than completely banning indecent programming and profane speech from television and radio broadcasts, the FCC limits such material to the hours of 10:01 p.m. to 5:59 a.m. The FCC prohibits indecent programming and profane speech between the hours of 6:00 a.m. and 10:00 p.m.

Even with these limits, the rating system, and V-chip technology in place, the general public may be accidentally exposed to material they deem indecent during primetime. Several hundred thousand individuals complained bitterly to the FCC after Janet Jackson and Justin Timberlake performed a song and dance routine for the 1 February 2004 Super Bowl half-time show. At the end of the routine, Timberlake sang the lyrics "I gotta have you naked by the end of this song" as he tore off part of Janet Jackson's top and exposed her bejeweled right breast for almost two seconds.

The performance resulted in personal consequences for both singers and increased penalties for the networks. Janet Jackson was dropped from starring in an ABC television movie based on the life of Lena Horne after Horne refused to cooperate with the production as long as Janet Jackson remained in the role. [Van Gelder, *Art Briefing.*] Timberlake cancelled his commitment to co-host ABC's *Motown 45* special with Lionel Richie after a coalition of African-American organizations protested the Timberlake connection. [*Id.*] Further, the Senate voted to increase fines tenfold to $275,000 per indecency violation, up to a maximum of $3 million. [Reuters, *Senate Panel to Consider New Indecency Bill.*]

After the Senate bill passed, FCC chairman Michael Powell proposed fining Viacom, CBS's parent company, $275,000 a second for each of the two seconds Janet Jackson's breast appeared on television. The FCC fine only applied to the 16 TV stations directly owned and operated by Viacom. Fox Television Stations appealed the fine, and the Supreme Court held that the FCC violated networks' due process rights by failing to give them fair notice that, in contrast to prior policy, a fleeting expletive or a brief shot of nudity could be actionably indecent. The Supreme Court vacated and remanded the case for further action. *See FCC v. Fox Television Stations*, 132 S.Ct. 2307 (2012).

In 2004, the FCC also issued a record fine of $1.75 million against Clear Channel for indecency complaints against Howard Stern and other radio personalities. [Shiver, *2 seconds of breast could cost CBS $550,000*]

In an effort to address sexually oriented programming on cable television, Congress passed Section 505 of the Telecommunications Act of 1996. It required cable television operators who provide channels "primarily dedicated to sexually-oriented programming" either to "fully scramble or otherwise fully block" those channels or to limit their transmission to hours when children are unlikely to be viewing, such as between 10:00 p.m. and 6:00 a.m.

Although cable companies use scrambling in the regular course of business, scrambling can be imprecise, leading to "signal bleed." The Supreme Court observed in *United States v. Playboy Entertainment Group*, 529 U.S. 803, 806 (2000), that the purpose of § 505 was to shield children from hearing or seeing images resulting from signal bleed.

To comply with § 505, cable operators adopted a "time channeling" approach, in which they eliminated the transmission of targeted programming outside the safe harbor period. Playboy challenged § 505 as "unnecessarily restrictive content-based legislation violative of the First Amendment." [*Id.* at 807.]

The Supreme Court agreed, affirmed the District Court's prior ruling, and declared that § 505 violates the First Amendment. The Court noted that unlike broadcast networks, cable television systems had the capacity to block unwanted channels on a household-by-household basis. This "targeted blocking enables the Government to support parental authority without affecting the First Amendment interests of speakers and willing listeners." [*Id.* at 815.] Since target blocking is less restrictive than banning, the Court concluded, "the Government cannot ban speech if target blocking is a feasible and effective means of furthering its compelling interests." [*Id.*]

2. TELEVISION VIOLENCE

In addition to complaining to Congress and the FCC, individuals have sued network broadcasters for showing violence on television that they believed led to tortious or criminal behavior, or both. In *Graves v. Warner Brothers*, 253 Mich.App. 486, 656 N.W.2d 195 (Mich.App. 2002), the parents of Scott Amedure sued *The Jenny Jones Show*, charging that one of its programs led to the death of their son.

On a show about secret crushes, Scott Amedure was invited to reveal his previously undisclosed affections toward Jonathan Schmitz. Three days after the taping, Amedure left a sexually charged note on

Schmitz's front door. Schmitz bought a 12-gauge pump-action shotgun, drove to Amedure's home, and fatally shot him in the chest. Schmitz was convicted of second-degree murder and sentenced to a prison term of twenty-five to fifty years.

Amedure's parents sought to lay the blame for Schmitz's behavior on *The Jenny Jones Show*, its producer, and owner. Amedure's parents argued that by intentionally withholding from Schmitz that the true topic of the show was same-sex crushes, the defendants knew or should have known that their actions would incite violence, with the sole purpose of increasing their ratings. A jury found in favor of Amedure's parents and awarded $29,332,686 in damages.

On appeal, the judgment was reversed and vacated. The Michigan Court of Appeals determined that *The Jenny Jones Show* did not owe a duty to protect Amedure from harm caused by Schmitz. The court said, "[T]here is no legal duty obligating one person to aid or protect another.... Moreover, an individual has no duty to protect another from the criminal acts of a third party in the absence of a special relationship." [*Id.* at 493.] The court observed, "Criminal activity, by its deviant nature, is normally unforeseeable." [*Id.*]

The court decided that *The Jenny Jones Show* "had no duty to anticipate and prevent the act of murder committed by Schmitz three days after leaving defendant's studio and hundreds of miles away." [*Id.* at 497.] The court perceived the relationship between *The Jenny Jones Show* and Schmitz as one of business invitor to invitee, which ended after the taping on March 6, 1995, three days before the murder. On March 6, both men peacefully left the studio. [*Id.*]

The Jenny Jones Show never aired the March 6 episode. On June 21, 2004, the United States Supreme Court denied the parents' request for a writ of certiorari, thus ending their appeals.

In an incident from the 1970s, teenagers attacked another adolescent after observing a brutal scene on the NBC drama *Born Innocent*. In the television movie, four girls violently raped an adolescent girl with a plunger. In the real life incident, a nine-year-old girl was attacked on the beach.

Olivia N. sued NBC, claiming that the television show incited the violence against her. After reviewing the entire film, the trial judge determined that it did not advocate or encourage violent and depraved acts, and entered judgment for the defendants. In *Olivia N. v. NBC*, 74 Cal.App.3d 383, 141 Cal.Rptr. 511 (Cal.App. 1 Dist. 1977), the California Court of Appeals overturned the ruling and ordered the trial court to impanel a jury and proceed to trial.

On remand, Olivia N.'s counsel admitted that he couldn't prove incitement in his opening statement. This led the trial court to grant NBC's motion for a nonsuit. When the counsel appealed that decision, the California Court of Appeals affirmed the nonsuit in *Olivia N. v. NBC*, 126 Cal.App.3d 488, 178 Cal.Rptr. 888 (Cal.App. 1 Dist. 1981). NBC was thus able to stop a full trial on the merits of Olivia N.'s case.

D. MUSIC CENSORSHIP

This section discusses music ratings, music violence, and issues concerning community standards.

1. MUSIC RATINGS AND VIOLENCE

The music industry has the simplest ratings system of all. Either the producer or distributor will stamp the CD, LP or cassette with the designation:

"Parental advisory: explicit content."

This alert, however, is not sufficient to stop individuals from suing songwriters, singers, producers, and distributors over music believed to cause death.

In *McCollum v. CBS*, 202 Cal.App.3d 989, 249 Cal.Rptr. 187 (Cal.App. 2 Dist. 1988), the parents of John Daniel McCollum sued John "Ozzy" Osbourne, CBS Records, and other individuals and companies for composing, performing, producing, and distributing an album they alleged caused the death of their son. Among the songs John listened to the night before shooting himself in the temple was "Suicide Solution," with the lyrics "suicide is the only way out." He was found wearing headphones with the stereo still running. [*Id.* at 995.]

While John's parents alleged that it was foreseeable that Osbourne's music would influence peculiarly susceptible individuals to act in a manner destructive to their person or body, the court disagreed. The court concluded that the First Amendment protected Osbourne's music. In order to constitute culpable incitement, the court said Osbourne's music must be (1) directed and intended toward the goal of bringing about the imminent suicide of listeners and (2) likely to produce such a result. After finding that Osbourne's music met neither test, the court ruled that Osbourne and the other defendants bore no responsibility for John's suicide. [*Id.* at 1000-1001.]

In a 1990 interview available at http://rockonthe net.com/artists-o/ozzyosbourne.htm, Osbourne said, "If I wrote music for people who shot themselves after listening to my music, I wouldn't have much of a following." Nevertheless, Osbourne was sued again when Michael Jeffery Waller committed suicide after repeatedly listening to Osbourne's music. Waller's parents claimed the song "Suicide Solution" contained subliminal messages. The District Court ruled in *Waller v. Osbourne*, 763 F.Supp. 1144 (M.D.Ga. 1991), that Osbourne's First Amendment rights protected him from being held liable for claims of negligence, nuisance, fraud, and invasion of privacy. The Court of Appeals affirmed in *Waller v. Osbourne*, 958 F.2d 1084 (11th Cir. 1992).

In a different case, *Davidson v. Time Warner*, 1997 WL 405907 (S.D. Tex. 1997), Ronald Howard attempted to avoid the death penalty by claiming that listening to *2Pacalypse Now* caused him to shoot Officer Bill Davidson. One song on the album contained the following lyrics: "My brain locks, my Glock's like a f--kin mop; The more I shot, the more mothaf--ka's dropped; And even cops got shot when they rolled up." The jury apparently did not believe that these lyrics were enough to cause someone to shoot a police officer because it sentenced Howard to death.

When the relatives of Officer Davidson sued Tupac Shakur, Interscope Records, and Time Warner, they also claimed the album was responsible for the officer's death. The court disagreed, finding the album protected by the First Amendment. The court observed that while Shakur's words offend, they "are not 'by their very nature' likely to cause violence." Further, the court said, "no reasonable jury could conclude that persons would reflexively lash out because of the language of Shakur's recording." Moreover, "Ronald Howard did not reflexively react based on Shakur's offensive speech." [*Id.* at *18.]

Even when the music industry is charged with targeting minors with violent lyrics, courts have been reluctant to allow lawsuits to proceed on First

Amendment grounds. Fifteen-year old Elyse Pahler was kidnapped, tortured, raped, and murdered by three adolescent males who said they planned to emulate the band Slayer's song lyrics. When her parents sued the band and their recording and distributing companies, the court dismissed the case of *Pahler v. Slayer*, 2001 WL 1736476 (Cal. Superior Ct 2001). The court stated, "Unless the products are harmful to children or incite imminent unlawful conduct, no statute or regulation specifically prohibits or restricts the sale or distribution of Slayer albums to children." [*Id.* at *2.]

These cases indicate the importance of parents paying attention to the music rating "Parental advisory: explicit content." Parents should preview the music before permitting their children to purchase particular albums. If the child already owns a substantial collection through gifts or purchase, parents should monitor all acquisitions to determine if their kids are listening to violently or sexually charged lyrics and confiscate the music if necessary.

Suing the music industry after parents have lost their children does not bring back offspring. Further, parents may receive no compensation if they are unable to maintain their lawsuit. These cases demonstrate that the First Amendment is a large hurdle to clear. Short of the music actually giving explicit instructions on how to commit murder, suicide, or other violent crimes, [*Rice v. Paladin Enterprises*, 128 F.3d 233 (4th Cir. 1997)], the parents may have no recourse against the industry. Policing the industry begins at home.

2. COMMUNITY STANDARDS

The first prong of the *Miller* test requires a court to apply contemporary community standards to determine whether the work, taken as a whole, appeals to prurient interest as part of determining whether it is obscene. At least one judge considered himself as a fitting representative of his community.

When a Broward county sheriff discouraged record stores from selling the 2 Live Crew album "As Nasty as They Wanna Be," the musicians filed suit to enjoin the sheriff from interfering with record sales. The District Court granted the injunction, but declared the song obscene in *Skyywalker Records, Inc. v. Navarro*, 739 F.Supp. 578 (S.D.Fla. 1990).

The Court of Appeals in *Luke Records v. Navarro*, 960 F.2d 134, 136 (11th Cir. 1992), found two problems with the case. First, the court noted the sheriff put in no evidence other than the "As Nasty As They Wanna Be" tape recording, while the plaintiffs put in substantial evidence concerning the three-part Miller test.

Second, the Court of Appeals expressed concern that the district judge tried the case without a jury, relying on his own expertise. The district judge determined that the relevant community was Broward, Dade, and Palm Beach Counties. He stated that he had resided in Broward County since 1958, had practiced law and been a judge in the community, and had personal knowledge of this area's demographics, culture, economics, and politics. He had attended public functions and events in all three counties and was aware of the community's concerns as reported in the media and by word of mouth. The judge also mentioned his personal knowledge of the nature of obscenity in the community obtained from viewing dozens, if not hundreds, of allegedly obscene films and other publications seized by law enforcement. [*Id.* at 137.]

The Court of Appeals said that it is difficult to review the value judgments of the judge as fact-finder. In reversing, the Court of Appeals stated that the sheriff failed to meet his burden of proving that the recording was obscene because he submitted no evidence to contradict the testimony that the work had artistic value. The court concluded, "A work cannot be held obscene unless each element of the Miller test has been met. We reject the argument that simply by listening to this musical work, the judge could determine that it had no serious artistic value." [*Id.* at 137-138.]

E. VIDEO GAME CENSORSHIP

This section considers efforts to rate interactive video games played on GameBoy, Nintendo, Play Station, Xbox, and other systems. An Electronic Software Rating Board applies the five ratings depicted in Table 5-3 to interactive video games. Manufacturers voluntarily submit their games

As discussed in Chapter 4, the Electronic Software Rating Board assigns these designations based on a submitted tape and questionnaire. The Entertainment Software Association estimates that 76 percent of all games sold in 2010 were rated "E" for Everyone, "T" for Teen, or "E10+" for Everyone 10+. [http://www.theesa.com/facts/index.asp]

TABLE 5-3: VIDEO GAME RATINGS	
Rating	*Applicable Ages*
eC: early childhood	3 and older
E: everyone	6 and older
T: teen	13 and older
M: mature	17 and older
Ao: adults only	18/21 and older
RP	Rating pending

The interactive game industry also uses phrases such as "animated violence," "comic mischief," "strong language," and "mature sexual themes" to refer to its content. Bushman and Cantor report, "According to the Interactive Digital Software Association's Website (www.idsa.com) 71% of video game titles are rated E (everyone), 19% are rated T (teen), and 7% are rated M (mature)." [Bushman and Cantor, *Media Ratings for Violence and Sex.*] They also report that "Sixty-five percent of parents with children under the age of 18 say that computer and video games are a positive addition to their children's lives." [*Id.*] The Family Online Safety Institute [http://www.fosi.org/] is a lobbying group that seeks to make the online world safer for children and their families.

Some of the more popular games, such as *Grand Theft Auto* and its progeny, come with a MA rating. Law student Chris Mills says the game teaches players "how to run a criminal operation and that business is at the point of a gun." [Author Interview with Mills.] When playing this game, individuals identify with the lead character as they choose from a variety of weapons (guns, machetes, knives, and baseball bats) to slay police officers, prostitutes, and persons pursuing ordinary lives.

Saints Row, an even more violent game, is described by the Official Xbox Magazine as "an unapologetic cop-killing, prostitute-beating third-person action game that's certain to generate reaction from concerned parents and spot-seeking politicians." [Mahood, *Saints Row*.] According to the Official Xbox Magazine, *Saints Row* sets up the player "as a tough street thug who falls in with the 3rd Street Saints, one of four vicious gangs running [an] underground economy." This game permits players to rise through the gang hierarchy, and increase their bankroll and intra-gang respect level by pulling off successful robberies, murders, and illegal activities. [*Id.*]

Seeking to protect children from exposure to game-depicted violence, several cities have passed ordinances that ban the sale of violent video games in their environs. However, the video game industry has successfully sued cities to keep them from enforcing the statutes.

The Interactive Digital Association sued St. Louis County [329 F.3d 954 (8th Cir. 2003)] to enjoin enforcement of an ordinance making it unlawful for any person to knowingly sell, rent or make available graphically violent video games to minors. The Court of Appeals held that the ordinance violated the First Amendment because video games are a protected form of speech. In a similar suit [American Amusement Machine Ass'n v. Kendrick, 244 F.3d 572 (7th Cir. 2001)], the Seventh Circuit Court of Appeals issued a preliminary injunction prohibiting Indianapolis from enforcing an ordinance banning the sale of video games. The Court of Appeals determined that Indianapolis had failed to show compelling grounds for restricting access to video games notwithstanding their literary character and the unrealistic appearance of their graphic violence.

Similarly, District Courts refused to enforce a Louisiana statute [The Coup Entertainment Software Ass'n v. Foti, 451 F.Supp.2d 823 (M.D.La. 2006)], an Illinois statute [Entertainment Software Ass'n v. Blagojevich, 404 F.Supp.2d 1051 (N.D.Ill. 2005)], and a Minnesota statute [Entertainment

Software Ass'n v. Hatch, 443 F.Supp.2d 1065 (D.Minn. 2006)], among many others. The Minnesota statute prohibited individuals under 17 years of age from renting or purchasing violent video games.

Although outright prohibitions against the selling of video games have run afoul of the First Amendment, one group successfully sought the removal of particular language. Take-Two Interactive Inc. removed the phrase "Kill the Haitians" from *Grand Theft Auto* after the Haitian American Coalition of Palm Beach Co. sued. [Baldas, *Video Game Industry Explodes with Legal, Regulatory Issues.*]

In *Brown v. Entertainment Merchants Ass'n* 131 S.Ct. 2729 (2011), the United States Supreme Court (in a 7-2 decision) struck down California's 2005 law banning the sale of violent video games to children without parental supervision. The Court ruled that video games were protected under the First Amendment, and thus California's ban of sales to minors was unconstitutional. In his majority opinion, Justice Scalia reasoned that since children's fairy tales and classic literature contain violence and gore, violent video game content is subject to the same First Amendment protection. To his dissent, Justice Breyer attached Appendix A listing 115 journal articles supporting the hypothesis that violent video games are harmful and Appendix B listing 34 journal articles rejecting the hypothesis.

Some individuals, like Norwegian Anders Behring Breivik, have murdered others after playing violent video games. Breivik killed 77 people in 2011. He said he played *Call of Duty: Modern Warfare 2* to practice shooting. On August 24, 2012, Breivik was sentenced to 21 years in prison. He did not appeal.

In the United States, several victims whose perpetrators practiced on video games before committing their crimes subsequently sued the manufacturers, claiming that their products incited the violence against them. For example, a lawsuit in Tennessee claimed that a man was allegedly killed by two teenagers who said they were inspired by the video game *Grand Theft Auto III*. [*Id.*] Parents of children murdered in Kentucky alleged that violent video games and other media trained a killer to point and shoot a gun. [James v. Meow Media, 90 F.Supp.2d 798 (W.D.Ky. 2000).] The District Court granted the defendants' motion to dismiss because they owed no legal duty of care since the killer's actions were unforeseeable. The Sixth Circuit affirmed. [James v. Meow Media, 300 F.3d 683 (6th Cir. 2002).]

Similarly, the District Court dismissed an action by survivors of a teacher who was shot and killed by two students in the shooting spree at Columbine High School. [Sanders v. Acclaim Entertainment, 188 F.Supp.2d 1264 (D.Colo. 2002)]. Again, the District Court found the defendants owed no duty of care to the shooting spree victim. It also noted that the ideas and expressive content contained in video games are not products contemplated by strict liability doctrines, and they are protected by the First Amendment.

The legal action of a Connecticut mother against Midway Games over the death of her son was also dismissed. The son's friend, who allegedly became addicted to and obsessed with a game, fatally stabbed him. In *Wilson v. Midway Games, Inc.*, 198 F.Supp.2d 167, 182 (D.Conn. 2002), the District Court found the First Amendment a complete bar to Wilson's negligent and intentional infliction of emotional distress claims against Midway.

Although a newer form of entertainment than films, television, and music, interactive video games are equally protected by the First Amendment. Cities are finding their ordinances restricting the sale of video games to minors are running afoul of the First Amendment. Parents experience difficulty in maintaining their suits charging that video games contributed to the death of their children.

F. INTERNET CENSORSHIP

It seems that catching Internet predators has become a national pastime. NBC routinely runs *Dateline* specials called "To Catch a Predator." These shows feature men caught in a sting after they venture forth to meet the 13-year-old girl or boy they thought they had been conversing with. In some instances, the men sent pictures of their private parts via the Internet. The men come from many communities and hold different types of jobs, including those of rabbi, priest, doctor, teacher, and student. When caught, they cry, deny, look horrified, and offer to go undercover to help police catch "real" predators.

Dateline NBC: To Catch a Predator has caused NBC to be sued on numerous occasions. In *Tiwari v. NBC Universal,* 2011 WL 5059505 (N.D.Cal. Oct. 25, 2011), Anuwag Tiwari alleged that he was lured to a sting house set up by NBC by a Perverted Justice Foundation decoy in August 2006, where he was surprised and confronted by NBC news reporter Chris Hansen and NBC cameras. He was arrested, charged initially with two felony criminal charges, later reduced to a misdemeanor, and convicted. On the first business day after the show aired, he was placed on administrative leave by his employer and forced to resign shortly thereafter.

The episode featuring Tiwari was rebroadcast in 2007, 2008, 2009, and 2010. In the October 2010 telecast, the epilogue stated Tiwari had been convicted of attempted lewd and lascivious acts with a child, which is a felony under California Law. Since he was convicted only of a misdemeanor, Tiwari sued for defamation, intentional infliction of emotional distress, and for violating several other rights. The court dismissed the defamation claim, finding that the epilogue when viewed in context was substantially true, but denied NBC's efforts to dismiss Tiwari's claim for intentional infliction of emotional distress.

In another case, *Armstrong v. NBC Universal*, 2011 WL 2193379 (W.D.Ky. June 6, 2011), a district court allowed a plaintiff's state law claims for invasion of privacy, intentional infliction of emotional distress, and negligence to proceed for further development. Armstrong claimed he was lured into a sting house in Bowling Green, Kentucky by a decoy claiming to be an underage female, and that the filming and broadcast of the incident caused him substantial mental anguish.

Oprah Winfrey hosted on her show a boy who began producing Internet porn in his bedroom through the use of a webcam. The boy, who initially told his story to the New York Times, repeated how men paid him using their credit cards to perform certain acts for them. They also sent gifts to his home. One man sent an airline ticket. When they met, he raped the boy. These incidents indicate that many dangers lurk on the Internet for unsuspecting children and their parents.

The Internet Content Rating Association was established as an independent organization to regulate the Internet. It claimed to empower parents to make informed decisions about electronic media by openly and objectively labeling the Internet's content. The ICRA website, www.icra.org, indicates that it has ceased existence, and refers individuals to the Family Online Safety Institute. FOSA, www.fosi.org, describes itself as an international, non-profit organization which works to make the online world safer for kids and their families.

Congress has also passed several laws that criminalized certain Internet content. The Communications Decency Act of 1996, 47 U.S.C. § 223, was declared unconstitutional by the Supreme Court in the case of *Reno v. ACLU*, 521 U.S. 844 (1997). The Supreme Court found the CDA unconstitutional because it was not narrowly tailored to serve a compelling government interest and less restrictive alternatives were available. [*Id.*]. Congress subsequently passed the Child Online Protection Act, 47 U.S.C. § 231, to protect minors from exposure to sexually explicit materials on the Internet. COPA imposes criminal penalties of a $50,000 fine and six months in prison for knowingly posting content harmful to minors on the Web for commercial purposes.

In reviewing a challenge to COPA, the Supreme Court concluded in *Ashcroft v. ACLU*, 542 U.S. 656 (2004), that least restrictive alternatives, such as blocking and filtering software, may be more effective than COPA. It affirmed the Court of Appeals decision that the District Court did not abuse its discretion by entering a preliminary injunction against the statute since it likely violated the First Amendment.

Nevertheless, Internet content providers who sell material deemed obscene under the *Miller* test may still be held liable for their actions. In *United States v. Ragsdale*, 426 F.3d 765 (5th Cir. 2005), the Fifth Circuit Court of Appeals upheld the conviction of a husband and wife who sold two videos deemed obscene through the Web. Garry Ragsdale, a Dallas police officer, and his wife Tamara offered "Brutally Raped 5" and "Real Rape 1" on their (now defunct) website www.gelschlecht.com. The tapes depicted sodomy, torture, and other violent acts. While the couple argued the tapes were not obscene and proffered expert testimony that the videos possessed scientific value to buttress their claim, the jury determined the videos obscene and convicted them. They were sentenced to jail time and fined. Mr. Ragsdale was fired from his job for conduct unbecoming a police officer. [*Id.* at 769.] The Court of Appeals affirmed the conviction.

Although the Internet seems to provide a veil of privacy when the individual gains access from their home or office, it does not. What people say, send, sell, and purchase may be seen by others. Parents must carefully monitor their children's viewing habits to limit access to harmful material. They can do so by employing the filters and blocking software mentioned in *Ashcroft v. ACLU*.

While ratings might be considered a form of voluntary censorship, they provide important information to parents. The ultimate goal is to guide parents in making decisions about the content of the entertainment their children experience. The entertainment industry is putting the onus on parents to be the final determinant of what entertainment forms their children see, listen to, surf, and play.

When surveyed by the Kaiser Foundation, parents were asked to report on their reaction to the various industry ratings. [Bushman and Cantor, *Media Ratings for Violence and Sex*.] Fifty-three percent of parents found movie ratings very useful and 40% classified them as useful. For television, 48% found the television ratings very useful, and 44% said they were useful. For music, 52% of parents found the single rating very useful and 40% somewhat useful. Interactive games received a similar reaction, with 52% finding the ratings very useful and 41% finding them somewhat useful. This indicates that the overwhelming majority of parents find industry ratings helpful.

CHAPTER 6
INTELLECTUAL PROPERTY

The entertainment industry depends on the law of intellectual property to shield its ideas, copyrights, trademarks, trade secrets, and patents from theft. This chapter focuses on the legal protection of ideas and fully realized products like films, books, video games, television shows, and albums or compact disks. Talent may capitalize on their intellectual property rights in a myriad of ways.

The Law of Ideas protects story snippets that become the source of films and television shows. Copyright law protects the expression of these ideas, as in a fully realized motion picture version of *Romeo and Juliet*, not just the idea of presenting a version of Shakespeare's play on the silver screen.

Trademarks are symbols or words that are used to designate a particular product, such as "R-Restricted." The Motion Picture Association of America (MPAA) uses this trademark to rate movies for the general public. Even the name of a film or television show may be trademarked if it is going to be applied to merchandise and sold in the marketplace. Some action films, such as *Batman*, may ultimately generate more revenue from selling merchandise than movie tickets.

Patent protection was used initially in the entertainment industry to protect camera, film, music, and television equipment and other innovations in merchandising. Companies obtain patents on the machines they create to display or perform the entertainment products. The general requirements to obtain a patent will be discussed below.

This chapter discusses the various components of intellectual property law and how they apply to the entertainment business.

A. THE LAW OF IDEAS

Ideas are the livelihood of the entertainment industry because the difference between one star-crossed lover story and another can be millions of dollars. In the film industry, for example, ideas are either pitched orally or submitted in a written treatment, which is a short summary of the story, its plotlines, and other important details.

Ideas are often presented as an intersection between two well-known films, such as "*Star Wars* meets *Romeo and Juliet*" or "*The Graduate* meets *Lord of the Rings*." One producer pitched former NBC executive Brandon Tartikoff the idea of "Noah's Ark: the Miniseries" as "*Roots* with animals." [Tartikoff, *Last Great Ride*, at 19.] Such shorthand gives the studio executive a sense of what the final product might look like.

Similarly, books and television shows may be presented as an idea. Authors often send agents and publishers a book proposal, which includes a one to two-page summary of their fictional or non-fictional manuscript. The proposal may also contain author background information, a statement of competitors, and an indication of where the book fits in the marketplace.

A writer, director, producer, show runner, or an ordinary person may present a television show idea to a studio executive with connections in the industry. Due to the limits to the 12-tone scale, it is rarer to pitch a music idea; thus, cases charging theft of musical ideas are uncommon compared to those filed in the other components of the entertainment industry. Plaintiffs are more likely to sue for violation of the copyright to the entire musical work, which will be discussed later in this chapter.

Legally, the Law of Ideas falls in the middle between no protection and full protection afforded by copyright, trademark, and patent law. The Law of Ideas restricts the free use of ideas by others and delays the benefit to society of having complementary access to the idea. It grants the creator the right to obtain compensation from those who benefit when he or she discloses an idea to another in confidence. The purpose of the compensation is to reward the creator.

While it may seem straightforward to say that those who generate ideas should be compensated for them, there can be a long legal road between the moment of disclosing the idea and the receipt of compensation. In *Desny v. Wilder*, 46 Cal.2d 715, 299 P.2d 257 (Cal. 1956), the court considered ideas to be "free as the air and as speech and senses, and as potent or weak, interesting or drab." Nevertheless, it observed that "there can be circumstances when neither air nor ideas may be acquired without cost."

Ideas may be protected by either express or implied contracts. With an express contract, the parties state in words the terms under which one will compensate the other for the disclosure and use of the idea. With an implied contract, it is the parties' conduct that indicates the contract exists. It thus becomes a question of fact as to whether the parties agreed that one would compensate the other for the use of an idea that was confidentially disclosed. Courts are left to decipher whether the parties intended to create a contract by either words or deeds.

In *Blaustein v. Burton*, 9 Cal.App.3d 161, 88 Cal.Rptr. 319 (Cal.App. 1970), the California Court of Appeals declared there were sufficient facts to imply that the defendants—Richard Burton, Elizabeth Taylor Burton and Franco Zeffirelli—had agreed to compensate the plaintiff Julian Blaustein for the use of his ideas. The court found that

Blaustein disclosed the following ideas to the Burtons, their agent, and to Franco Zeffirelli:

(a) to produce a film based on William Shakespeare's *The Taming of the Shrew*;

(b) to cast Richard Burton and Elizabeth Taylor Burton as the stars;

(c) to have Franco Zeffirelli, a stage director unknown in the United States who at that time had never directed a motion picture, direct the film;

(d) to eliminate the so-called "frame" (i.e., the play within a play device which Shakespeare employed), and begin the film with the main body of the story;

(e) to include in the film version the two key scenes (i.e., the wedding scene and the wedding night scene) which in Shakespeare's play occur offstage and are merely described by a character on stage; and

(f) to film the picture in Italy, in the actual Italian settings described by Shakespeare.

The court found that all these ideas were eventually incorporated into the film *The Taming of the Shrew*, which starred Elizabeth Taylor and Richard Burton, was directed by Franco Zeffirelli, and was filmed in Italy. The court reversed the grant of summary judgment to the defendants, holding that there was sufficient evidence to raise a triable issue of fact as to whether there was an implied contract to compensate Blaustein at the going rate of a producer for the use of his ideas.

The most difficult idea to protect is one based on copyrighted fictional characters. Timothy Burton Anderson wrote a thirty-one page treatment entitled "Rocky IV" after seeing the film *Rocky III*. Anderson met with a member of the MGM board of directors and MGM's president to discuss his treatment, which incorporated characters created by Sylvester Stallone and named Stallone as co-author. At the meeting, the MGM people had Anderson sign a release form, relieving MGM from liability for the use of the treatment, but supposedly promising him "big bucks" if they used his treatment.

After *Rocky IV* was made into a feature film, Anderson saw a screening and sued. In *Anderson v. Stallone*, 1989 WL 206431 (C.D. Cal. 1989), a United States District Court declared Anderson's treatment to be an infringing work not entitled to copyright protection. The court found Stallone's characters to be so highly delineated that they warranted copyright protection. Anderson had in essence created nothing of real value.

Individuals like Anderson who develop ideas in the entertainment industry must be careful about the conditions under which they disclose an idea. If the person blurts the idea out, he or she may lose all rights to the idea. To establish the conditions to create an implied contract, there must be some semblance of confidentiality in the relationship. As Anderson found out, the individual must have something worthy of protection. Even that may not be enough.

Anderson had signed a release agreement with MGM, which is a common practice in the entertainment industry as Hollywood production companies seek to protect themselves from charges of idea theft. Barry Spinello signed a similar release agreement to get Steven Spielberg's former production company, Amblin Entertainment, to look at his script, "Adrien and the Toy People." Amblin rejected Spinello's script by a letter dated April 24, 1990. In April 1992, *Daily Variety* announced that Amblin had purchased "Small Soldiers" from Gavin Scott, a British screenwriter.

Based solely on the *Daily Variety* article, Spinello concluded that "Small Soldiers" was based on his "Adrien and the Toy People" and sued. In *Spinello v. Amblin Entertainment*, 34 Cal.Rptr.2d 695 (Cal.App. 2 Dist. 1994), the court addressed the question of whether the release agreement, which required arbitration in the event of a dispute, was a contract of adhesion. The court concluded that it was not. It observed, "Spinello had the opportunity to negotiate and simply failed to do so." [*Id.* at 1397.] The court then found that the agreement was "patently fair to all parties" and remanded with directions to the trial court to compel arbitration. [*Id.* at 1399.]

For several decades up until the year 2000, New York state law required a property interest in an idea to make it protectible. To obtain that property interest, the idea must be novel, original, and unique. This concept was illustrated in *Murray v. NBC*, 844 F.2d 988 (2nd Cir. 1988), when Hwesu Murray sued NBC, claiming that it stole his idea for "Father's Day" when it created *The Cosby Show*. The Second Circuit held that Murray's idea lacked novelty and originality as Bill Cosby himself had discussed the idea of creating a Black television family in non-stereotypical roles. While the court acknowledged that Murray's idea could be considered a breakthrough, the idea represented the achievement of many Black Americans, including Bill Cosby himself. [*Id.*]

In *Nadel v. Play-By-Play Toys and Novelties, Inc.*, 208 F.3d 368 (2nd Cir. 2000), the Second Circuit held that New York law had abrogated *Murray v. NBC* by adopting a "novelty to the buyer" standard when it comes to protecting ideas by contract law. The court stated, "While an idea may be unoriginal or non-novel in a general sense, it may have substantial value to a particular buyer who is unaware of it and therefore willing to enter into a contract to acquire and exploit it." [*Id.* at 377.] The novelty to the buyer is much easier to prove than general novelty and originality, although the *Nadel* court was careful to point out that there may be some ideas that are "so unoriginal or lacking in novelty that its obviousness bespeaks widespread and public knowledge of the idea, and such knowledge is therefore imputed to the buyer." [*Id.* at 378.] The *Nadel* court concluded that a finding of novelty provides sufficient consideration to support contract claims.

The idea case that received the most notoriety was submitted by columnist Art Buchwald in the form of an eight-page treatment to Paramount Pictures. At the time, Paramount was seeking projects for Eddie Murphy. In early 1982, Buchwald prepared the treatment called "It's a Crude, Crude World" after observing a state visit by the Shah of Iran. He acknowledged that the title was inspired by "It's a Mad, Mad, Mad, Mad World."

Later in 1982, the eight-page treatment was reduced to three pages and the title was changed to "King for a Day." In 1983, Paramount registered the title with the Motion Picture Association of America. On March 22, 1983, the two parties entered into an agreement to have Paramount purchase the rights to Buchwald's story and concept. At the later trial, a Paramount executive testified that in his ten years at the company, they had never optioned a treatment, though they frequently optioned screenplays. [Buchwald v. Paramount Pictures, 13 U.S.P.Q.2d (BNA) 1497 (Cal. Superior Ct. 1990).]

In September and October 1983, Paramount extended the option by paying Buchwald $2500. On 16 October 1984, Paramount paid Buchwald an additional $10,000 to extend the option for a third time. The contract specified that if Paramount produced a feature-length theatrical motion picture based upon Buchwald's treatment, it would pay him a percentage of net profits.

Paramount hired Tad Murphy to write the screenplay, but it did not like his first draft. It then hired French writer and director Francis Veber to draft another screenplay and paid him $300,000. On March 29, 1985, Paramount decided to abandon "King for a Day" after investing over $418,000 to develop it. Buchwald optioned his "King for a Day" treatment to Warner Brothers in May 1986. It cancelled the project in January 1988 after discovering that Paramount was shooting *Coming to America* with Eddie Murphy.

Because Buchwald had an express contract with Paramount, he was in a superior position to sue Paramount than those plaintiffs who try to establish the existence of a quasi-contract based on oral agreements. For Buchwald, his case turned on whether Paramount had breached his contract by basing *Coming to America* on "King for a Day" and not compensating him. The court ruled that it had in the first phase of the trial. The next two phases of the trial, which addressed the nature of Buchwald's compensation, will be discussed later in Chapter 8 on Credits and Compensation.

B. COPYRIGHT

Congress is empowered under Article 1, Section 8, Clause 8 of the U.S. Constitution, "to Promote the Progress of Science and useful Arts, by securing for limited Times to Authors and Inventors the exclusive Right to their respective Writings and Discoveries." Congress first implemented this provision with the Copyright Act of 1790, which was modeled on England's Statute of Anne [8 Anne, c.19 (1709)]. By implementing the first copyright law, England produced a breakthrough against piracy that arose after the invention of the first printing press in 1450 by German Johannes Gutenberg and the second 26 years later by Englishman William Claxton.

Prior to the invention of these printing presses, monks and scriveners copied books by hand, averaging a book a year. With this slow process of producing books, authors worried little about others stealing their work. Indeed, the book that was reproduced most often was *The Bible*. The printing press revolutionized the manufacture of books, permitting mass reproduction and theft of original works.

The Statute of Anne protected authors' works for 14 years, after which they fell into the public domain. The U.S. Copyright Act of 1790 gave authors an initial 14 years of protection with the option to renew for an additional 14 years. Since that time, the duration of copyright has been extended numerous times to the current lifetime of the individual author or entertainer plus 70 years. In the case of joint owners, the copyright expires 70 years after the death of the last surviving author or entertainer. Corporate, anonymous, pseudonymous, and work for hire authors and entertainers enjoy protection for a flat 95 years.

While Congress initially protected only books, charts, and maps, it has expanded coverage of new forms of art and technology as they have been invented. Congress began protecting photographs in 1865, motion pictures in 1912, sound recordings in 1972, and computer disks in 1976.

1. COPYRIGHT REQUIREMENTS

There are three requirements for an item to be copyrightable. It must possess all the following:

1. Copyrightable subject matter

2. Fixation in a tangible medium of expression

3. Originated with or created by the author

Books, motion pictures, television shows, music, theatrical plays, and choreographic notes are listed among the items that qualify as copyrightable subject matter under the statute. They are fixed in tangible media of expression because they can be physically touched and handled. Theaters show movies from reels and buyers can purchase them in DVD or

VHS formats. Television shows are also played from tapes or digital format in studios, or downloaded from a satellite feed. Music can be physically rendered in sheet music, on tapes, or CDs. Video games are mounted in boxes and viewed through screens.

The necessity that a work originate with the author produces some disputes, particularly when an allegation of plagiarism surfaces. In bringing an action for theft, the plaintiff maintains that the defendant's work originated with the plaintiff. Originality can have a dual meaning when it comes to derivative works. The courts also ask whether the newcomer contributed anything new or novel to the first work.

In *Gracen v. Bradford Exchange*, 698 F.2d 300 (7th Cir. 1983), Jorie Gracen won a competition to paint figures from the MGM film *The Wizard of Oz*. When she didn't like the contract, she refused to sign it and later sued after Bradford Exchange copied her painting. The court ruled that her painting, derived from MGM movie stills, was not sufficiently original to warrant copyright protection. Because Gracen produced a derivative work, the court seemed to impose a higher originality standard, requiring substantial differences between the original and the derivative to make the latter copyrightable.

2. COPYRIGHT FORMALITIES

Copyright formalities include providing a notice that ownership is claimed in the work and registering the work with the Copyright Office, which is housed in the basement of the Library of Congress in Washington, D.C. To give notice to the world that an author claims copyright to a given item, he or she must include the following information on the work:

Copyright or ©, name, and year.

In books, this information is normally printed on the first inside page, known as the copyright page. For movies and television shows, the copyright credit is usually the last to be shown on the screen. For music, notice is written on the CD in the form of the letter p in a circle to indicate that a performance copyright is claimed. Visual artists may place the notice on the back of a painting or on the bottom of sculpture because they do not want to ruin the artistic presentation of their work. This notice form alerts the world that copyright protection is claimed.

Until 1989, the United States required that notice be placed on the work by the author or the work fell into the public domain, which permitted anyone to use the work without compensating the author. The author had a five-year period to cure the problem by republishing with notice. During this time, notice was completely optional in most other countries in the world.

After Congress passed the Berne Implementation Act amendments to the Copyright Law, which became effective on 1 March 1989, copyright notice became optional. Works are automatically protected whether or not authors place a notice on them. The U.S. law continues to provide incentives to encourage citizens to apply notice to their works. By applying a notice to the work, the copyright holder eliminates the innocent infringer defense, whereby someone claims they did not know that the work was subject to copyright protection. Notice makes it clear that copyright law covers the work.

Another copyright formality is to register the work with the U.S. Copyright Office. To do so, the author must fill out the copyright forms, pay the applicable fee, and deposit two copies of the best edition of the work. The forms to register the work can be found at www.copyright.gov.

The forms are set up by category. Form TX is used to register books, brochures, computer programs, games, poetry, and speeches. Form PA is appropriate for television shows and accompanying teleplays, motion pictures and screenplays, and musical works for motion pictures. Form SR is employed for all "fixation of a series of musical, spoken, or other sounds, but not including the sounds accompanying a motion picture or other audiovisual work."

While registering the work is optional, it remains a prerequisite before U.S. nationals can initiate a suit in U.S. courts. Under the Digital Millennium Copyright Act, signed into law by President Clinton on October 28, 1998, foreign works are exempt from this requirement.

Registration does, however, provide *prima facie* evidence that the author owns the work. Depositing two copies of the best edition of the work (i.e., two DVDs, CDs, or books) is also no longer a prerequisite to suit, but fines may be imposed if the Library of Congress requests the work and the author declines to send it. The fines are often the equivalent of what it would cost the Library of Congress to purchase two copies of the work.

3. COPYRIGHT OWNERSHIP

In most instances, the person who actually creates the work is considered the owner of the copyright, and will be the sole owner of the copyright. Copyright ownership can also be joint or a work for a hire.

a. Joint Works

Two or more individuals may collaborate to create a joint work. The copyright statute defines a "joint work" as a work prepared by two or more authors with the intention that their contributions be merged into inseparable or interdependent parts of a unitary whole.

For example, law professors Kevin McMunigal and Kate Bloch agreed to write a criminal law casebook together in 2000. They signed an agreement with Aspen Publishers in 2003, and the book was printed in 2005. Their relationship deteriorated and their Teacher's Manual came out in 2006 with his and her portions published as Part I and Part II. In 2007, Aspen offered them separate contracts if they agree to separate in writing. A Separation Agreement was prepared by McMunigal's Attorney. After Bloch refused to sign it, Aspen withdrew its contract offer to McMunigal who then sued Block.

McMunigal claimed that the casebook was a collective work and not a joint work, which would permit him to own his individual contributions. The Copyright Act, 17 U.S.C. §101, defines a collective work "as a periodical issue, anthology, or encyclopedia, in which a number of contributions, constituting separate and independent works in themselves, are assembled into a collective whole." By contrast, the Copyright Act, 17 U.S.C. §101 defines a "joint work" as "a work prepared by two or more authors with the intention that their contributions be merged into inseparable or interdependent parts of a unitary whole."

When considering how the casebook was created and published, the Court found it to be a joint work as a matter of law in *McMunigal v. Block*, 2010 WL 5399219 (N.D.Cal. Dec. 23, 2010). First, there was a contract evidencing McMunigal and Block's objective manifestation of their intent to be coauthors. The authors were jointly and severally liable for their obligations in the agreement. The authors received $4,000 to be used by them for expenses. Second, both parties supervised the casebook by exercising control. They may have independently selected and edited cases and written original text, but their intent was to merge the parts into a unitary whole. Third, the audience appeal can be attributed to both McMunigal and Block, and the share of each in its success cannot be separately appraised. The casebook lists the authors in alphabetical order. By contrast the teacher's manual identified plaintiff as the author of Part I and the defendant as the author of Part II.

A joint author issue can also arise when others feel their collaboration is worthy of author credit, but the copyright owner disagrees. The question then centers on the nature of the contributions and the intent of the parties.

In *Aalmuhammed v. Lee*, 202 F.3d 1227, 1233 (9th Cir. 2000), the court noted that in film, "Everyone from the producer and director to casting director, costumer, hairstylist, and 'best boy' gets listed in the movie credits because all of their creative contributions really do matter." Nevertheless, they are not all entitled to proclaim themselves as authors or coauthors of the film. In this instance, the court declared that "neither Aalmuhammed, nor Spike Lee, nor Warner Brothers, made any objective manifestations of an intent to be coauthors.... Aalmuhammed offered no evidence that he was the 'inventive or master mind' of the movie." [*Id.* at 1235.]

Film, television, music, games, theater and dance, and jointly authored books are collaborative processes with two or more creative people contributing to the final output. On any given film, for example, the following supply their talent: writers, actors, directors, producers, set designers, wardrobe designers, make-up artists, camera operators, editors, soundtrack composers, stunt performers, special effects supervisors, animators, and lighting designers. Music may be produced with the assistance of sound engineers and composers.

Without copyright ownership defined by contracts, customs, and statutes, anyone who contributed to the final output of an entertainment product could claim authorship of the film and inhibit its exploitation. The work for hire doctrine resolves problems concerning authorship and copyright ownership.

b. Work For Hire

Section 101 of the U.S. copyright statute defines a work made for hire as:

(1) a work prepared by an employee within the scope of his or her employment; or

(2) a work specially ordered or commissioned for use as a contribution to a collective work, as a part of a motion picture or other audiovisual work, as a translation, as a supplementary work, as a compilation, as an instructional text, as a

test, as answer material for a test, or as an atlas, if the parties expressly agree in a written instrument signed by them that the work shall be considered a work made for hire.

In the film industry, for example, contributions to motion pictures fall under subsection 2. Although screenwriters, for example, will be given credit for writing the film and can copyright the script individually, once they sell the script, their work becomes incorporated into the film and is considered a work made for hire. The studio or production company will copyright the film in its corporate name.

While no written instrument is required in the case of an employee work, a written instrument is required in the case of a work prepared on special order or commission to make it a "work made for hire."

This requirement of a writing for specially ordered works under subsection (2) means that the creator of that type of work must consciously-- assuming the contract is read--give up the copyright to the work that he or she would normally possess. By contrast, with employee works produced within the scope of employment under subsection (1), the act presumes the employer to be the author and requires an express written instrument signed by both parties for the employee to retain any of the rights comprised in the copyright.

4. BUNDLE OF RIGHTS

The copyright holder is entitled to the following exclusive rights under Section 106 of the U.S. Copyright Act, subject to the limitations found in sections 107 through 121:

(1) to reproduce the copyrighted work in copies or phonorecords;

(2) to prepare derivative works based on the copyrighted work;

(3) to distribute copies or phonorecords of the copyrighted work to the public by sale or other transfer of ownership, or by rental, lease or lending;

(4) in the case of literary, musical, dramatic, and choreographic works, pantomimes, and motion pictures and other audiovisual works, to perform the copyrighted work publicly;

(5) in the case of literary, musical, dramatic, and choreographic works, pantomimes, and pictorial, graphic, or sculptural works, including the individual images of a motion picture or other audiovisual work, to display the copyrighted work publicly; and

(6) in the case of sound recordings, to perform the copyrighted work publicly by means of a digital audio transmission.

[17 U.S.C. § 106.] These rights can be simplified as the right to copy or reproduce, the right to adapt or prepare derivative works, the right to distribute or transfer the work through sale, lending, or lease, the right to publicly perform the work, the right to publicly display the work, and the right to digitally transmit audio works. Some of the rights that have led to litigation include the assignment, termination, performance, and moral rights.

a. Transfer and Assignment Right

Section 201(d) of the Copyright Act provides that "ownership of a copyright may be transferred in whole or in part by any means of conveyance or by operation of law, and may be bequeathed by will or pass as personal property by the applicable laws of intestate succession." Further any of the bundle of rights may be transferred individually or together. Thus, an author of a pre-existing work may assign to another the right to use it in a derivative work.

In *Stewart v. Abend*, 495 U.S. 207 (1990), the author of a pre-existing work agreed to assign the rights in his renewal copyright term to the owner of a derivative work, but died before the commencement of the renewal period. The Supreme Court considered whether the owner of the derivative work infringed the rights of the successor owner of the pre-existing work by continued distribution and publication of the derivative work during the renewal term of the pre-existing work.

The Court decided that since the grant of rights in the pre-existing work lapsed, "the derivative work owners' rights to use those portions of the pre-existing work incorporated into the derivative work expired." It concluded that thus "continued use would be infringing."

In *Gary Friedrich Enterprises, LLC v. Marvel,* 837 F.Supp.2d 337 (S.D.N.Y. 2011), a freelance author who had developed the "Ghost Rider" comic book character and story filed suit against Marvel for copyright infringement for allegedly using his character in films, toys, video games, and other products without his authorization. The district court held that the freelance author relinquished any rights to his character by signing a check from Marvel which contained an assignment legend. This assignment, which conveyed whatever remaining renewal rights the author had to Marvel, was not unconscionable and was supported by sufficient consideration, according to the court.

b. Termination Right

Section 203 of the Copyright Statute provides that with the exception of a work made for hire, "the exclusive or nonexclusive grant of a transfer or license of copyright ... is subject to termination." The termination may be made (1) by the author, or majority of joint authors, or (2) by the surviving author's spouse, children, and grandchildren. Further, the statute provides that the right to terminate may be effected at any time during a five-year period beginning at the end of 35 years from the date of execution of the grant. If the grant covers publication, the period begins at the end of 35 years from date of publication, or 40 years from the date of execution of the grant, whichever term ends earlier.

To affect termination, the party must serve advance notice in writing signed by the owners or their agents. The effect of termination is the reversion of rights to the author(s) or other persons owning the termination interest.

In *Mills Music v. Snyder*, 469 U.S. 153 (1985), the Supreme Court queried whether the termination of a publisher's copyright interest also terminated the publisher's contractual right to share in royalties of a derivative work, i.e. the song "Who's Sorry Now." The 1976 Copyright Act gave Snyder's heirs the statutory right to reacquire the copyright that Snyder had previously granted Mills. The Act also stated that "a derivative work prepared under the authority of the grant before its termination may continue to be utilized under the terms of the grant after its termination." The Supreme Court ruled that Mills Music is entitled to a share of the royalties despite the termination. It reasoned that Mills Music's prior licenses remained intact under the Copyright Act. Nothing in the language of Copyright Act reassigned the contractual rights granted by licenses to Mills Music to Snyder's heirs.

c. Performance Rights

Performance rights societies were discussed in Chapter 3. These institutions license the right of public performance to others seeking to use copyrighted works. In the United States, ASCAP and BMI operate under a consent decree. If a potential licensee is dissatisfied with the proposed fee for a blanket license, it may sue to have a federal court review and set the fee.

In *United States v. American Society of Composers*, 616 F.Supp.2d 447 (S.D.N.Y. 2009), the Court set interim fees for a blanket license for the public performance of ASCAP's more than two million musical compositions on YouTube's streaming video service on the Internet. ASCAP proposed interim fees of $1.5 million for 2005–2006, $3.5 million for 2007, $7.0 million for 2008 and $7.0 million for 2009. ASCAP did not explain how it arrived at the figures, but merely argued that they are "conservative" when compared to the fees paid to ASCAP by Yahoo! Inc. as set by the court in the prior case of *In re AOL, Realnetworks and Yahoo! Inc.*, 562 F.Supp.2d 413 (S.D.N.Y. 2008), and the fees YouTube has agreed to pay to the record companies for the right to stream their music videos.

YouTube proposed an interim fee of $79,500 for the period from its launch in 2005 through the end of 2008 and $20,000 per quarter thereafter. After stating that the assessment of interim fees is "intended as a temporary measure to ensure a reasonable flow of funds to ASCAP . . . while the parties negotiate or litigate a binding fee," the district court set blanket license interim fees of $1,400,000 for the period from YouTube's launch in 2005 through 2008 and $70,000 per month for the period commencing January 1, 2009 and continuing until the determination of final fees were reasonable in all respects. [*See U.S. v. ASCAP*, 616 F.Supp.2d at 455.]

d. Moral Rights and Colorization

The concept of moral rights originated in France where they are known as *droit moral*. They are explained in Table 6-1.

TABLE 6-1: MORAL RIGHTS	
MORAL RIGHT	*PERMITS/PROHIBITS*
Right to Create	prohibits the completion of works from being judicially mandated
Right of Disclosure	permits authors to determine when to make works public
Right to Withdraw Work after it has been disclosed	permits authors to withdraw published works so long as they indemnify publishers for losses
Right of Name Attribution (or Authorship)	entitles authors (a) to be recognized as creators of their work, (b) to anonymously or pseudonymously publish works, (c) to prevent works from being attributed to others, and (d) to stop their names from being used on works they did not create or that later became distorted;
Right of Integrity	allows authors to prevent alterations, distortions or destructions of their work;
Right of Protection from Excessive Criticism	permits authors to publish replies to unjustified criticism

The United States officially recognizes the Right of Authorship and the Right of Integrity in 17 U.S.C. § 106A, but only gives these rights to visual artists. [Burr, *Introducing Art Law*.] The enter-

tainment industry has looked to other aspects of
U.S. law for protection.

For example, the "Right to Create" can be found
in the prohibition against specifically enforcing personal service contracts. The "Right of Disclosure"
relates to the Copyright Act's grant of the right to
copy under 17 U.S.C. § 106. Entertainers who seek
the "Right of Protection from Excessive Criticism"
may find it in U.S. libel law. As for protection
against distortions, sometimes entertainers have
found relief under 15 U.S.C. § 1125 of the Lanham
Act, which prohibits false designation of origin and
false description.

In *Gilliam v. ABC*, 538 F.2d 14, 24 (2nd Cir. 1976),
for example, the British writers and performers
known as Monty Python sued ABC to restrain the
network from broadcasting edited versions of three
separate programs that allegedly violated the Lanham Act. Monty Python argued that the cuts for
commercials and U.S. censorship standards
amounted to a mutilation or misrepresentation of
their work. The court found that the Lanham Act
could be used "to prevent misrepresentations that
injure plaintiff's business or personal reputation."
[*Id.*] The court quoted another case to augment its
point that "[t]o deform his work is to present him to
the public as the creator of a work not his own, and
thus makes him subject to criticism for work he has
not done." [*Id.*] The Second Circuit directed the Dis-

trict Court to issue a preliminary injunction against ABC.

The *Gilliam* case exemplifies how the moral rights principle of the "Right of Integrity" can be found in other aspects of U.S. laws, which protect entertainers from having others distort their work. ABC had omitted 24 of the original 90 minutes of script, leaving segments that were disjointed and difficult to follow. In one segment, the court noted, "The ABC edit eliminates [the] middle sequence so that the father is comfortably dressed at one moment and, in the next moment, is shown in a soaked condition without any explanation for the change in his appearance." [*Id*. at 25.]

Moreover, due to the global nature of the entertainment industry, some U.S. citizens have sought moral rights relief in France. In *Turner Entertainment v. Huston*, 16 Ent. L. Rptr. 10:3 (1995), the children of director John Huston sued Turner Entertainment for colorizing Huston's work *Asphalt Jungle*. Huston's heirs argued that it was a violation of his moral rights to add color to a film that Huston had deliberately chosen to film in black and white to create the right atmosphere. Huston said about another one of his black and white films, *The Maltese Falcon*, "I wanted to shoot it in black and white like a sculptor to work in clay, to pour his work in bronze, to sculpt in marble."

Turner Entertainment fought for the right to colorize the film, claiming that as the copyright holder, it was "the author" of the film. The French court separated the economic rights in the film, which were held by Turner Entertainment, from the moral rights, which were held by Huston. The French court enjoined the showing of the film on French television. The court also ordered Turner Entertainment to pay 200,000 French francs in damages and costs.

5. COPYRIGHT INFRINGEMENT AND REMEDIES

Section 501(a) provides, "Anyone who violates any of the exclusive rights of the copyright owner . . . is an infringer of the copyright or right of the author, as the case may be." [17 U.S.C. § 501(a).] To prove copyright infringement, the plaintiff must establish (1) that he or she owns the copyrighted work; and (2) that the defendant copied the work or took another exclusive right of the plaintiff.

To determine whether a defendant has infringed a plaintiff's copyright, courts use words such as theft or plagiarism to refer to the unauthorized taking of one party's work by another. The plaintiff may offer either direct or circumstantial evidence to prove the unauthorized taking. Circumstantial evidence consists of showing that the defendant had access to the copyrighted work and that there exists a substantial similarity of ideas and expression between the plaintiff's and defendant's works.

In copyright infringement cases, courts primarily analyze facts. It is crucial to track the major and some of the minor similarities between the two works and compare them to public domain works. To succeed, a plaintiff must show that the defendant could only have produced his work by copying the plaintiff's work.

The following subsections explore how copyright infringement cases relate to film, television, music, publishing, and interactive games.

a. Film Infringement

With film infringement cases, the original copyright holder may be the author of a book, a screenplay, a play, a treatment, or even another film. The question becomes whether the defendant's work came from the plaintiff's copyrighted piece or a public domain source, such as an expired copyrighted work or factual material.

In *Sheldon v. MGM Pictures*, 81 F.2d 49 (2nd Cir. 1936), the court considered whether the movie *Letty Lynton* starring Joan Crawford came from the book by the same name or the plaintiff's play. Both the book and the play were based on a true story of a Scottish girl name Madeleine Smith who was tried for attempting to and actually poisoning her French lover, Emile L'Angelier, after he threatened to reveal their relationship to her new fiancé. L'Angelier died after drinking arsenic-laced hot chocolate. Smith was acquitted when her sister testified that on one of the poisoning occasions, they had slept together in a bed throughout the night. On the other alleged poisoning occasion, Smith's fiancé swore that she had been with him at the theater.

The court found the defendants' film *Letty Lynton* to be substantially similar to the plaintiff's play named "Madeleine Cary," which the defendants initially sought to purchase and turn into a movie. When the head of an association of motion pictures thought the play obscene, MGM purchased instead the movie rights to the book *Letty Lynton*.

The court said, "The defendants took for their *mis en scène* the same city and the same social class; and they chose a South American villain." [*Id.* at 54.] The court also noted that Letty Lynton "tracked" Madeleine Cary in her passion at the beginning, her errant parent, the death scenes, and the district attorney investigation at the end. Both lovers use Gaucho songs to woo the heroines and both die of strychnine, not arsenic as in the original story and the book. The court concludes, "[I]f the picture was not an infringement of the play, there can be none short of taking the dialogue." [*Id.* at 56.]

Other film cases have questioned whether commercials infringed a film, and whether film advertising was stolen from magazine covers. In *MGM v. American Honda Motor Co.*, 900 F. Supp. 1287 (C.D. Cal. 1995), MGM claimed that Honda violated its copyrights to sixteen James Bond films and infringed its rights to the James Bond character through the commercial for the Honda del Sol automobile. The court ruled in MGM's favor, finding that film scenes and characters were copyrightable.

In *Steinberg v. Columbia Pictures*, 663 F.Supp. 706 (S.D.N.Y. 1987), Saul Steinberg claimed that Columbia Pictures violated the copyright in his illustration for the 29 March 1976 issue of *The New Yorker* magazine that Columbia Pictures used to advertise its film *Moscow on the Hudson* starring Robin Williams. In ruling for Steinberg, the court found the Columbia Pictures' poster substantially similar to Steinberg's because it symbolized the same myopic view of the world, used the same typeface, spiky lettering, and whimsical, sketchy style as the plaintiff's illustration. [*Id.* at 710.]

Nevertheless, when Paramount Pictures Corp. was inspired by Annie Leibovitz's *Vanity Fair* cover of a pregnant Demi Moore to create a movie poster with actor Leslie Nielsen's face attached to a pregnant body, the court in *Leibovitz v. Paramount Pictures*, 137 F.3d 109 (2nd Cir. 1998), determined that it was not infringement. Rather, it found it an acceptable parody under the fair use doctrine, which will be discussed in more detail later in this chapter.

More recently, downloading films via the Internet has led to numerous lawsuits, as the Motion Picture Association of America and individual companies have sought to stem the piracy of their films. In one lawsuit, the defendant admitted downloading the plaintiffs' movies and making them available to others. The court in *Universal City Studios v. Bigwood*, 441 F.Supp.2d 185 (D.Maine 2006), granted the plaintiffs' request for statutory damages of $3,000 for each violation.

b. Television Infringement

The challenges to television infringement determine whether a defendant has taken a particular type of television show. In *Sid and Marty Krofft Television Productions v. McDonald's Corp.*, 562 F.2d 1157 (9th Cir. 1977), the plaintiffs charged that the defendants infringed their "H. R. Pufnstuf" children's television show by the production of "McDonaldland" television commercials. The District Court found that the defendants had infringed and the Court of Appeals affirmed that decision, finding that there was sufficient proof of infringement.

In *Ringgold v. Black Entertainment Television*, Inc., 126 F.3d 70 (2nd Cir. 1997), artist Faith Ringgold sued Black Entertainment Television for copyright infringement after it used a poster depicting her work "Church Picnic Story Quilt" as set decoration on the television sitcom series "ROC." BET argued that its use of the Ringgold poster was either de minimis or protected by fair use. Ringgold countered that she had an exclusive right to make and distribute copies and derivative work, and to collect royalties from those who use her copyrighted work.

Ringgold claimed that BET violated her copyright in a derivative work by failing to ask permission and pay a royalty for its use of the "Church Picnic Story Quilt" as set decoration.

The Court of Appeals found that BET's use of Ringold's work was not de minimis, that the use of the poster for same decorative purpose for which poster was sold weighed against BET on fair use, and that the district court erroneously assessed fair use factor addressing effect of use on potential market for artist's work.

The Los Angeles News Service (LANS) sued Reuters Television for re-broadcasting its copyrighted video and audio tape recording of the Reginald Denny beating during the April 1992 riots. LANS licensed the work to NBC to be used on the *Today* show. A group of Reuters defendants and their partner Visnews International simultaneously re-transmitted the *Today* show to Europe and Africa by satellite. While the Court of Appeals noted in *Los Angeles News Service v. Reuters Television*, 149 F.3d 987 (9th Cir. 1998), that the Copyright Act does not apply extraterritorially, it does apply to initial infringing acts that take place in New York. The Court of Appeals considered the satellite transmissions to be "merely a means of shipping the unlicensed footage abroad for further dissemination." [*Id*. at 991.] The Court of Appeals held that LANS could recover damages "flowing from exploitation abroad of the domestic acts of infringement committed by defendants." [*Id.* at 992.]

c. Music Infringement

During Mozart's era, composers constantly took other musicians' themes and composed variations. In the movie *Amadeus*, Mozart tells Salieri upon their first meeting that he once composed variations on one of Salieri's themes.

Salieri bows and says, "You do me great honor."

Mozart responds, "Funny little theme but it yielded some great results."

Salieri grimaces.

This exchange illustrates that during that time, imitation was considered a means of flattery, not theft. Eventually, that attitude would change as more and more musicians associated copyright protection with their ability to earn a living. [Burr, *The Piracy Gap*, at 247.]

There have been several famous music infringement cases, from the 1947 *Arnstein v. Porter* to the 2005 *MGM v. Grokster*. Along the way, George Harrison was sued in the 1970s for lifting "He's So Fine" from The Chiffons to create his "My Sweet Lord." Vanilla Ice was alleged to have stolen a song from the British group Queen to make his 1990 hit "Ice Ice Baby." Biz Markie was accused of sampling or incorporating three words from Gilbert O' Sullivan's "Alone Again (Naturally)" in his "Alone Again."

In Biz Markie's case, the first sentence of Judge Duffy's opinion cited *The Bible*'s Seventh Commandment, "Thou shalt not steal." [Grand Upright Music Ltd. v. Warner Bros. Records, Inc., 780 F.Supp. 182, 183 (S.D.N.Y. 1991).] Judge Duffy expressed concern that "the defendants in this action for copyright infringement would have this court believe that stealing is rampant in the music business and, for that reason, their conduct here should be excused." However, Judge Duffy noted that Biz Markie's conduct violated "not only the Seventh Commandment, but also the copyright laws of this country." [*Id.*] Because Biz Markie and his collaborators had their attorney contact the brother/agent of O'Sullivan in search of consent, the judge deemed this as evidence that the "defendants knew they were violating the plaintiff's rights." [*Id.* at 185.]

In another sampling case, *Bridgeport Music v. Dimension Films*, 410 F.3d 792 (6th Cir. 2005), there was no dispute that the filmmaker's recording of a rap song contained a sample of a copyrighted guitar solo. While the trial court determined that the sample was *de minimis* and did not rise to the level of legally cognizable appropriation, the Court of Appeals disagreed. It determined that where there was no authorization, infringement was established.

Ira Arnstein claimed Cole Porter stole several of his compositions, some of which had already been made public, but others of which were private. The court acknowledged that some of Arnstein's claims seemed "fantastic," such as his allegation that Porter "had stooges right along to follow me, watch me, and live in the same apartment with me." [Arnstein v. Porter, 154 F.2d 464, 467 (2nd Cir. 1947)] Nevertheless, the court felt that Arnstein's credibility should be left up to a jury.

The *Arnstein* court established the Lay Audience test: "whether defendant took from plaintiff's work so much of what is pleasing to the ears of lay listeners who comprise the audience for such popular music is composed, that defendant wrongfully appropriated something which belongs to the plaintiff." [*Id.* at 473.] The court felt that this was "an issue of fact which a jury is peculiarly fitted to determine." [*Id.*] The court reversed a grant of summary judgment and remanded the case for a jury trial.

Judge Thomas Tang, writing for the Ninth Circuit, followed similar logic in his opinion reversing summary judgment for MCA and remanding the question of whether the theme from the motion picture *ET: The Extra-Terrestrial* came from Les Baxter's copyrighted song "Joy." [Baxter v. MCA, 812 F.2d 421 (9th Cir. 1987)] Baxter claimed that Academy Award-winning composer John Williams was familiar with his work, having played "Joy" in the

Hollywood Bowl in the 1960s before creating "Theme from E.T." in the 1980s.

MCA attached the following items to their motion for summary judgment: (1) cassette tape recordings of "Joy" as it appeared on the album "The Passions" and the movie soundscore of "Theme from E.T."; (2) the twenty-three page written instrumental sheet music of "Joy" that was copyrighted; and (3) the five-page piano score of the "Theme from E.T." Baxter introduced expert testimony and five comparison tapes by Professor Harvey Bacal regarding the degree of similarity between the two works.

In granting summary judgment for Williams and MCA, the District Court judge had written,

> This court's 'ear' is as lay as they come. The Court cannot hear any substantial similarity between defendant's expression of the idea and plaintiff's. Until Professor Bacal's tapes were listened to, the Court could not even tell what the complaint was about. Granted that Professor Bacal's comparison exposes a musical similarity in sequence of notes which would, perhaps, be obvious to experts, the similarity of expression (or impression as a whole) is totally lacking and could not be submitted to a jury.

[*Id.* at 423.]

The Court of Appeals reversed, holding "[W]e cannot say that "Joy" and "Theme from E.T." are so dissimilar that reasonable minds could not differ as to a lack of substantial similarity between them." The court was careful to reject defendants' contention that "any similarity between the works can be reduced to a six-note sequence which is not protectible under the copyright laws."

In *Three Boys Music Corp. v. Bolton*, 212 F.3d 477 (9th Cir. 2000), the Isley Brothers claimed that Michael Bolton's 1991 pop hit, "Love is a Wonderful Thing", infringed on their copyright of a 1964 song with the same name. The Court of Appeals found that Bolton had access to the Isley Brothers' song, and that the two songs were substantially similar. Bolton testified that he was a great fan and collector of the Isley Brothers' music. Both songs also shared the same title hook phrase, same shifted cadence, same instrumental figures, same verse/chorus relationship, and same fade ending.

Another important issue is whether providing musical equipment can lead to charges of contributory infringement. The standard for contributory infringement is that the secondary infringer "know or have reason to know" of direct infringement. [A & M Records v. Napster, 239 F.3d 1004, 1020 (9th Cir. 2001).]

On December 6, 1999, A & M Records and seventeen other record companies filed a complaint for contributory and vicarious copyright infringement and sought an injunction against Napster, Inc., an

Internet start-up company. [A & M Records, Inc. v. Napster, 114 F.Supp.2d 896, 900 (N.D. Cal. 2000).] The District Court enjoined Napster from "engaging in, or facilitating others in copying, downloading, uploading, transmitting, or distributing plaintiffs' copyrighted musical compositions and sound recordings, protected either by federal or state law, without express permission of the rights owners." [*Id.* at 927.]

While Napster did not directly copy music from other computers, the Ninth Circuit Court of Appeals found in *A & M Records v. Napster*, 239 F.3d 1004, 1011 (9th Cir. 2001), that it had designed and operated a system that permitted "the transmission and retention of sound recordings employing digital technology." The Ninth Circuit noted the District Court's determination that as much as "eighty-seven percent of the files available on Napster may be copyrighted and more than seventy percent may be owned or administered by plaintiffs." Napster did not challenge the District Court's conclusion that the plaintiffs could establish Napster's liability as a contributory infringer. The Court of Appeals agreed that Napster had knowledge, both actual and constructive, of direct infringement, and materially contributed to the infringing activity by providing "the site and facilities" for direct infringement. [*Id.* at 1020-1022.]

Grokster, Ltd. and StreamCast Networks, Inc. marketed themselves as Napster alternatives. They distributed free software products that permitted users to share electronic computer files through peer-to-peer networks. These networks can be used to share any type of digital file, but were primarily used to share copyrighted music and video files without obtaining authorization from the copyright holder. Grokster and StreamCast made money through advertising. As the number of their software users increased, their advertising opportunities were worth more.

MGM Studios sued Grokster for vicarious copyright infringement in *MGM v. Grokster*, 259 F. Supp.2d 1029 (C.D. Cal. 2003). The District Court granted summary judgment in Grokster's favor after determining that distributing the software did not give rise to liability. The Court of Appeals [380 F.3d 1154 (9th Cir. 2004)] affirmed, finding that Grokster and StreamCast did not monitor or control the use of the software, did not supervise its use, and did not possess an independent duty to police infringement. The Supreme Court [125 S.Ct. 2764] reversed. It held that "one who distributes a device with the object of promoting its use to infringe copyright, as shown by clear expression or other affirmative steps taken to foster infringement, is liable for the resulting acts of infringement by other parties."

Grokster subsequently shut down. Its website www.grokster.com now provides the following notice:

The United States Supreme Court unanimously confirmed that using this service to trade copyrighted material is illegal. Copying copyrighted motion picture and music files using unauthorized peer-to-peer services is illegal and is prosecuted by copyright owners.

There are legal services for downloading music and movies. This service is not one of them.

YOUR IP ADDRESS IS [XXX.XX.XX.XX] AND HAS BEEN LOGGED. Don't think you can't get caught. You are not anonymous. In the meantime, please visit www.respectcopyrights.com and www.musicunited.org to learn more about copyright.

While the Grokster litigation was pending, the Recording Industry Association of America sued thousands of music downloaders for direct copyright infringement. The RIAA was able to identify downloaders through their computer's Internet protocol addresses. In *BMG Music v. Gonzalez*, 430 F.3d 888 (7th Cir. 2005), the user unsuccessfully argued that her activities constituted fair use of BMG's copyrighted material. She had downloaded and saved more than 1300 songs to her computer. She was convicted, fined $22,500, and had an injunction issued against her.

On appeal, the Seventh Circuit refused to accept her arguments for reversal that she was downloading to try out the music before buying it or that the injunction should be vacated because she had learned her lesson. The Seventh Circuit said, "A private party's discontinuation of unlawful conduct does not make the dispute moot." [*Id.* at 893.]

d. Publishing Infringement

Book authors and freelance writers have also sued or been sued for copyright infringement. In *Hoehling v. Universal City Studios*, 618 F.2d. 972 (2nd Cir. 1980), A.A. Hoehling claimed that another author and a movie company lifted his theory that the Hindenburg was sabotaged by Eric Spehl to please his lady friend. Michael McDonald Mooney, another author, consulted Hoehling's book *Who Destroyed the Hindenburg?* while writing his literary version of the Hindenburg disaster called *The Hindenburg.* Mooney sold the movie rights to his book to Universal Studios. The court said that notwithstanding Hoehling's valid copyright in his work, he could not protect his historical interpretation of facts or a number of specific facts, as these were not copyrightable as a matter of law. [*Id.*]

In *New York Times v. Tasini*, 533 U.S. 483 (2001), six freelance authors sued the New York Times for copyright infringement for placing their articles in its computer database without their consent. The freelance authors charged that their contracts with the Times did not include the right to place their articles in an electronic database.

The Times claimed that it could republish the articles in its database under 17 U.S.C. § 201 (c), which provides:

Copyright in each separate contribution to a collective work is distinct from copyright in the collective work as a whole, and vests initially in the author of the contribution. In the absence of an express transfer of the copyright or of any rights under it, the owner of copyright in the collective work is presumed to have acquired only the privilege of reproducing and distributing the contribution as part of that particular collective work, any revision of that collective work, and any later collective work in the same series.

The Times maintained that section 201 accorded it, as copyright owner of collective works, a privilege to reproduce and distribute the authors' works. [*Id.* at 488.] The Supreme Court disagreed, holding that the publishers infringed the author's copyrights by reproducing and distributing the articles in a manner not authorized by the authors and not privileged by § 201 (c).

In *Feist Publications v. Rural Telephone Service Co.*, 499 U.S. 340 (1990), the Supreme Court considered whether telephone directories were copyrightable in light of the fact/expression dichotomy that affects writers of nonfiction works. As discussed in *Hoehling*, because facts are not original to a particular author, they cannot be copyrighted.

The Supreme Court noted that while the copyright statute does not protect facts, it does protect compilations if the author demonstrates originality.

In a prior decision, the Supreme Court established that "originality requires independent creation and a modicum of creativity" and defined "author" as "he to whom anything owes its origin."

The copyright laws protect writings that are the fruit of intellectual labor embodied in the form of books, prints, engravings, and the like. The Supreme Court observed, "[S]ince facts do not owe their origin to an act of authorship, they are not original and, thus, are not copyrightable." [*Id.* at 1285.] Nevertheless, writers of factual compilations may choose:

A. Which facts to include

B. In what order to place them

C. How to arrange the data so that readers use it effectively

[*Id.* at 347.] This selection and arrangement entails a minimal degree of creativity. A work can be copyrighted, but some parts not protected. Facts must be clothed with original expression, as copyright protection extends only to those elements that owe their origin to the author. Subsequent compilers of facts may use facts contained in another's work.

Compilations, like phone books, are an expression of facts and thus can be copyrighted. Here, Feist took names, telephone numbers, and towns from the Rural phone book that Rural may have been the first to report. However, these items did not owe their origin to Rural. Therefore, Rural could not own them.

In *Allen v. Scholastic Inc.*, 739 F.Supp.2d 642 (S.D.N.Y. 2011), Paul Gregory Allen claimed J.K. Rowling's *Harry Potter and the Goblet of Fire* unlawfully appropriated protected expression from *The Adventures of Willy the Wizard – No 1 Livid Land* by Adrien Jacobs. As the trustee of Jacob's Estate, Allen sued Scholastic for copyright infringement.

The Court found that Allen failed to demonstrate substantial similarity between *Harry Potter and the Goblet of Fire* and the protected elements of Jacob's *Willy the Wizard* book. As a 34-page illustrated book, *Willy the Wizard* combined equal parts text and illustration. The protagonist is an adult wizard seeking to win admission to "Stellar Land" for retirement. *Harry Potter and the Goblet of Fire* is a 734-page book, the fourth in a seven-part installment, following the adventures of a famous boy wizard named Harry. The Court did not fine similarities between the total concept and feel, theme, characters, plot and sequence, pace, and setting of the two books. For example, the Court described the character of Willy as too rudimentary to be infringed. "Because Willy's character does not display any creativity, it does not constitute protectable expression." [739 F.Supp.2d at 661]

e. Video Game Infringement

As interactive games have become a popular form of entertainment, so too have evolved their problems with copyright infringement. In *Lewis Galoob Toys v. Nintendo*, 964 F.2d 965 (9th Cir. 1992), *cert denied* 507 U.S. 985 (1993), the Ninth Circuit addressed whether Game Genie violated Nintendo's copyrights.

Simply summarized, Nintendo of America markets a home video game system called Nintendo Entertainment System. The player inserts a Nintendo cartridge containing a video game to use the system. The player controls one of the game's characters and progresses by pressing buttons and manipulating a control pad. Galoob manufactures Game Genie, which the player can use to alter up to three features of a Nintendo game by increasing the lives, the speed, and versatility of the Nintendo characters. Game Genie's altering affects on the Nintendo characters are temporary. [*Id.* at 967.]

Nintendo charged that Lewis Galoob Toys infringed its §102 (2) rights to prepare derivative works. The Ninth Circuit, however, disagreed, finding that Game Genie was not a derivative work because its audiovisual display was not fixed. While Game Genie generated a $150 million market, the court concluded,

> [T]he existence of a market does not, and cannot, determine conclusively whether a work is an in-

fringing derivative work. For example, although there is a market for kaleidoscopes, it does not necessarily follow that kaleidoscopes create unlawful derivative works when pointed at protected artwork. The same can be said of countless other products that enhance, but do not replace, copyrighted works.... The Game Genie does not physically incorporate a portion of a copyrighted work, nor does it supplant demand for a component of that work.

[*Id.* at 969.] In holding that Game Genie was not a derivative work, the Ninth Circuit stated, "The Game Genie is useless by itself, it can only enhance, and cannot duplicate or recast a Nintendo game's output." [*Id.*]

In *Bissoon-Dath v. Sony Computer Entertainment*, 694 F.Supp.2d 1071 (N.D.Cal. 2010), the copyright owners of a screenplay filed an action against a video game manufacturer. The District Court held that the plots, themes, and mood between the copyrighted screenplays and the accused video game were not substantially similar. Further, it found that screenplay's statements made by Zeus to Athena and Ares and the notion of war on earth leading to war among the gods were not protectable under Copyright Act.

Thus, video games are held to the same infringement standards as other entertainment media. In *Dream Games of Arizona, Inc. v. PC Onsite*,

561 F.3d 983 (9th Cir. 2009), the Ninth Circuit affirmed the award of statutory damages to Dream
Games of Arizona after its "Fast Action Bingo," an
electronic video bingo game, was infringed by PC
Onsite. The Court decided that (1) the district court
properly allowed the jury to see unprotectable elements of the game without identifying the protectable elements; (2) the jury should have been allowed
to hear evidence that Fast Action Bingo was operated illegally in two states; (3) statutory damages
were available to Dream Games despite the illegal
operation; and (4) the district court properly dismissed claims against PC Onsite's majority owner
for lack of evidence of direct infringement.

In *Incredible Technologies, Inc. v. Virtual Technologies*, 400 F.3d 1007 (7th Cir. 2005), the Seventh
Circuit considered whether a video golf game had
been infringed. The facts indicated that Golden Tee,
made by Incredible Technologies, Inc. (IT), was one
of the most successful coin-operated games of all
time, beating classic games like PAC–MAN and
Space Invaders. Forty thousand Golden Tee games
(in a dedicated cabinet) were sold between 1995 and
August 2003 to taverns all over America and in other countries.

The Seventh Circuit affirmed the district court's
finding that when Global VR created its game PGA
Tour Golf, it had access to and copied IT's original
instruction guide and the video display expressions
from Golden Tee. Even so, the Court determined

that IT's expressions on its control panel were not dictated by creativity, but rather were simple explanations of the trackball system. At best, the Court noted that the control panel expressions were entitled to protection only from virtually identical copying. It also asserted that the video displays contained many common aspects of the game of golf and that IT's trade dress was merely functional because something similar is essential to the use and play of video games. Thus, the Seventh Circuit concluded that (1) copyright in instructions was not infringed; (2) copyright in video display was not infringed; and (3) the game's cabinet did not infringe manufacturer's trade dress.

6. DEFENSES

a. Fair Use

Once the plaintiff has put forth his *prima facie* case of copyright infringement, the burden then shifts to the defendant to refute the evidence that he stole the plaintiff's work. The defendant can offer proof of independent creation (he or she created his or her own work), that he only took noncopyrightable items from the plaintiff, or that the use was somehow authorized, such as making a fair use of the plaintiff's work.

Section 107 of the U.S. Copyright Act requires courts to balance the following four factors to determine whether a defendant has made a fair use of the plaintiff's work:

(1) the purpose and character of the use, including whether such use is of a commercial nature or is for nonprofit educational purposes;

(2) the nature of the copyrighted work;

(3) the amount and substantiality of the portion used in relation to the copyrighted work as a whole; and

(4) the effect of the use upon the potential market for or value of the copyrighted work.

The fair use statute seems uncomplicated on its face, yet it has generated considerable litigation. The statute does not tell how to weigh the factors, although courts consider some factors more important than others. Through judicial decisions, the fourth factor has become the most important.

Because of the balancing requirement, no one can ever be absolutely certain whether he or she has used a work fairly until the use has been litigated and decided by a court. Unfortunately, what the District Court may consider fair, the Court of Appeals may find unfair, and the Supreme Court may ultimately decide it fair. This split happened when music publisher Acuff Rose decided to sue the 2 Live Crew over its rap version of "Pretty Woman." The Supreme Court held that because it was a parody, it might be considered fair so long as the parodist took no more than necessary to conjure up and critique the original. [Campbell v. Acuff-Rose Music, Inc., 510 U.S. 569 (1994).]

In *Harper & Row v. Nation Enterprises*, 471 U.S. 539 (1985), the Supreme Court wrote the golden rule of copyright as "take not from others to such an extent and in such a manner that you would be resentful if they so took from you." It also indicated that fair use is predicated on the author's implied consent to "reasonable and customary" use. Harper & Row sued Nation Enterprises for leaking an excerpt of *A Time to Heal: The Autobiography of Gerald Ford* in the Nation magazine before the autobiography was published. The Nation received the manuscript from an undisclosed source. The Court ruled that such use was not covered by the doctrine of fair use.

In *Suntrust Bank v. Houghton Mifflin Co.*, 268 F.3d 1257 (11th Cir. 2001), the trustee of the Mitchell Trust sued the publisher of the fictional work *The Wind Done Gone* for copyright infringement of *Gone With the Wind*. The author claimed fair use. The Eleventh Circuit determined that *The Wind Done Gone* was a parody of *Gone With the Wind*, and did not infringe upon the copyright in *Gone With the Wind* held by the Mitchell Trust. Alice Randall, the author of *The Wind Done Gone*, persuasively argued that her novel critiques *Gone With the Wind*'s depiction of slavery and the Civil War-era American South. Although Randall appropriated characters and plot lines from Gone with the Wind, the Court found there was unlikely to be any market confusion between the two works or negative market impact on *Gone With the Wind*.

b. Innocent Infringer Defense

In addition to claiming fair use, a defendant may also claim that the use of a particular copyrighted work was innocent. In *Maverick Recording Co. v. Harper,* 598 F.3d 193 (5th Cir. 2010), Whitney Harper was found to have infringed the copyrights to 37 sound recordings. She claimed that she was an innocent infringer when she downloaded the recordings.

The Court of Appeals disagreed. It found Harper was responsible for sharing 544 copyright protected audio song files with other computer users on a peer-to-peer network. In 2005, Harper reinstalled her operating system, at which time she installed three file sharing programs and downloaded an additional 700 new recordings since the new operating system installation. Harper asserted that she did not understand the nature of the file sharing programs she used, and that she believed her use of these programs was like listening to music on non-infringing Internet radio stations.

The Court of Appeals found that the innocent infringer defense was unavailable to Harper as a matter of law because it was limited by 17 U.S.C. §402 (d), which states that when a copyright notice appears on the published phonorecords "to which a defendant in a copyright infringement suit had access, then no weight shall be given to a defendant's interposition of a defense based on innocent infringement in mitigation of actual or statutory damages." Proper notice existed on each of the phonorecords from which the digital files were created. Harper's lack of knowledge of copyright law did not affect the application of 17 U.S.C. § 402(d).

7. REMEDIES

In 17 U.S.C. §§ 502-513, the remedies are set out for infringement. Section 502 provides that any court may issue "temporary and final injunctions on such terms as it may deem reasonable to prevent or restrain infringement of copyright." The injunction may be served anywhere in the United States and shall be operative throughout the United States. This has been one of the most useful remedies employed in successful infringement cases as it keeps the copyright holder from sustaining further losses due to the defendant's actions.

Section 503 permits a court to impound and dispose of all copies, including "plates, molds, matrices, masters, tapes, film negatives, or any other article" used to produce the infringing article.

Section 504 provides that the copyright owner may receive damages and any profits that accrued to the infringer. The awarding of both is meant to make it expensive for infringers. They lose any profits that accrued to them and must reimburse the copyright owner for injuries. In some instances, the profits may be apportioned to account for the extent of the plaintiff's work in defendant's final product.

In *Sheldon v. Metro-Goldwyn Pictures Corporation*, 309 U.S. 390 (1940), the Supreme Court considered whether, in computing an award of profits against a copyright infringer, there may be an apportionment so as to give the owner of the copyright only that part of the profits found to be attributable to the use of copyrighted materials as distinguished from what the infringer has supplied. The district court had awarded Sheldon MGM's entire net profits of $587,604.37. The Court of Appeals reversed, fixing Sheldon's share at one-fifth of the net profits. The Supreme Court affirmed, holding that the apportionment of profits was appropriate.

Section 504 (c) permits the copyright owner to elect to receive statutory damages instead of proving actual damages. The court can award not less than $750 or more than $30,000, as it considers just. If the infringement was particularly willful, the court may, in its discretion, award a sum of up to $150,000. This can be valuable where, as in the case of *Marcus v. Rowley*, 695 F.2d 1171 (9th Cir. 1983), the plaintiff suffered only $23 in actual damages. The infringement was, nevertheless, egregious because defendant Rowley directly copied eleven pages of plaintiff's twenty-four page cake decorating book and did not give her credit or acknowledge her copyright. The Ninth Circuit remanded for a determination of damages.

In *BMG v. Gonzales,* 430 F.3d 888 (7th Cir. 2005) a woman downloaded 1,370 copyrighted songs that she kept for a few weeks. The dispute focused on 30 songs that she kept on her computer and acknowledges owning. The Seventh Circuit affirmed the statutory damages award of $20,000 for the 30 songs. Although she argued that the injunction should be vacated1 because she had learned her lesson and given up broadband, the Court said that "A private party's discontinuation of unlawful conduct does not make the dispute moot. ... An injunction remains appropriate to ensure that the misconduct does not recur as soon as the case ends."

Infringing conduct may be so willful as to give rise to enhanced statutory damages. In *Zomba Enterprises, Inc. v. Panorama Records,* 491 F.3d 574 (6th Cir. 2007), a music publisher sued the manufacturer of karaoke discs for copyright infringement. The Court of Appeals held that the manufacturing and selling of karaoke packages of copyrighted songs on profit-making basis without paying royalties could not be considered a transformative use, but rather was copyright infringement of entire compositions. Moreover, the Court found the conduct to be willful, and awarded a ratio of 44:1 in statutory damages to compensatory damages. The Court determined that this ratio was not sufficiently oppressive to constitute deprivation of due process, and that the district court did not abuse its discretion by also imposing attorney fees.

Successful copyright holders may also sue under Section 505 to obtain their costs and attorneys fees. Any court has discretion to award these fees.

In some instances, individuals may be held criminally liable under section 506 if they infringe a copyright willfully for purposes of commercial advantage or private financial gain. This section also applies to reproducing and distributing copyrighted works valued at more than $1000. The criminal penalties include fines of not more than $250,000 or imprisonment for not more than five years, or both. The infringing copies may also be seized and forfeited under section 509.

C. TRADEMARKS AND MERCHANDISING

A trademark can be a word, design, or combination thereof, used by a manufacturer to identify its goods. Trademarks may also describe the product. Table 5-1 depicts the 2012 top global brands.

Table 5-1: Top Global Brands			
Rank	*Brand*	*2012 Value (in millions)*	*2011 Value (in millions)*
1	Apple	70,605	29,543
2	Google	47,463	44,294
3	Microsoft	45,812	42,805
4	IBM	39,135	36,157
5	Walmart	38,320	36,220

[http://brandirectory.com/league_tables/table/global-500-2012/]

Trademarks identify the source of the commercial object, guarantee the constancy of the quality, advertise the manufacturer, and attract customers. The top four brands are technology companies that have an entertainment component to their enterprise. Apple and IBM sell hardware, such as iPods and computers, for the viewing of films and television shows. Google provides the leading Internet search engine and owns YouTube. Microsoft sells the Xbox 360 and other hardware used to play video games.

Brand names give rise to expectations. For example, consumers anticipate seeing a family film when they view a movie with the Disney label. For that reason, Disney does not permit its subsidiaries to distribute films rated NC-17. Valued at $15.4 billion in 2012, down significantly $34 billion in the year 2000, the Disney brand name is still considered one of the world's most valuable trademarks. The value comes from a range of Disney products and services, which include theme parks, motion pictures, and television networks.

There are several different types of trademarks. Service marks identify services, such as the H&R Block tax preparation company. Certification marks identify goods or services meeting certain qualifications, such as the previously discussed Motion Picture Association of America rating marks. When a picture receives a "R-Restricted" rating, the film has been branded with a certification that the film is not suitable for children 17 and under. A collective mark identifies goods, services, or members of a collective organization, such as the MPAA. Its membership derives from the major Hollywood Studio Association. Trade names identify the corporation, such as the Walt Disney Company.

Manufacturers provide a notice to indicate that they claim a trademark on a good. If the mark is unregistered at the federal level, the claimant will use a common law trademark such as: TM or SM. SM is use to designate a service mark. If the mark has been federally registered, then it will look like one of these: ®, or "Registered U.S. Patent and Trademark Office," or "Reg. U.S. Pat. and TM. Off." While applying one of these notices to the product is not mandatory, it is necessary to obtain damages and eliminate the innocent infringer defense that someone may claim if they did not know about the trademark.

Newspapers may sometimes use a trademark name without obtaining permission. The Ninth Circuit permitted News America Publications to use the name of New Kids on the Block to conduct a survey asking which one of the New Kids was the most popular. When the New Kids sued claiming trademark infringement, the court ruled for the news organization. The court noted in *New Kids on the Block v. News America Publications, Inc.*, 971 F.2d 302 (9th Cir. 1992), that the news organizations use did not imply sponsorship or endorsement.

In *Columbus Rose Ltd. v. New Millennium Press*, 2002 WL 1033560 (S.D.N.Y. May 20, 2002), author David Baldacci claimed that New Millennium's promotion of its sports mystery anthology, which included his story "The Mighty Johns," constituted false advertisement under the Lanham Act. Section 43(a) prohibits, as false advertising, the use of an author's name in connection with a work in which the author's true participation or contribution is misrepresented.

The Court required Baldacci and his loan-out corporation Columbus Rose to show that "either 1) the challenged advertisement is literally false, or 2) while the advertisement is literally true it is nevertheless likely to mislead or confuse consumers." In this case, the Court determined that the plaintiffs demonstrated a likelihood of success on the merits of their Lanham Act claim because although they did not prove that the book cover was literally false, they produced extrinsic evidence indicating that the current cover was likely to confuse or mislead the public.

1. FILM MERCHANDISING

Merchandising the products shown in a film or television program can generate considerable revenue for the film's owner. Producers and advertisers count on the public's interest in their fictional characters to sell products based on the character or that the character is seen using in the film.

In a typical James Bond film, for example, the character will drive a fancy new car, wear an exclusive watch, or utilize other merchandise. Producers sell product placements in their films to generate additional revenue to offset costs in their production budget. The 1997 James Bond film *Tomorrow Never Dies* reportedly secured $110 million in product placement, promotional, and merchandising deals, roughly the same amount as its domestic box office earnings. [Weiler, *Entertainment Media and the Law*, at 511.]

As CNN reported, Bond has evolved from a suave, English super spy to a flashy, moving billboard for global advertisers such as BMW, Omega watches, Martini vodka, and even construction machinery. [*CNN, From Omega to Caterpillar*.] All those products are prominently featured in the Bond film, *The World is Not Enough*. The Bond attraction is such that companies have been building entire advertising campaigns around products featured in the movie. BMW has made its Bond car an integral part of its marketing strategy, for instance.

2. TELEVISION MERCHANDISING

Television producers sell advertising in the form of product placement, while networks sell advertisements to intersperse with shows. With product placement, advertisers pay to have a popular television character drink their brand of soda or eat their brand of fast foods. They may also pay for characters to visit particular resort locations or use their personal care products. The producer receives revenue that helps offset the production budget, which pays star and crew salaries, set design expenses, and so forth.

A corollary is to create merchandise based on a popular show. Cartoons and comic books, for example, can generate toys, apparel, bedroom furniture, and posters for the walls. These items are usually produced under a license agreement.

When Margaret Rey initially licensed her children's book *Curious George* to become 104 television episodes, she retained ancillary rights. [Rey v. Lafferty, 990 F.2d 1379 (1st Cir. 1993).] In January 1983, she signed an Ancillary Products Agreement (APA) with the Canadian investment firm LHP to give the company the right to license "Curious George" spin-off productions for all tangible goods except, in certain instances, books, films, tapes, records, or video productions. In return for the rights, Rey was to receive one-third of the royalties on the licensed products, with a guaranteed minimum annual payment, later increased to one-half with no guaranteed minimum payment. She retained the right to disapprove any product, so long as the right was not unreasonably withheld.

Conflict developed over the contract after Rey disapproved of certain products and the royalty revenue declined. Rey sued the companies responsible for exploiting her ancillary rights. She alleged that the companies had wrongfully withheld royalties on the Houghton Mifflin books and Sony videos. She also contended that LHP could not recover damages from her withholding approval of certain ancillary products. The Court of Appeals ruled in Rey's favor, finding that she was entitled to royalties that had been wrongfully withheld and to refuse to give approval of licensed ancillary products on reasonable grounds. [*Id.*]

Rey had a contract with LHP to license the use of her characters on merchandise. *Curious George* became a feature film in 2006, and its movie soundtrack developed into one of the top-selling albums of that year.

In certain instances, individuals may use characters without obtaining approval. Cartoonists, for example, have been known to parody the products of manufacturers without their permission.

After Jim Henson Productions created "Spa'am," the high priest of a tribe of wild boars that worship Miss Piggy as Queen Sha Ka La Ka La for the movie *Muppet Treasure Island*, the Hormel Corporation sued. [Hormel Foods Corp v. Jim Henson Productions, 73 F.3d 497 (2nd Cir. 1996).] Hormel claimed the "Spa'am" character violated its trademark SPAM, which it used to sell luncheon meat. Hormel expressed concern that "Spa'am" the boar would make consumers worry about the quality of its meat products and that sales of SPAM will drop off if linked with "evil in porcine form." [*Id.* at 501.]

The court, however, disagreed, finding Henson's "Spa'am" to be a parody, which distinguished it from Hormel's products. The court did not accept Hormel's arguments that consumers would be confused between merchandise carrying the SPAM logo and products featuring "Spa'am" the wild boar. [*Id.* at 505.]

3. MUSIC MERCHANDISING

Bands tend to sell their merchandise while on tour as fans seek mementos to memorialize the evening. At live music events, be it a rap or rock concerts, bands or their licensed agents sell t-shirts, programs, hats, and posters along with CDs. Even at classical music concerts, fans will have opportunities to at least purchase CDs.

At a Seal concert, fans could purchase thong underwear bearing the musician's name. The vendor reported that he sells even more merchandise to young girls at Britney Spears concerts because they want to imitate the star. At a Barbra Streisand concert in Philadelphia, fans could pay $5 for a key chain, $20 to be photographed next to an official tour poster, $375 for a leather jacket, and up to $700 for a giclée, a canvas print made on an ink jet printer to resemble fine art. [Gardner, *Happy Days here again for Barbra.*]

Some companies license the use of musicians' names to apply to concert merchandise in anticipation of a certain number of attendees. Great Entertainment Merchandising (GEM) paid Vince Neil Merchandising (VNM) a $1,000,000 advance against royalties in anticipation of a Vince Neil concert tour before 800,000 paid attendees. The contract was signed with VNM, a loan-out company created the day before to enter into the agreement. It specified that VNM was to cause Neil to play before 800,000 paid attendees, or VNM would have to repay the advance. By the time Neil completed his tour, he had only performed before 533,032 paid attendees. GEM demanded a refund. When he refused to pay, GEM sued him.

VNM conceded that a breach of contract had occurred and the District Court granted summary judgment for GEM. [Great Entertainment Merchandising, Inc. v. VN Merchandising, 1996 WL 355377 (S.D.N.Y. 1996).] However, the District Court refused to grant summary judgment against

Vince Neil personally because he did not sign the agreement. Neil proved once again the value of loan-out companies to shield entertainers from personal liability.

Another challenge for musicians, musical groups, and their companies is to stop the flow of the unauthorized use of their names. Elvis Presley Enterprises (EPE) sued Barry Capese for applying the name "The Velvet Elvis" to his Houston, Texas nightclub. In *Elvis Presley Enterprises, Inc. v. Barry Capese*, 141 F.3d 188 (5th Cir. 1998), EPE declared that it was the assignee of all trademarks, copyrights, and publicity rights belonging to the Elvis Presley estate. It asserted that merchandise sales brought in over $20 million in revenue over a five-year period and accounted for the largest portion of its revenue. [*Id.* at 191.]

EPE claimed that Capese's nightclub "The Velvet Elvis" infringed its trademarks. While the District Court held that it was a parody of the trademark, the Court of Appeals disagreed, finding infringement and issuing an injunction. The Court of Appeals said that parody was not a defense against trademark infringement, but rather a factor to be considered in determining whether there is a likelihood of infringement. The Court of Appeals found that "The Velvet Elvis" mark was similar in appearance, sound, and meaning to the Elvis trademarks. [*Id.* at 200.]

Further, the nightclub had made every effort to link itself to Elvis Presley. Its menu included a frozen drink called "Love Me Blenders" and a hot dog called "Your Football Hound Dog." The nightclub also advertised with slogans such as "The King Lives," "Viva La Elvis," and "Elvis has not left the building." The court considered these uses as attempts to profit from the good will associated with the Elvis name and trademark. Moreover, these uses were likely to cause consumer confusion and lead consumers to think the Elvis estate officially sponsored them.

Finally, just like television, video game, and film productions, musicians can make money from selling companies the opportunity to place brands in their music videos. In 2011, Rolling Stones Magazine reported that Britney Spears made $500,000 from charging manufacturers to place products in her music video for "Hold It Against Me." The products placed included Sony televisions and monitors, Make Up Forever eye shadow, the Plenty of Fish dating website, and Spear's Radiance Perfume. Lady Gaga's "Telephone" video also featured product placement for the website Plenty of Fish. [http://www.rollingstone.com/music/news/britney-spears-made-500-000-from-product-placement-in-hold-it-against-me-video-20110222]

D. PATENT LAW

A patent grants exclusive rights to prohibit others from making, using, and selling inventions to the absolute exclusion of others. It does not automatically grant the right to exploit the patent as it may be an improvement patent based on another patent. In such a case, the patentee must obtain permission from the other patent holder in order to use his invention based on the other one. The patent term is 20 years from the date of filing.

To patent an invention, the creator must prove that it meets five substantive requirements. First, the invention must be patentable subject matter under 35 U.S.C. Sec. 501. This means the invention or discovery must be a new and useful process, machine, manufacturer, composition of matter, design, or plant, or it can be a new or useful improvement thereof. Second, the invention must be original, which is defined as new. Third, the invention or discovery must fulfill the novelty requirement, which means it is new and was not developed before a certain date. Fourth, the invention must be useful and confer a demonstrated benefit to society. The invention also must not be illegal, immoral, ineffective, dangerous, or merely curious. Finally, the invention or discovery must be non-obvious to those skilled in the arts. There must be synergism so that two plus two equals more than four.

Patented inventions enabled the entertainment industry to grow. An important early patent in the film industry was earned by Thomas Edison. The famed inventor of the light bulb also created the camera and the movie camera. Edison sued the

Biograph Company for infringing his patent for a kinetographic camera. Although the language of the patent claim was broad enough to cover a camera device, the District Court found no infringement because, in considering the practical utility and substantial identity, there were differences in parts, in action, and in result. On appeal, the Second Circuit reversed in *Edison v. American Mutoscope and Biograph Co.*, 151 F. 767 (2nd Cir. 1907).

The patent system strikes a bargain similar to the copyright law. It encourages the development of technology by giving monopoly rights to exploit the invention, while demanding ultimate disclosure of the information to the public. Unlike copyright law, where rights accrue once the material is fixed in a tangible means of expression, a patent must be issued from the federal government before the creator obtains these monopoly rights. Patents also differ from trademark law, where rights accrue on using the mark in commerce and permitting consumers to associate the particular designation with goods.

E. TRADE SECRETS

An old adage proclaims, "A secret is only a secret if one of the two parties is dead." [Burr, *Protecting Business Secrets*, at 282.] Fortunately, death is not a prerequisite to keeping secrets in the entertainment business.

Maintaining undisclosed ideas, information, and technology is important to talent, producers, studios, networks, and recording companies. Toward this end, companies have individuals sign release agreements before sharing ideas. They may also require business partners to sign nondisclosure agreements that keep them from revealing business information given to them in confidence. Some high profile celebrities have their pizza delivery boy sign a confidentiality agreement prohibiting him from informing the media about what he learned while briefly in their homes.

Trade secret law protects information that is concealed and gets its value because it is not readily available or known. Initially, courts protected business secrets within their respective jurisdictions on a case-by-case basis using tort theories. This court-made law was eventually expressed in the Restatement of Torts. At least forty-five states have adopted Uniform Trade Secrets Act (UTSA), sponsored by The National Conference of Commissioners on Uniform Laws, which approved the UTSA initially in 1979 and revised it in 1985.

Under the UTSA, such information may include "formulas, patterns, compilations, programs, devices, techniques or processes" that

(1) Derive independent economic value (actual or potential) from not being generally known or readily discoverable by proper means by others who would obtain an economic value from its disclosure or use; and

(2) Is the subject of efforts that are reasonable under the circumstances to maintain its secrecy.

Entertainment companies may consider a variety of information, from plot formulas to special effects, as secrets. The key is to limit disclosures of the information to only those who receive it in confidence. Companies have to keep in mind that there are two types of culprits most likely to steal such secrets: competitors and employees.

The goal of trade secret law is to secure a level playing field among all competitors, who can acquire information through proper means (such as individual discovery and effort), but not improper means (such as theft). With employees, who may someday become competitors, trade secret law seeks to balance the rights of individuals to pursue the knowledge acquired from their careers with the rights of a business to be protected from unfair competition.

The controlling factor is how the person first learned of the information. Even if the information could have been reverse engineered, the fact that it was first learned in confidence will give rise to legal action. By permitting reverse engineering, the law seeks to reward individual efforts, while not encouraging theft.

Once theft has occurred, individuals and companies can seek injunctions, damages and attorneys' fees in civil courts. Some states permit criminal sanctions. For federal law, global entertainment companies may rely on The Economic Espionage Act of 1996, which Congress adopted to discourage theft of trade secrets in foreign commerce. This act permits criminal sanctions.

In conclusion, all forms of intellectual property can prove valuable to entertainers, studios, and producers. The most recently created form of intellectual property—the right of publicity—will be discussed in Chapter 10.

CHAPTER 7

REPRESENTING ENTERTAINERS

This chapter explores the relationships between entertainers and those who represent them, namely agents, managers, lawyers, and unions. These representatives provide services to entertainers and assist in growing their careers.

The primary job of an agent is to solicit and obtain employment for their clients or material for future exploitation. Entertainers need agents to advance their careers as most studios and production companies will not accept and look at unsolicited manuscripts and projects sent directly from unknown talent. The State of California caps agents' fees at ten percent. In New York and elsewhere, literary agents routinely charge their clients fifteen percent.

Managers in the film and television industry may assist talent in picking scripts that diversify their abilities. Managers in the music industry may be responsible for everything from running the band to taking care of their tours and personal matters. Managers may receive 5 to 25% of the talent's income. If the manager belongs to a management conglomerate, he may be responsible for several entertainers' careers.

Attorneys draft and review contracts. They may also offer advice on setting up businesses. Some lawyers create pre- and post-nuptial agreements for clients. Others draft their client's wills and participate in estate planning. Still others may handle criminal matters. When entertainers like Robert Blake and the late Michael Jackson are charged with crimes, their lawyers must possess special skills in media relations to accompany their understanding of the criminal justice system.

Unions negotiate agreements with studios and agents that provide minimum fees and working conditions for talent, which are known as minimum basic or collective bargaining agreements. Once they become eligible to join a union such as the Screen Actors Guild (SAG), the Directors Guild (DGA), the Writers Guild (WGA), International Alliance of Theatrical Stage Employees (IATSE), Actors' Equity Association, American Federation of Television and Radio Artists (AFTRA), or the American Federation of Musicians, talent must pay membership initiation fees and ongoing dues. The challenge for lawyers entering the entertainment law field is to know what the unions have negotiated for their clients so that they do not waste time haggling over rights the talent already possesses.

Entertainers may also have other professionals in their lives, like accountants to manage their finances and publicists who assist talent in selling their image. Some publicists specialize in quieting matters for talent, like Paris Hilton or Mel Gibson, who commit errors in judgment.

This introduction to the role of representatives sets the stage for a more detailed discussion below. This chapter presents disputes that have arisen about or between talent and their agent, manager, lawyer, and union representatives.

A. AGENTS

William Goldman, the author of *Adventures in the Screen Trade*, writes, "[S]tars come and go. Only agents last forever." Agents (or talent agents) endure because the system is set up to guarantee their survival. New film artists may find themselves caught in a paradox—they cannot get work without an agent, and they cannot get an agent to look at them until they demonstrate their talent.

Anyone, including licensed attorneys, seeking to become a talent agent with a conglomerate may have a tough road ahead. Typically, the big agencies like Creative Artist Agency, International Creative Management, United Talent Agency, and William Morris, hire and place recruits in the mailroom sorting the incoming correspondence and making deliveries. After succeeding in the mailroom job, they may move on to become desk and personal assistants to other agents. This apprentice rotation can take two years before the recruit becomes an assistant agent or full agent.

Wally Amos, who would later become renowned for launching "Famous Amos Cookies," began his agent career earning $50 a week as a trainee in the mailroom of the William Morris Agency in 1961. [Amos and Murray, *The Cookie Never Crumbles*, at 37.] In his book, *Man With No Name*, Amos describes his initial duties as "sorting mail and running errands." [Amos, *Man with No Name,* at 43.]

Amos immersed himself in learning about the business and was promoted to substitute secretary within two months. By the end of his first year, he was elevated to talent agent and became the founding member of a new rock and roll division. He brought in Simon and Garfunkel when they were unknown and playing in small clubs. In his five and a half years as an agent, he also booked and promoted The Supremes, The Temptations, Dionne Warwick, Helen Reddy, and Marvin Gaye. [*Id.* at 44-45.] For Amos, a perk to becoming an agent, i.e., the opportunity to fraternize with available women, turned into a pitfall. He divorced twice during these years.

The current economic rewards associated with succeeding as an agent are potentially huge with income exceeding $1 million a year, as one Los Angeles agent privately said. The downsides are equally enormous. This agent said that he fields over 100 calls and 125 e-mails daily. A desk assistant sits in his office to make and receive phone calls and to instantly check facts. Sometimes while he is on the phone with one person, he will have his desk assistant call another agent to verify the truth of what the person on the phone is telling him. He said it is harder for others to lie to him because he has access to a wealth of knowledge.

He confessed that other downsides are the long hours and his inability to take more than two or three days off from work at a time. When he travels to nice places like the Cannes Film Festival, he works. This agent was also aware that no matter how much effort he contributes to building an artist's career, the artist might leave him at any moment for another agent. When asked whether a gentlemen's agreement keeps agents from poaching each other's clients, he barked, "You steal from us; we steal from you."

For many individuals, the rewards of becoming an agent are worth the risks. Over the years, California and New York have passed legislation regulating agents. California talent agents are regulated by the California Labor Code, a few provisions of which are reprinted below, and by the Screen Actors Guild to the extent that they represent film artists.

Section 1700.4 of the California Labor Code defines talent agents and artists as follows:

(a) "Talent agency" means a person or corporation who engages in the occupation of procuring, offering, promising, or attempting to procure employment or engagements for an artist or artists, except that the activities of procuring, offering, or promising to procure recording contracts for an artist or artists shall not of itself subject a person or corporation to regulation and licensing under this chapter. Talent agencies may, in addition, counsel or direct artists in the development of their professional careers.

(b) "Artists" means actors and actresses rendering services on the legitimate stage and in the production of motion pictures, radio artists, musical artists, musical organizations, directors of legitimate stage, motion picture and radio productions, musical directors, writers, cinematographers, composers, lyricists, arrangers, models, and other artists and persons rendering professional services in motion picture, theatrical, radio, television and other entertainment enterprises.

[Cal. Lab. Code § 1700.4 (2003), "Talent agency"; "Artists."] One of the goals of the Talent Agencies Act is to prevent improper persons from becoming talent agents and to regulate such activity for the protection of the public.

* The entire Talent Agencies Act [Lab. Code, §§ 1700-1700.47] is considered a remedial statute designed to protect artists and correct abuses, which have been the subject of both legislative action and judicial decision. The Act voids contracts between an unlicensed agent and an artist.

In *Waisbren v. Peppercorn Productions*, Inc., 48 Cal.Rptr.2d 437 (Cal.App. 2 Dist. 1995), a personal manager sued his former client, a company special- ized in the design and creation of puppets for use in the entertainment industry, for breach of contract and for failure to pay him a percentage of its profits. In return for managing certain business affairs and occasionally procuring employment for Peppercorn, Waisbren was to receive 15 percent of its profits. After Peppercorn terminated its relationship with him, Waisbren filed suit to recover unpaid amounts.

The California Court of Appeal distinguished an agent's duties to procure employment from a man- ager's responsibilities to advise and direct artists in the development of their careers. [*Id.* at 438.] The court concluded that because Waisbren had func- tioned as a talent agent, by procuring employment for Peppercorn, he was required to be licensed under the Talent Agencies Act. The court affirmed the trial court's voiding of the parties' oral agreement be- cause Waisbren had not obtained the necessary li- cense under the Talent Agencies Act.

In *Matthau v. Superior Court*, 60 Cal.Rptr.3d 93 (Cal.App. 2 Dist. 2007), The California Court of Ap- peal considered whether William Morris Agency could compel arbitration with actor Walter Mat- thau's son regarding his failure to pay the Agency's 10% commission on Matthau's contracts. William Morris Agency represented the actor from 1960 un- til his death in 2000. Although Matthau and the

Agency had no written agency contract after 1970, Matthau routinely paid 10% of earnings under contracts that Agency procured and negotiated.

The court determined that the relationship between Matthau and the Agency was governed by the collective bargaining agreement between the Screen Actors Guild and the Association of Talent Agents (ATA). After his death, Matthau's son succeeded to Matthau's and his wife's rights in profit participation payments. The son stopped paying commissions to the Agency in January 2004, and it filed a motion to compel arbitration, as per SAG rule 16(g). The Court ruled that the Agency could not compel arbitration because the son was not a party to the agreement. As a non-signatory successor-in-interest, the son could not be bound by his father's agreement to arbitrate.

New York rules regulating agents also apply to booking agents who secure lectures and engagements for film and theater clients. In Friedkin v. Harry Walker, 90 Misc.2d 680, 395 N.Y.S.2d 611 (N.Y. City Civ. Ct. 1977), director William Friedkin (*The French Connection*, *The Exorcist*) sued Harry Walker, seeking the return of $4,743.32 in commissions. As an unlicensed agent, Walker managed, directed, and promoted lectures, talks and addresses by well-known personalities. He charged Friedkin a 30% commission to secure lecture engagements. Although he booked 23, Friedkin only performed three and paid commissions on those. The court ruled in Friedkin's favor because Walker was an unlicensed agent.

A properly licensed agent must be careful how she engages employment for talent. Director Stephen Frears (*The Grifters*, *The Queen*) had an agent accept money and commit him to a picture before he had reviewed the script. [Author Interview with Frears.] After he read the script, he realized the film wasn't for him and decided to back out of his oral agreement. His attorney advised him that he might have a claim against his agent for taking the money. He learned from that experience that "[t]aking money creates a contract and expectations that you are really going to do the picture." [*Id.*]

Actor Kelsey Grammer experienced the opposite problem with his agent. He became dissatisfied with his representatives at the Artist Agency because they failed to secure film work for him. His two television shows, *Cheers* and *Frasier,* were obtained before he joined the Artist Agency. He sought freedom from his agreement with Artist Agency by negotiating an interim deal whereby Artist Agency would continue to represent him on his television projects and he could seek other representation on film deals. After a year, Grammer completely terminated his relationship with the Artist Agency. The Agency then sued him for $2 million in unpaid commissions on his television work. A three-member union arbitration panel decided in favor of the Agency.

When Grammer appealed the panel's ruling to federal courts, both the District Court and the Court of Appeals affirmed. In *Grammer v. Artists Agency*, 287 F.3d 886 (9th Cir. 2002), the actor argued that his interim contracts violated SAG Rule 16(g) § IV(C)(1), which provides that all "contracts ... not complying with these Regulations ... shall be void except as hereafter provided." SAG initially rejected the interim contract, but eventually accepted it after the Artist Agency faxed a copy of the settlement agreement to prove the interim contract was in Grammer's best interest. The arbitration panel found that Grammer had waived the Rule 16(g) violations, and the courts agreed with that finding.

Grammer turned his problems with agents into humor. From *Frasier's* earliest beginnings in 1993 until its conclusion in 2004, actress Harriet Sansom Harris hammed up the recurring character Bebe Glazer as an unscrupulous agent who would do anything for money and to advance her own interests. Bebe's shenanigans were often to the detriment of her client's welfare.

Agents have been subjected to considerable ridicule over the years, yet for many talented individuals they remain a potent force in the industry, as long as they can continue to secure deals for clients. When the industry is a global recession or retrenchment, as it was in 2006 when studios began canceling production deals, agents can become even more valuable to stars.

Comedy superstar Jim Carrey fired his long-term agent Nick Stevens with United Talent Agency in September 2006 and moved to Creative Artists Agency. The change occurred after Fox Studios pulled the plug on his futuristic comedy "Used Guys" in May 2006 and Paramount suspended production of "Ripley's Believe It or Not." The New York Times reported that both studios were concerned about ballooning budgets. [Waxman, *Not So Funny Anymore*.] The loss of two films in short order sent Carrey searching for a bigger agency.

B. MANAGERS

What exactly are the responsibilities of an artist's manager? According to the court in *Raden v. Lauri*, 20 Cal.App.2d 778, 262 P.2d 61, 64 (Cal. Ct. App. 1953), "[O]ne is not an artist's manager unless he advises, counsels, and directs artists in the development of their professional careers...."

The HBO hit *Entourage* portrays a rising movie star with both an agent and manager. The agent obtains movie roles and negotiates deals for his client. The live-in manager (a home-town buddy) is depicted reviewing scripts, giving advice on what offers the client should accept, and making sure the client shows up on time to meetings.

It is not uncommon for talent to select managers from among their close personal friends. Tennis legend Andre Agassi asked Perry Rogers, a childhood buddy, to become his manager right after Rogers graduated from the University of Arizona College of Law. Since there are no bar requirements to become a manager, Rogers was able to immediately step into that role and begin negotiating endorsement contracts for his new client.

Singer Nancy Wilson advises musicians to get a lawyer first to negotiate their contract with their manager and for the manager to find the agent. "I've had the same manager since 1959 and I feel well represented," she says. She cautions young people to surround themselves with people who care about them. She believes that it's important to have a good manager to run interference for her. She says, "I never had to meet the booking agent and promoters. My manager took care of all that. I could just show up and sing. Back in the day, I didn't sign any contracts with the band and club owners. If things were not right, I could just end things then. I'm easy going. I like doing my job. I don't like a lot of stress. That is what managers are for." [Jazz Workshop Interview with Wilson.]

In *Crown v. Kiedas*, 27 Va. Cir. 371 (Va.Cir.Ct. 1992), the issue arose as to whether a management company can be held responsible when a band member behaves reprehensibly. Anthony Kiedas, a member of the Red Hot Chile Peppers, allegedly committed assault and battery against a woman while she was waiting in the hallway of the George Mason University Student Union Building.

The court examined whether the relationship between manager Lindy Goetz and Kiedas required the manager to control Kiedas' behavior. The plaintiff maintained that Lindy Goetz had knowledge of Kiedas' history of violent and sexually abusive conduct toward women.

According to the Restatement (Second) of Torts, a master is under a duty to exercise reasonable care to control a servant who is acting outside the scope of his employment as to prevent him from intentionally harming others if the servant is upon the premises and the master knows or has reason to know that he has the ability to control the servant. In this case, the court determined that Lindy Goetz functioned more as the servant, and could not be held liable for the conduct of the master.

The jobs of agents and managers may overlap when managers begin securing employment for their clients. As indicated in the *Waisbren* (1995) and *Friedkin* (1977) cases, managers risk not being paid when they act as an agent without procuring the appropriate license.

In *Wachs v. Curry*, 13 Cal.App.4th 616, 16 Cal.Rptr.2d 496 (Cal.App. 2 Dist. 1993), Wachs and X Management Inc. lost their suit against actor and television host Arsenio Hall. The parties' personal management contract required Hall to pay 15% of his earnings from all of his activities in the entertainment industry. Despite the contract's statement that Wachs had not promised to obtain employment or engagements for him, the company did so. Hall successfully sought the return of all moneys collected from him and his employers in connection with his activities in the entertainment industry.

The court in *Wachs v. Curry* discussed the California Talent Act's exemption of recording contracts. The California Entertainment Commission recommended the exemption permitting managers to secure a recording contract for a musician because "[i]n the recording industry, many successful artists retain personal managers to act as their intermediaries, and negotiations for a recording contract are commonly conducted by a personal manager, not a talent agent." [*Id.* at 625.] The Commission also observed that the "managers frequently contribute financial support for the living and business expenses of entertainers. They may act as a conduit between the artist and the recording company." [*Id.*]

In *Buchwald v. Superior Court*, 254 Cal.App.2d 347, 62 Cal.Rptr. 364 (Cal. Ct. App. 1967), the musical group Jefferson Airplane sued their personal manager Matthew Katz. Their written agreement stated that Katz was neither authorized, nor would he obtain employment for the group. [*Id.* at 351.] Jefferson Airplane claimed that, despite the contractual language, Katz did indeed procure bookings for them. Katz argued that the written agreement established that he was not subject to statutory regulation.

In rejecting Katz's contention, the court looked to the illegality lying behind the contract to determine whether the contract was prohibited. [*Id.* at 355.] *Buchwald* held generally that procurement efforts require a license and that the substance of the parties' relationship, not its form, is controlling. [Waisbren v. Peppercorn Productions, Inc., 48 Cal.Rptr.2d 437 (Cal.App. 2 Dist. 1995)]

The *Waisbren* court noted that when the *Buchwald* case was decided, Labor Code section 1700.4 used the term "artists' manager" instead of "talent agency" and was part of the Artists' Managers Act. [Stats.1959, ch. 888, § 1, pp. 2921, 2922.] Then, an "artists' manager" was defined as "a person who engages in the occupation of advising, counseling, or directing artists in the development or advancement of their professional careers and who procures, offers, promises or attempts to procure employment or engagements for an artist. . ." [Stats.1959, ch. 888, § 1, p. 2921.] The Legislature changed the name of the statutory scheme in 1978 and amended section 1700.4 to use the term "talent agency." [Stats.1978, ch. 1382, §§ 3, 6, pp. 4575, 4576.] These changes did not alter the statute's remedial purpose. [Waisbren, 48 Cal.Rptr.2d at 442, n.7]

More recently, in *Marathon Entertainment, Inc. v. Blasi*, 42 Cal.4th 974 (Cal. 2008), the issue arose as to whether illegal conduct could be severed from the lawful purposes of an agreement to provide personal management services. In 1998, Marathon Enter-

tainment and actress Rosa Blasi entered into an
oral contract for Marathon to serve as Blasi's personal manager. In return for counseling Blasi and
promoting her career, Marathon was to receive 15%
of Blasi's earnings.

Over the next three years, Blasi had two roles,
one in film and the other as a lead in the television
series *Strong Medicine*. Marathon argued that Blasi
reneged on their agreement by not paying their
commission for Blasi's employment on *Strong Medicine*. Blasi claimed that Marathon violated the Talent Agencies Act by procuring employment for her
without a talent agency license.

The trial court granted Blasi's motion for summary judgment, holding the entire oral contract in-
valid because Marathon lacked a talent agency license. The Court of Appeals reversed in part because under the law of severability of contracts the
parties' agreement had a lawful purpose of providing personal management services that was unregu-
lated by the Talent Agencies Act.

The California Supreme Court affirmed the Court
of Appeals' judgment. It reasoned that the California Talent Agencies Act requiring anyone who solic-
its or procures employment for artists to obtain a
talent agency license applies to managers based on
function, not title. As such, Marathon is subject to
the Act. However, when a manager engages in unlawful procurement of employment, the manager is

still due compensation for lawfully provided services, such as career advice and counseling under the doctrine of severability.

While managers lost the regulatory battle that would have permitted them to procure employment for artists, the Los Angeles Times reported in 1998 that agents were becoming obsolete. [Wallace, *Hollywood Agents Lose the Throne*.] The Wallace article noted that many agents were turning themselves into personal managers to charge higher fees, 15% instead of 10%, of the client's earnings. It also observed that some of the biggest stars do not have agents. It said that Leonardo DiCaprio and Jackie Chan, for example, were represented solely by managers, and that "Kevin Costner and Sharon Stone use lawyers to close deals." [*Id.*]

C. LAWYERS

An individual trained in the law and who passes the bar possesses advantages if he or she seeks employment in the entertainment industry because they can work as agents, managers, or lawyers. To work in the entertainment industry, it is helpful if the lawyer acquires knowledge about corporate and business law, tax law, labor law, criminal law, family law, contracts, immigration and intellectual property law.

Lawyers at studios often begin their career on the legal side and some eventually migrate to the business side if they demonstrate sufficient skill. Studio lawyers are paid a salary, while law firms may charge hourly fees or by the job. In some instances, lawyers enter into contracts to do all the talent's legal work (including contracts, divorces, adoptions, wills, and criminal defense) in return for 5% of the talent's gross dollar revenue.

Contemporary lawyers in the entertainment industry have been known to package deals, shop talent and creative material, and offer advice on financial matters, according Gary Devlin. He says, they often cross over into the definitional realms of agent and manager. [Devlin, *The Talent Agencies Act*.]

1. U.S. COUNSEL

An entertainment attorney's career within the United States can consist of multiple jobs counseling various types of clients. Frank I. Davis, for example, began working for the law firm of Donovan, Leisure right after he graduated from Harvard Law School in 1948. [Author Interview with Davis.] He subsequently joined producer David (*Gone With The Wind*) Selznick's business as general counsel of his production company. Two years later, Davis became the company's president. In 1956, Davis moved to California to join Famous Artists Agency, which at that time represented actors John Wayne, William Holden, and Susan Hayward, as well as prominent directors and producers. Davis moved to MGM in 1966 as the executive in charge of talent. He stayed until 1999.

Among the challenges that lawyers, like Davis, face in representing clients in the entertainment industry is dealing with strong egos. Frank Davis advises young attorneys to seek entertainment law for its career aspects, not its glamorous aspects. He says, "The glamour is superficial. It's not substantive. And you can't rely on it for a career."

Rebel Steiner, a partner at Loeb and Loeb, for over 20 years, laments the impact of technology on his entertainment clients. He says it has become more difficult for new talent to get record deals because recording companies "don't want to take chances." [Author Interview with Steiner.] Nevertheless, Steiner believes he has some advantages as an independent lawyer who doesn't work at a studio. "Creative people overrule lawyers at studios," he says. Because he has a lot of different clients, Steiner is not beholden to one client.

One of attorneys' most important duties is to protect confidential communications with their clients. The case of *Geragos v. Borer*, 2010 WL 60639 (Cal.App.2 Dist. 2010), involved Jeffery Borer, a private jet owner, secretly videotaping singer Michael Jackson and his two criminal defense lawyers, Mark Geragos and E. Pat Harris, while flying on Borer's private charter jet. Borer planned to sell the tape to media for a lot of money, but Geragos sued him for invasion of privacy, and use of name and likeness, in violation of Civil Code section 3344. Geragos received an injunction prohibiting the sale and, at a bench trial, a judgment of $2.25 million in compensatory damages and $9 million in punitive damages.

The Court of Appeals held that the trial court's damages judgment was not supported by sufficient evidence, and remanded the case for a new trial on damages unless the parties agreed to an alternative judgment with significantly reduced damages. The Court reasoned that there was no evidence regarding the videotape content since it lacked audio, was never sold or viewed by several people, and did not make a profit for Borer. As such, the Court ruled that the damages were excessive as a matter of law.

2. INTERNATIONAL ATTORNEYS

Lawyers specializing in entertainment law can be found around the globe, working in large law firms, small firms, and government offices. Because entertainment law has mostly been created in the United States, these attorneys must also master U.S. intellectual property and contract law. They represent foreign companies seeking to do business with U.S. companies or U.S. talent visiting their country.

Klaus Beucher, a German attorney who received an LL.M from the University of Wisconsin, works for Freshfields Bruckhaus Deringer, a large German firm with offices throughout Asia and the United States. Beucher represents cable television conglomerates. He reports that because most agreements are based on U.S. law, this makes it easier for someone who has mastered U.S. entertainment law to practice internationally. He reports that "Americans don't like to litigate in Europe and Europeans don't like to litigate in America." Beucher describes his job as "fun." He says, "I haven't been to the office for a day when I'd say I'd rather not go.... It's really cutting edge." [Author Interview with Beucher.]

Beucher's colleague at Freshfields, Dr. Jan-Holzer Arndt, specializes in film financing. He represents German close-end funds who invest in Hollywood films by taking a portfolio approach. They may finance three films at once, one with big names and two smaller ones with no stars. They lost hundreds of millions of dollars when they initially invested in films because they did not understand Hollywood accounting methods. Indeed, Arndt says that in the early days German film funds were called "stupid money" in Hollywood. "Now," Arndt says, "We focus on the gross." [Author Interview with Arndt.]

Melbourne, Australian attorney Bruno Charlesworth was sleeping comfortably in his bed when the phone rang early one morning. "It's Courtney Love," said the voice on the other end. [Author Interview with Charlesworth.] Charged with assault after an altercation on an airplane to Australia, Love sought representation from one of Australia's best known entertainment lawyers. Charlesworth began his legal career primarily as a music lawyer representing Australian acts. In addition to Love, he has also represented American musical artists Kiss and Marilyn Manson. Charlesworth believes that "success breeds success breeds success" because musicians talk among themselves. He says to become a thriving music lawyer, the person has "to love music. Your chance of getting a client exponentially increases by getting to know the band, what they play, and their manager." He listens to their tunes when he hears that a band is seeking a lawyer. To maintain a client, he recommends that lawyers try to pick those who "are going to be successful, value your opinion, and achieve." Eventually, a lawyer may be able to charge clients with flourishing careers their "full rate." [*Id.*]

Toronto attorney Paul Sanderson personifies the music attorney who is also a musician. His "Blue Room" band plays 1-2 gigs a month, and he composes original music. He finds practicing law a tough business because people often surprise him by "some of the fact situations they get into. There is always some new twist and turns, some new aspect to the negotiation. As a lawyer, I am not here to judge. I just work with the facts. How can I help solve this dilemma?" [Author Interview with Sanderson.] His Toronto colleague Tony Duarte says, "It takes a long time to cultivate a client. You have to get everything right. You have to cultivate them over a long period of time. Your current clients are your best source of new clients. [Author Interview with Duarte.]

3. CLIENT VIEWS

When asked on the cable television show *Arts Talk* what was the most difficult aspect of being an entertainment lawyer, Johnnie Cochran replied, "Having to say no to people who are not used to having people say no to them." [Author Interview with Cochran.]

This is an important admonition since talented individuals seek out lawyers to strongly represent their interests. From the client viewpoint, screenwriter Duncan North (*The Tao of Steve*) defines good attorneys as those who "most assiduously fight" for their clients' rights. He says, "Lawyers and agents are not [our] spiritual mentors. But if they are really, really good, then they make it easier for [us] to be that way." [Author Interview with North.]

Author and screenwriter Max Evans says his long-term lawyer Norma Fink has "never had a client that doesn't honor her as if she's a bishop." "She's mean to me," he adds. "She's mean to everybody. She's just mean. But the point of it is she's going to be mean for you. There's no way a studio can buy her out or intimidate her. She has a very powerful clientele." [Author Interview with Evans.]

Actor and documentary filmmaker Jason Miller retained representation from an entertainment lawyer after he wrote a letter asking for representation. Miller observed the lawyer giving a presentation at a seminar. After Miller began filming *Project Ever-*

lasting (about long-lasting marriages) with his best friend Mat Boggs, the lawyer agreed to represent Boggs, their film, their book, and other entertainment products in return for 5% of their revenue. The lawyer put together an extensive release agreement for Miller and Boggs to give to subjects prior to interviewing them. [Author Interviews with Miller and Boggs.] Even after signing the agreement, some married couples sought to keep personal information (such as how they overcame adultery or dealt with their child's homosexuality) from being depicted in the film or book.

Academy Award-winning actress Shirley MacLaine stresses the importance of lawyers to the success of actors. She says, "Actresses and actors don't worry too much about the law. Their lawyers and agents do that. When actresses hire lawyers, they expect the lawyers to do everything. We usually just follow their recommendations." Ultimately, MacLaine said, "Sometimes lawyers help, sometimes they don't." [Author Interview with MacLaine.]

D. UNIONS

In the film and television industries, the Screen Actors Guild (SAG)-American Federation of Television and Radio Artists (AFTRA), the Directors Guild of America (DGA), the Writers Guild of America (WGA), Producers Guild and the International Alliance of Theatrical Stage Employees (IATSE) are the major unions that represent actors, directors, screenwriters, producers, and crew respectively. SAG, DGA, WGA, and IATSE negotiate minimum basic agreements with studios and producers to obtain minimum scale wages, acceptable working conditions, creative rights, and credits for their members. The American Federation of Musicians (AFM) negotiates master agreements with symphony orchestras, and Actors' Equity Association negotiates with Broadway producers on behalf of talent.

Who is bound by guild agreements? In *Hollywood Online* (1996), Allen R. Grogan and Sam C. Mandel wrote the following:

> Guild agreements are contracts. Typically, they bind guild members and producer signatories to the agreement.... Once the producer is a signatory to a guild agreement, he or she may hire members of that guild to provide services.... Furthermore, although the exact rules will differ with each guild agreement, most guild agreements contain cross-affiliation provisions which, in the case of an individual producer signatory, bind not only the individual but also all companies controlled by such individual and in the case of a corporate signatory, bind all subsidiaries of such entity....

Unions are now trying to organize reality TV shows. Because television series like *The Bachelor* and *Survivor* are not unionized, they do not pay scale wages, do not provide insurance, and do not entitle participants, writers, and directors to residuals unless specifically negotiated. [Rendon, *Unions Aim to Share in the Success of Reality TV*.] The following subsections discuss issues that have arisen with each of the guilds.

1. SAG-AFTRA

The Screen Actors Guild (SAG) and the American Federation of Television and Radio Artists (AFTRA) and Actors' Equity merged on 30 March 2012. SAG represented film talent, and AFTRA represented 70,000 television and radio performers, journalists and other artists working in the entertainment and news media. The new union is called SAG-AFTRA. According to its website www.sagaftra.org, the merger will increase their bargaining leverage, improve their ability to organize, and protect health, pension/retirement benefits, and the future of their members.

SAG's Global Rule One, which requires that "No member shall work as a performer or make an agreement to work as a performer for any producer who has not executed a basic minimum agreement with the Guild which is in full force and effect" is to remain. It is similar to AFTRA's "No Contract No Work Rule."

In prior SAG litigation, conflict arose if an actor or actress accepted a part before joining SAG or paying SAG dues. Part-time actress Naomi Marquez accepted a one-line role in an episode of the television series *Medicine Ball*. Lakeside Productions, a signatory to SAG's collective bargaining agreement, produced the show. Lakeside called SAG to confirm Marquez's eligibility and was advised that she needed to pay her union dues. After Marquez learned that her dues would be $500, she tried to negotiate with SAG to permit payment of her dues after she received compensation for her film work. Because she had not resolved her conflict with SAG the day before her appearance, Lakeside recast the role. SAG later faxed a letter saying it did not object to Marquez playing the part, but it arrived too late. Marquez then sued SAG and Lakeside.

In *Marquez v. Screen Actors Guild*, 525 U.S. 33 (1998), Marquez alleged that SAG breached its duty of fair representation under the National Labor Relations Act (NLRA) by negotiating and enforcing a flawed union security clause and by failing to truthfully notify her about her NLRA rights. Marquez argued that SAG should have provided and notified her of a 30-day grace period following her new employment before she was required to pay her dues. The Supreme Court disagreed, holding that SAG had not breached its duty of fair representation. SAG's union security clause appropriately tracked the language of §8(a)(3) of the NLRA, and it did not have to notify Marquez of specific rights.

The results of such a case would apply to both SAG and AFTRA since it addresses a union's relationship with its members.

2. DIRECTORS GUILD

The DGA negotiates working conditions and minimum salaries for directors depending on the size of the budget. The size of the budget also determines minimum salary scale for preparation and post-production editing time. The DGA also hosts annual awards recognizing the talent of its members, who frequently go on to win the Best Director Oscar®.

Labor unions sometimes bring legal actions to enforce their members' contracts. The DGA sued Millennium Television Network when it failed to pay several directors for their work in a 1999 New Year's Eve telecast called the "Millennium World Broadcast." In *Directors Guild of America v. Millennium Television Network*, 2001 WL 1744609 (C.D. Cal. 2001), the District Court found that because the directors did perform the work and labored on the telecast they were owed payment for their services, despite the fact that Millennium cancelled the show on December 23, 1999. An arbitrator awarded the directors $64,846.13 in compensation and $14,864.65 in pension and health contributions, plus late charges.

In this action, DGA also sued Frontier Insurance Company (Frontier) and NAC Reinsurance Corporation (NAC). DGA argued that these two companies were liable for the arbitration award obtained against Millennium, which had gone out of business. Frontier and NAC had executed a payment bond with Millennium making them liable as co-sureties to "any and all persons, corporations who perform work or labor on the *Millennium World Broadcast* scheduled for December 31, 1999." [*Id.*]

In its defense, NAC argued that the express terms of the bond did not encompass the plaintiffs' arbitration award against Millennium because the plaintiffs did not actually "perform work or labor on" the cancelled telecast. NAC also argued that the plaintiffs failed to mitigate their damages following the cancellation of the telecast. The District Court, however, disagreed with this argument. It found that the plaintiffs had "performed work" or "labored on" the telecast and were therefore owed the amounts set forth in the arbitration award. It granted DGA's motion for summary judgment. [*Id.* at *6.]

3. WRITERS GUILD OF AMERICA

The Writers Guild has two divisions, the Writers Guild East and the Writers Guild West, who divide the country along the Mississippi River. The WGA West represents screenwriters who live west of the Mississippi. Under the contract that both Guilds negotiated in 2001, screenwriters receive a minimum of $50,100 for an original screenplay, including the treatment. [Writers Guild, *Schedule of Minimums.*]

Since the WGA represents employees, writers must be employed before they can join and yet the signatories are limited to hiring only WGA members. To evade this Catch-22, new screenwriters must find someone who wants to buy their script and is willing to sign the minimum basic agreement. In the event of a dispute over which screenwriters are entitled to credit on a film, the WGA will arbitrate the dispute and award credit. An ampersand (&) indicates two writers wrote the script as a joint work; a written "and" indicates writers who worked independently of each other.

The WGA sometimes allocates screen credits after 17 writers contributed to a screenplay. Greg Brooker, who became one of two credited writers on *Stuart Little*, said, "A lot of [the 17 writers] were brought in to write a line or two for the animals.... You could say that *Stuart Little* was written by committee. After we went through the Writers Guild credit arbitration, only two writers received credit: me and M. Night Shyamalan. I was the first writer, and he was the third. I spent a lot of time writing my letter to the WGA explaining how I created my screenplay and what was mine. I didn't claim the whole picture because the concept changed." [Author Interview with Brooker.]

According to screenwriter Walon Green (*The Wild Bunch*, *Eraser*), the Writers Guild is a mixed blessing for writers because it performs legal services that writers cannot afford to do on their own and decides credit arbitration. He reports, "I've arbitrated four times and lost once. Only three of my 13 credited films went through arbitration. Arbitration can occur in strange ways. I'm adapting a book now that has been through three prior screenplay adaptations. While I haven't seen the prior adaptations, it's possible that we will all have similar scenes since we are working from the book. This is the kind of situation that could easily end in arbitration to determine who is entitled to the credit for writing the film." [Author Interview with Green.]

When writers are unhappy with the results of the arbitration process, they can bring legal action. Nick Marino sued the WGA, Francis Ford Coppola, and Mario Puzo, charging that the arbitration procedures used to determine the screenwriting credit to *Godfather III* were fundamentally unfair. Marino objected to the WGA practice of keeping the arbitrators' identities confidential and claimed that the WGA breached its duties of fair representation.

In 1985, Marino and Thomas Wright co-wrote a treatment for *Godfather III*. Paramount Pictures Corporation purchased the treatment and hired Marino to write a screenplay based on his treatment. Marino completed the screenplay in 1985, but Paramount chose not to produce it at that time. In 1987, Marino wrote a second treatment and sent it unsolicited to executives at a production studio owned by Coppola. They did not purchase Marino's 1987 treatment. In 1989 and 1990, Coppola and Puzo co-wrote a screenplay for *Godfather III*, which was produced and completed in 1990. Prior to the film's release, Marino was notified that the WGA would be conducting an arbitration to determine the writing credits for *Godfather III*. Accordingly, Marino, Coppola, and Puzo submitted written materials and statements for review.

In *Marino v. WGA*, 992 F.2d 1480, 1482 (9th Cir. 1993), the Court of Appeals outlined the three stages of the WGA arbitration process. In the first phase, a committee conducts a hearing to decide disputes as to "authenticity, identification, sequence, authorship or completeness of any literary material to be considered." These arbiters, whose names are kept confidential from the writers, the public, and each other, conduct the second phase. The three arbiters individually read material submitted by the film company and the writers to decide who is entitled to screen credit. A majority vote decides the issue. The third phase is conducted by a Policy Review Board (PRB) which hears requests from writers concerned that there has been a dereliction of duty by the arbiters or that they have misinterpreted, misapplied, or violated WGA policies. The court noted that the entire process must occur within 21 business days or the producer's own selection may become final. [*Id.*]

On November 5, 1990, the WGA informed Marino that Coppola and Puzo would receive sole writing credit for *Godfather III*. Marino requested a hearing before the PRB. At the event, he objected to the arbitration procedure. [*Id.* at 1482.] The PRB telephoned the three arbiters and presented Marino's allegations to them. The PRB discovered that one arbiter had not read Marino's 1985 treatment. That arbiter was sent the 1985 treatment for review, and the arbiter then reaffirmed the prior conclusion. The PRB subsequently informed Marino that a new arbitration was unnecessary and that the arbitration decision was final.

The Court of Appeals found that Marino had waived his right to object to the arbitration proceedings by his failure to protest the procedure before arbiters were selected and performed their task. The Court of Appeals also concluded that Marino had failed to establish that the union breached its duty of fair representation in its conduct of the arbitration proceedings.

4. PRODUCERS GUILD

The Producers Guild of America (PGA) is a voluntary association that many producers elect to join. The PGA determines, similar to the WGA, who is entitled to which producer credits on a film. The Academy of Motion Pictures abides by PGA credits when it awards the Best Picture Oscar®.

At the annual Academy Awards ceremony, producers are the individuals who collect the Oscar® for Best Picture. Bob Yari sued the PGA and the Academy of Motion Picture Arts and Sciences in 2006, alleging that the process by which producer credits are awarded is "secretive, arbitrary, and unfair." [Shprintz, *Claim Jumpers: Suits fly over*

'Crash' Credits.] Yari claimed that he had been denied the recognition and prestige that goes with the producer credit for the film *Crash*. [*Id.*] *Crash* subsequently won the Best Picture Oscar, and Yari did not receive an award. Months following the ceremony, several of the film's stars, directors, and producers claimed that Yari had failed to share profits with them.

In 2008, The California Court of Appeal in *Yari v. Producers Guild*, 161 Cal.App.4th 172 (Cal.App.2 Dist 2008), affirmed the trial court's judgment that the right of fair procedure does not apply to the decisions private organizations make about their own awards. Further, Yari's application for an award did not create a contract, or a promise on which reliance was reasonable.

5. IATSE

IATSE's full name is the International Alliance of Theatrical Stage Employees, Moving Picture Technicians, Artists and Allied Crafts of the United States, Its Territories and Canada. IATSE was formed in 1893 by representatives of stage hands. With a membership of over 113,000, IATSE boasts that it is the largest labor union in the entertainment industries. [http://www.iatse-intl.org/about-ia]

According to its website, IATSE members work in all forms of live theater, motion picture and television production, trade shows and exhibitions, television broadcasting, and concerts as well as the equipment and construction shops that support all these areas of the entertainment industry. IATSE says it represents virtually all the behind the scenes workers in crafts ranging from motion picture animator to theater usher.

Like other entertainment unions, IATSE has been sued for failure to provide fair representation. In *Wills v. Walt Disney Pictures and Television*, 173 F.3d 862 (9th Cir. 1998), Michael Wills and Robert Thurlwell charged that IATSE unfairly represented them in their dispute with Disney. Wills and Thurlwell claimed that Disney employed fewer senior craft services workers in violation of the collective bargaining agreement, and that Thurlwell had been unfairly terminated after the dispute arose.

The Court of Appeals said to establish that a union breached its duty of fair representation, the employee "must show that the union's conduct toward him was 'arbitrary, discriminatory, or in bad faith'." To be arbitrary, the union's conduct must lack a rational basis and demonstrate "egregious disregard" for the rights of its members. [*Id.*]

The Court of Appeals split its decision. It first held that IATSE did not breach its duty in failing to follow-up on Wills and Thurlwell's claim that they were discriminated against because of age. After investigating, the union determined that the two men were unavailable when the initial craft positions were filled on *In the Army Now*. When a junior worker filled a later available position that the two men could have taken, the union negotiated a $400 settlement on their behalf.

Second, the Court of Appeals decided that IATSE did breach its duty by not pursuing the issue of whether Thurlwell resigned, as Disney contended, or was fired, as he maintained. The court decided that the IATSE representative should have followed up to determine how Thurlwell had left after working 30 years for Disney. The court affirmed the summary judgment on the age discrimination issue and reversed on the resignation claim.

6. AMERICAN FEDERATION OF MUSICIANS

The American Federation of Musicians (AFM) was founded in 1896 to improve the professional lives of musicians. The union considers any individual who receives pay for his musical services as a professional musician. Within its first ten years, the AFM represented 45,000 musicians throughout North America. It currently has over 250 local chapters, representing over 100,000 members. The local chapters negotiate with management on behalf of musicians.

"Our basic reason for existing is to protect the interest of musicians in the working field," says Larry Wheeler, president of the New Mexico branch of the AFM, Local #618. The cost to join AFM depends on where the musician is located. The New Mexico local charges fees to join the federal union and the local union as well as yearly dues. Wheeler says, "The main benefit is that musicians have local representation if they believe they are unduly let go." He also says that the union makes available individual contracts and represents union members to produce collective bargaining agreements with management. Among other activities, the AFM and its locals file grievances or lawsuits, or both, against symphonies on behalf of their members.

In *American Federation of Musicians v. St. Louis Symphony,* 203 F.3d 1079 (8th Cir. 2000), the union brought an action in the District Court to compel the symphony to arbitrate a grievance pursuant to the parties' collective bargaining agreement. The union was granted its motion for summary judgment, but was denied its motion for attorneys' fees. The Eight Circuit affirmed.

The dispute arose after violinist Louis Kampouris, who had initially been hired to perform in 1949, was informed when he reported to work on 2 September 1997 that he could no longer rehearse or perform with the orchestra. Kampouris, who was 68 at the time, sued the symphony for age discrimination and intentional infliction of emotional distress after it discontinued his salary and benefits. [*Id.* at 1080.]

The Eight Circuit affirmed the denial of attorneys' fees because the union's proposed arbitration panel included arbitrators from outside the St. Louis metropolitan area. In a different arbitration, the union and symphony had agreed to limit themselves to local arbiters. The court found that the symphony's reliance on the previous agreement was not unreasonable.

In *Michigan Employment Relations Commission v. Detroit Symphony Orchestra*, 393 Mich. 116, 119, 223 N.W.2d 283 (Mich. Sup. Ct. 1974), Allen Chase claimed that the Detroit Symphony Orchestra fired him from his position as a trombonist because of his participation in union activities. Chase rejected an offer of a $10 a week raise by telling the orchestra's general manager, "Get yourself another boy. I do not accept." Contacted a week later, he indicated he had not changed his mind. The orchestra declared the position vacant and began auditioning for a new trombonist. When Chase eventually tried to accept the offer, he was told it was withdrawn. He auditioned for the vacancy but was not rehired.

Chase charged that the orchestra had discharged him because of his union activities. The trial examiner disagreed. After conducting an evidentiary hearing and listening to testimony from the parties, he concluded that Chase quit the orchestra when he rejected the contract and the raise with the abrupt, "Get yourself another boy." [*Id.*] The Michigan Employment Relations Commission (MERC) Board reversed the trial examiner's ruling, finding there was union animus. The Michigan Court of Appeals reversed the MERC board. The Michigan Supreme

Court affirmed the Court of Appeals, concluding that the MERC Board's finding was not supported by "substantial evidence." [*Id.* at 121.]

Diane Bredesen, a house contractor for the Detroit Opera House, sued the Detroit Federation of Musicians Local 5 for breach of duty of fair representation, and for violating Michigan's sexual discrimination laws while negotiating her salary. As a house contractor, Bredesen was responsible for hiring the "pick up" orchestras that perform traveling shows at her theatre, and acting as the musicians' liaison to the conductor and the theatre. Bredesen was the only woman among three house contractors in Detroit Federation of Musicians Local 5. When she was hired in 1996, she asked the Union to negotiate a "double scale" contract. The Union told her all house contractors were paid the same as side musicians' scale rate. Bredesen accepted the Union's response. Three years later, she learned that this information was false. The same year her contract was negotiated, other Detroit venues paid male house contractors double the side-musician's scale rate that she received.

The Union sought summary judgment in *Bredesen v. Detroit Federation of Musicians*, 165 F.Supp. 2d 647 (E.D.Mich.2001), on both the breach of duty of fair representation and sex discrimination claims. The Court granted the Union's motion for summary judgment in regard to Bredesen's breach of duty of fair representation, but denied summary judgment with respect to her sex discrimination claim.

The Court found that Bredesen did not exhaust internal Union remedies in regard to her breach of duty of fair representation claim, as required by Article 12, Sect. 27 of the Bylaws of American Federation of Unions. Bredesen's state law sex discrimination claim, however, was not preempted by federal labor law. Section 301 of the Labor Management Relations Act does not apply to state laws that "Grant nonnegotiable rights that are shared by all state workers".

In a reflection of an era, the American Federation of Musicians was once segregated by race. Two years after Pittsburgh jazz legend Errol Garner joined a band led by saxophonist Leroy Brown in 1937, he qualified for the African-American Local 471 of the Musician's Union. [Community Voices, Pittsburgh Jazz Legends 8] When trumpeter Walter Fuller was asked to join the San Diego local chapter in the 1940s, he insisted on a change in the format of the union's directory, which he said "had a page for white musicians up front and a list of colored musicians in the back." [McLellan, Walter Fuller, 93 Miller, Karl E., "*Children's Behavior Correlates with Television Viewing*," 67, No.3 *American Family Physician* 593-4 (Feb. 1, 2003) (herein referenced as "Miller, *Children's Behavior Correlates with Television Viewing*")]. Fuller successfully convinced the local union boards to integrate and alphabetize all members on the list, and eventually the policy was adopted by every union chapter in the state. [*Id.*]

7. ACTORS' EQUITY ASSOCIATION

Actors' Equity Association negotiates collective bargaining agreements with major theatrical producers on behalf of stage actors and actresses throughout the United States. Similar to SAG-AFTRA, Actors' Equity negotiates minimum conditions of employment for its members, while permitting the performer to negotiate more favorable terms of employment.

For example, on December 4, 1969, actor Robert DeNiro signed an Actors' Equity Association "Standard Resident Theatre Contract for Dramatic Productions" to play the part of Stott in the production of "The Basement." At the top of the contract, it states that it is "to be issued only to Equity members in good standing" and that it must be signed before the actor goes into rehearsal. The contract specified that DeNiro was to report to the Theater Company of Boston in time for the first rehearsal on December 4, 1969 and the opening date of December 17, 1969. He was to receive $200 per week in compensation on Saturday of each week, and that the contract could be terminated by either party upon two weeks' written notice to the other party. [Contract Courtesy of the Harry Hansom Humanities Research Center, the University of Texas at Austin]

In summary, agents, managers, lawyers, and unions play a vital role in the entertainment industry. They assist entertainers in achieving their goals, and sometimes are sued by entertainers for failure to represent them in a fair manner. Chapter 8 will address in more detail the issues of credits and compensation, which representatives negotiate for and on behalf of talent.

CHAPTER 8

CREDITS AND COMPENSATION

Credit and compensation issues intertwine in the entertainment industry. Credit accords recognition to the talent who contributes to the final product. Talent is then compensated according to the value of his or her work. This chapter discusses the importance of credit and the intricacies of the compensation system in the film, television, and music industries.

A. CREDITS

In the publishing industry, the placing of the author's name on the book supposedly indicates who penned the manuscript. However, for the book *It Takes a Village*, former First Lady, Senator, and Secretary of State Hilary Clinton received sole author credit, although Barbara Feinman Todd ghostwrote it. While Feinman Todd was compensated for her services, there was no indication anywhere within the manuscript of her contributions to the book, which became a bestseller. Had Feinman Todd received direct credit, those who liked the book might have looked up and purchased other works that she wrote or co-wrote.

Credits are important because people receive acknowledgements for their contributions, and the acknowledgements can lead to increased compensation. Dan Brown wrote *Angels and Demons* before *The Da Vinci Code*, but it was only after the latter became a runaway bestseller that the former climbed to the top of bestseller lists.

This phenomenon happens throughout the entertainment industry. An entertainer who performs well creates demand for his or her services. Television actor Kelsey Grammer began performing the Frasier character on *Cheers* in 1984. After the demise of that sitcom in 1993, he starred in the show *Frasier* from 1993 to 2004. By sticking with the same character for 20 years, he tied James Arness, who starred as Matt Dillon on *Gunsmoke*, for playing the longest ongoing TV character. Similarly, in the music industry, musicians want to receive credit for the notes they write and sing.

1. FILM CREDITS

Credits roll or blink in and out on screen at the beginning and end of films. Credit refers to the listing of a person's name next to the function he or she performed in the entertainment project. The "story by" credit indicates the person who developed the story but did not write the screenplay. That credit is denoted as "written by" and may go to one or more people. An ampersand (&) indicates two or more writers who worked together to create a joint work. The word "and" designates two or more authors who contributed to the script after the first author finished the original script. The "script supervisor" took detailed notes (scene number, take number, camera position, and dialogue running time) during the filming, which aids the director and editor in deciding which cuts to add to the final product.

Depending on the size of the project and the amount of special effects, several hundred credits may scroll across the screen at the end. The last three credits at the beginning of the film are usually the producer, the writer, and the director. The director credit may also be the first credit listed on screen at the beginning of the movie, such as "A film by Alfred Hitchcock" or "A Spike Lee Joint." While national audiences tend to depart the theater when the credits commence, L.A. audiences often stay until the last frame, usually as the copyright indicator, is shown. This occurs out of deference to those who participated in the venture.

Crediting talent for their contributions was a slow developing concept in the film industry. During the era of silent films, studios did not indicate which actors starred in their films. According to William Goldman, if fans wanted to write actors, they sent letters to "The Butler with the Mustache" or "The Girl with the Curly Blonde Hair." [Goldman, *Adventures in the Screen Trade*, at 5.] Viewers saw only the names of the film and the production company until executives recognized that giving credit improved the selling of films, as audience members were likely to return to see a particular actor in his next picture. Similarly, if viewers liked the writing in *Casablanca* they might rush out to see *Arsenic*

and Old Lace once they realized that Julius J. Epstein penned both pictures.

Credits have both financial and psychological
consequences. Talent and crew find that their pay
rises as their credit increases from "Best Boy or
Girl" (first assistant electrician who adjusts lighting) to "Gaffer" (chief electrician) or from "Grip" (a
laborer who creates and breaks down stage sets) to
"Key Grip" (the head of the crew). Further, pay increases as the talent's reputation for producing excellent work in the industry grows. Likewise, the
psychological reward comes from the acknowledge-
ment of the person's role in the project, that no matter how small the task may have been, it added value to the film.

Billing, which relates to order of credit placement,
is particularly important to actors as their stature
may be based on whether their name is placed before or after the title of the film. In *Smithers v.
MGM Studios*, 139 Cal.App.3d 643, 189 Cal.Rptr.
20, 23 (Cal.App. 2 Dist. 1983), the court said that
billing "reflects the actor's stature in the industry,
and affects his negotiations for roles, since it reflects
what his status and compensation has been in the
past. Billing reflects recognition by the producer and
the public of the actor's importance or 'star quality,'
and in turn affects the author's compensation in
present and future roles." If the actress is not the
star, the sooner her name appears after the star the

better. Another desired credit is to receive the final listing, such as "and starring Catherine Zeta-Jones."

For some actors, billing issues can generate lawsuits. Sophia Loren sued Samuel Bronston Productions for breaching an agreement that required "in all paid advertising of 'El Cid' Miss. Loren is to be accorded 'second (2nd) star billing above the title, 100% the same size and type of the title on the same line, same size, same prominence as that used for Charlton Heston, who received first (1st) star billing'." [Loren v. Samuel Bronston Productions, 32 Misc.2d 602, 224 N.Y.S.2d 959 (N.Y. Supreme Ct. 1962).] Ms. Loren claimed the production company violated the agreement by placing her name below that of Charlton Heston on electrically illuminated upright signs. The defendants claimed that this was in keeping with the billing clause.

The court agreed, questioning whether Loren was "really in danger of suffering the loss of prestige and other damage attributed to [the] non-observance" of the agreement. [*Id.* at 604.] While the judge scheduled the dispute for trial, he made clear how he was leaning in the opening paragraph of his opinion when he used words such as "egocentricity" and "vanity" to refer to Miss. Loren. He indicated that such vanity was "due in measurable part to the adulation which the public showers on the denizens of the entertainment world in a profusion wholly disproportionate to the intrinsic contribution which they make to the scheme of things when seen in cor-

rect perspective. For that matter often in disproportionate to any true talent, latent or apparent." [*Id.*
at 602.] Since there are no further references to this
case, it likely settled before trial.

The unions have a say in credit issues. SAG negotiates minimum credit requirements for actors who
can, by contract, negotiate for size and placement of
the credit. The Writers Guild also establishes minimum requirements to receive a screenwriter's credit. When several screenwriters contribute to the final movie, the WGA arbitrates to determine who is
entitled to receive the writing credit.

The arbitration to determine who is entitled to
credit is done before the release of the film. However, a lawsuit may occur after the release, particularly if the film is a hit.

Sometimes directors and writers seek to limit
their credit on films they deem unworthy. The Wall
Street Journal reported in 1996 that directors hide
behind the pseudonym Alan Smithee to disassociate
themselves from a dud. Director David Lynch sub-
stituted the name "Alan Smithee" for his own when
his *Dune* was re-cut to appear on television.
[Shapiro, *Movies: Despite Disdain, a Legendary Director Endures.*]

When Tristar Pictures cut 22 minutes from the
film *Thunderheart* starring Val Kilmer to show it on
commercial television, the director Michael Apted
objected and requested his name be removed. Sec-

tion 8-211 of the DGA's collective bargaining agreement with Tristar entitled the director to a pseudonym if he persuaded the DGA's Director's Council. The Council, an arbitrator, and the courts ruled in Apted's favor. [Tristar v. Director's Guild of America, 160 F.3d 537 (9th Cir. 1997).] When Tristar aired *Thunderheart* on Fox, it carried the label "An Adam Smithy Film." [*Id*. at 539.]

In 1992, Stephen King sought an injunction to prohibit the use of his name in connection with the film adaptation of *The Lawnmower Man*. King wrote a short story by the same title in 1970 and assigned the motion picture and television rights to Great Fantastic Picture Corporation in 1978. In 1990, Great Fantastic transferred its rights to Allied, a London production company, which set about making a picture it described as "Stephen King's The Lawnmower Man," thus according King possessory credit. [King v. Innovation Books, 976 F.2d 824 (2nd Cir. 1992).]

King learned of the picture in early October 1991 from a film magazine article. He protested the possessory credit given him in a letter dated 9 October 1991, and stated that he did not want this credit. He objected to the possessory credit as a misrepresentation since the film was very different from his short story. On 20 May 1992, King expressed concern that the "based upon credit," which usually indicates the original source of the film material, was misleading. In his lawsuit, King claimed that both credits violated Sec. 43(a) of the Lanham Act, which prohibits false designation of origin.

The District Court agreed and granted an initial injunction prohibiting both credits. It concluded that "the possessory credit was false on its face [and] that the 'based upon' credit was misleading." [*Id.* at 828.] The Court of Appeals let stand the possessory credit injunction, but overturned the injunction as to the "based upon" credit, finding that the core of the short story was used in the film. The court wrote, "We think that King would have cause to complain if he were *not* afforded the 'based upon' credit." [*Id.* at 831.]

In a subsequent case, *King v. Allied Vision*, 65 F.3d 1051 (2nd Cir. 1995), the Second Circuit affirmed one District Court ruling that held New Line Cinema in contempt and vacated another. It agreed that New Line had not complied with a consent decree provision requiring it to use certified, instead of first class, mail to correct the references. It vacated the portion of the District Court's 1994 order requiring New Line to contact all its retailers to determine their inventory of the film. [*Id.* at 1063.]

This case indicates the value of credits to the production company, which clearly thought it could sell more tickets by closely linking Stephen King to the film. However, because King did not think well of the film, he preferred to limit his involvement rather than develop a reputation for producing films he deemed to be of low quality.

The possessory credit, which may be indicated as "a film by Hitchcock," "a Hitchcock film," or "Hitchcock's *The Birds*," is rarely granted to writers. It is more often accorded to directors, such as D.W. Griffith or Cecil B. DeMille, who shape the final product from start to finish. Even so, the possessory credit can be controversial, given the number of contributors to the film.

In recent times, this credit appears more frequently on the big screen. The *Chicago Tribune* reported it has been "taken by any director whose agent can successfully negotiate for it." [Caro, *The Director or the Writer*.] This article cites the possessory credit as appearing frequently on bombs, such as Bruce Paltrow's *Duets*, or even for a directorial debut, such as Sally Field's *Beautiful*.

Director David Lean makes the case for his possessory credit in relation to *Dr. Zhivago*:

> I worked one year with the writer. Unlike him [the writer], I directed not only the actors but the cameraman, set designer, costume designer, sound men, editor, composer and even the laboratory in their final print. Unlike him, I chose the actors, the technicians, the subject and him to write it. I staged it. I filmed it. It was my film of his script, which I shot when he was not there.

[*Id.*] Some directors, like Kevin Smith (*Clerks, Dogma, Jersey Girl*), refuse to take the "film by" credit. Smith said, "A film is probably the most collaborative art form there is…. No one person makes a movie. So taking that 'A film by' [credit] kind of leaves everybody out…. [This] means that there were no grips, there was no crew, there was no producer, [and] there was no PA production assistant that got the star to the set when you needed them." [*Id.*]

Producers have also sued to be accorded credit for their contributions to a film, as they are often the ones who find the initial project, secure the financing, and put the film together. For their efforts, the persons with the producer credit can win the Academy Award for Best Picture.

In *Tamarind Lithography Workshop v. Sanders*, 143 Cal.App.3d 571, 193 Cal.Rptr. 409 (Cal.App. 2 Dist. 1983), Terry Sanders asserted that he acted as writer, director, and production manager by personally hiring and supervising personnel comprising the film crew for the film *Four Stones for Kanemitsu*. When the film screened at Tamarind's 10th anniversary celebration, however, it lacked the screen credit "A Film by Terry Sanders." At trial, the jury awarded Sanders $25,000, which was not contested on appeal. Rather, the California Court of Appeals expressed concern as to whether this award could compensate "Sanders not only for past or preexisting injuries, but also for future injury (or injuries) as well." [*Id.* at 574.]

The court noted that the value of a film that is "favorably received by its critics and the public at large, can result in valuable advertising or publicity for the artists responsible for that film's making. Likewise, it is unquestionable that the nonappearance of an artist's name or likeness in the form of screen credit on a successful film can result in a loss of that valuable publicity. 'By its very nature, public acclaim is unique and very difficult, if not sometimes impossible, to quantify in monetary terms'." [*Id.* at 576.]

The court concluded that "pecuniary compensation for Sanders' future harm is not a fully adequate remedy." It reversed the judgment denying Sanders' request for injunctive relief to have his name added to the screen credits. [*Id.* at 577, 579.] In footnote 6 of the opinion, the court quoted three experts who opined in the 1983 case that the "a film by" credit for documentaries could be worth between $50,000 and $150,000. [*Id.* at 577.]

Even receiving credits on Internet databases have become an issue as talent strives for recognition. Founded by Col Needham in 1990, the Internet Movie Database, www.imdb.com, is now used by over 100 million unique users worldwide each month. At the 2011 Cannes Film Festival, audience members questioned Needham at the American Pavilion about how to become profiled on imdb.com. He recommended signing up through IMDb Pro.

One purported film producer sued IMDb when he was not given credit for certain productions. In *Kronemyer v. Internet Movie Database, Inc.,* 150 Cal.App.4th 941 (Cal.App. 2 Dist. 2007), David E. Kronemyer claimed he was an executive producer of the motion pictures "My Big Fat Greek Wedding" and "Wishcraft" and the television production "Stand and Be Counted," but that IMDb.com did not attribute credits to him for these productions. He claimed to have followed the procedures established by IMDb to correct credit mistakes on the site, but received no response to his queries. He asked the court to require IMDb to identify him as an Executive Producer of these productions.

The Court held that Kronemyer did not have a cause of action against IMDb because its policy was to list credits exactly as they appeared on screen was protected by the First Amendment, and it followed its own policy. Kronemyer could not provide proof to support his claim of producer credits for the productions.

2. TELEVISION CREDITS

Similar to the film industry, a person's billing position in a television project determines his importance to the project and affects his future compensation. In *Smithers v. MGM Studios*, 139 Cal.App.3d 643. 189 Cal.Rptr. 20, 22 (Cal.App.

1983), William Smithers sued MGM for breach of contract for failure to honor his "Most-Favored-Nations" billing arrangement. This provision read:

> Except for the parts of DON WALLING, HELEN WALLING, and HOWARD RUTLEDGE, this deal is on a Most Favored Nations basis, i.e., if any other performer receives greater compensation than Artist, Artist shall receive that compensation.
>
> Additionally, no other performer shall receive more prominent billing or a better billing provision than Artist (except with respect to where his name is placed in the crawl).

[Id.] The billing provision was to offset Smithers' agreement to accept a lower than usual compensation rate. MGM said that it used this provision to "get some good people to work for reasonably low money and to not have to take up a great deal of space in the main titles." [Id.]

When the pilot was screened, Smithers saw that there were *four* actors with 'up-front' billing, instead of the agreed upon three actors…. Ultimately, ten or eleven actors were given 'up-front' billing, while Smithers' end-of-the-show-name-only billing remained the same. [Id.] In September 1976, Smithers complained that his billing was not in conformity with his contract. In mid-December 1976, he was told that his role was to be written out of the series.

MGM also tried to get Smithers to waive the clause, which he refused to do and instead sued MGM.

At trial, the jury ruled in favor of Smithers and awarded him damages of $3 million on four counts. It also found that MGM had committed the tort of breach of duty of good faith and fair dealing, breached its contract, and perpetrated fraud. Smithers agreed to reduce the verdict to $1,800,001 in return for denying MGM's motion for a new trial. On appeal, the judgment was affirmed. The Court of Appeal observed that there was sufficient evidence to support the jury's determination. On the fraud claim, for example, the Court of Appeal said the evidence indicated that MGM "had no intention of living up to its most-favored-nations provision, which was offered to induce Smithers to accept a lower than usual compensation rate."

The *Smithers* case was subsequently transferred to the California Court of Appeal for reconsideration in light of a ruling in another employment case. With no further case history, the parties most likely settled their dispute.

3. MUSIC CREDITS

In the music industry, musicians may fight over who is entitled to songwriter credit and who warrants the performance credit. Composers who contribute the music, the lyrics, or both are typically entitled to receive the songwriter credit.

In Mozart and Beethoven's era, composers received glory, some compensation, and immortality. While current songwriters may receive a measure of glory, they most importantly receive mechanical and performance royalties, which can sometimes result in a lifelong income stream. As a result, songwriters often make more money than performers because they get paid not only every time the song is performed, whether on a concert stage or on the radio, but also for each song that is sold.

Some producers and singers may seek to add their names to the writing credit as a means of receiving some of the royalties. The bigger the producer or singer, the more he or she can bargain for or demand this credit. Producers who are known for crafting hit after hit bring together the right backup musicians and sound crew. They have even more power. However, songwriters with little clout may sometimes be left out of the credits and have to sue to have their names added.

In *Goodman v. Lee*, 815 F.2d 1030 (5th Cir. 1987), Shirley Goodman claimed that she co-wrote "Let the Good Times Roll" with Leonard Lee and sought to have the copyright registration changed to reflect her co-authorship. Goodman and Lee grew up in the same neighborhood and began composing songs together in 1952. The singers who recorded the 1956 "Let the Good Times Roll" included Barbra Streisand, Ray Charles, Roy Orbison, and Jerry Lee Lewis. They made it Goodman and Lee's biggest hit.

Lee, who was responsible for their business affairs, registered the copyright in their early songs in both names, but registered later songs, including "Let The Good Times Roll," in his name alone. Goodman received no publishing royalties for songs registered solely under Lee's name. [*Id.* at 1031.] As the court noted in a footnote, publishing companies typically pay royalties, usually around 50%, to the author listed on the copyright registration. [*Id.* at 1031 n.1.]

Goodman did not learn of the error until the original copyrights were up for renewal in 1984. When she sought to have the copyright office add her name, she was informed that only the proprietor of the copyright could change the name. She then sued, requesting the court to include her name as co-author with Lee and to order an accounting of the royalty income. While the District Court granted summary judgment for Lee's family, the Court of Appeals reversed, finding that Goodman was entitled to a trial to prove her claim of co-authorship of the song. [*Id.* at 1032.]

The jury agreed with Goodman and awarded her damages. After several post-trial hearings, the District Court entered a final judgment declaring Goodman a joint owner of the copyright of "Let The Good Times Roll," ordering the Register of Copyrights to identify her as co-author and joint owner of the copyright registration, and awarding her one-half of royalties received by the Lees from 1976 to

1993, together with prejudgment interest. The Fifth Circuit affirmed [78 F.3d 1007, 1009 (5ᵗʰ Cir. 1996)], and the Supreme Court denied the Lees' request for an appeal [519 U.S. 861 (1996)].

In *C & C Entertainment v. Rios-Sanchez*, 208 F.Supp.2d 139 (D.Puerto Rico 2002), the court declared that "A co-authorship claimant bears the burden of establishing that each of the putative co-authors (1) made independently copyrightable contributions to the work; and (2) fully intended to become co-authors." [*Id.* at 142.] Further, the court noted that in *Edward B. Marks Music Corp. v. Jerry Vogel*, 140 F.2d 268 (4ᵗʰ Cir. 1944), "a lyricist and composer were found to be coauthors where the lyricist wrote the words for the song ('December and May'), intending that someone else would eventually compose the music for those particular words."

This court made a point of noting that authors do not have to work in concert, or even know each other to become joint authors. Rather, "it is enough that they mean their contributions to be complementary in the sense that they are to be embodied in a single work to be performed as such." [*Id.*]

Performance credits are listed on the album, CD, or cassette. Both the cover and the actual item will list the name of the group or individuals who performed the song(s). The group Milli Vanilli, composed of Rob Pilatus and Fabrice Morvan, was credited with the 1989 hit "Girl You Know It's True," which sold seven million copies in the U.S. and 30 million singles internationally. In 1990, Milli Vanilli won the Grammy Award for Best New Artist.

While performing a concert, the sound system broke. The duo didn't realize it and continued to mouth the lyrics, exposing to the world that Milli Vanilli was a fraud created by German producer Frank Farian. Pilatus and Morvan were merely the public face for a group of anonymous musicians that included female singer Gina Mohammed and several other male singers including Charles Shaw, Johnny Davis, and Brad Howell. After the truth was revealed, Milli Vanilli became the first group ever stripped of a Grammy Award.

In *Freedman v. Arista Records*, 137 F. R. D. 225 (E.D. Pa. 1991), several buyers sued in federal District Court, charging Arista Records with fraud, misrepresentation, and breach of warranty for promoting Milli Vanilli. The plaintiffs sought certification of a class to include all US purchasers of Milli Vanilli recordings prior to November 15, 1990. The plaintiffs argued that seven million people purchased the album because they believed Pilatus and Morvan personally sang the songs contained in the album.

The District Court refused to certify the class, finding that the motion could not be granted under Rule 23 (b)(3), which requires class issues predominate over the individual ones. The court stressed the individualized reasons for purchasing music. The court observed:

> What causes a person to respond positively to a performance is a complex matter, especially in these modern times where popular musical performances involve visual as well as auditory stimulation. One's response to art is personal and as such it is not susceptible to a class based determination of inducement.

While Arista won the lawsuit, the Milli Vanilli band disbanded. Pilatus and Morvan formed another group, called Rob and Fab, to prove they really could sing, but their debut sold only 2000 copies. Pilatus committed suicide in April 1998. [Huey, *Milli Vanilli*.]

Milli Vanilli's downfall revealed an open secret about live concerts. Many fans often wonder while listening to a performance, "Is it live, or is it Memorex?" Lip-synching rumors have plagued musicians as diverse as Ashlee Simpson, Britney Spears, Madonna, and Janet Jackson. Nevertheless, since they are mouthing the words to their own voices, these musicians do not create the performance credit problems of a Milli Vanilli.

B. COMPENSATION

As the discussion above has demonstrated, credit and billing are intricately linked to compensation. As noted in the *Smithers* case, actors will trade pay for credit to appear in a film that could help their careers. While unions negotiate the minimum compensation due talent in the film and television industries, the American Federation of Musicians primarily assists musicians who are employed under collective bargaining arrangements, such as symphony orchestras. The AFM also offers sample contracts to aid bands and solo artists in negotiating their own compensation.

Much publicity is given to film actors like Harrison Ford (*K-19*) and Will Smith (*I, Robot*) who make upwards of $25 million a picture. They have hit the lottery, while the scale actor makes $2541 a week, a set painter $2,889 per week, and a key grip $3,018 per week as scale wages. (Brady, *What Hollywood Makes.*] Similarly, the upper tier television stars that make $1 million or more an episode are rare.

That said, film stars have been known to trade compensation for credit by appearing in lower budget films that showcase their talent in other genres. By augmenting their acting range, stars may receive a higher quality choice of scripts. After getting his start in sexually explicit films (*The Italian Stallion*) and then becoming known for action flicks (*Rocky*, *Rambo*, and *Cliffhanger*), which earned him as much as $20 million per picture, Sylvester Stallone received union negotiated scale wages to play a chubby, passive sheriff driven to action in a New Jersey town full of rogue New York cops in *Copland*. That film offered Stallone the opportunity to prove he could act alongside luminaries such as Academy Award winner Robert De Niro.

Above-the-title actors, such as Jim Carrey and Robin Williams who sometimes make $25 million a picture, have their compensation based on a cut of the box office gross receipts. Jack Nicholson, for example, received total compensation approximating $60 million for playing the role of The Joker in the 1989 film *Batman*, which was far more than the one million dollars Michael Keaton earned for playing the title role.

The pay of stars often increases with the box office gross of their pictures. Bruce Willis, for example, was paid $20 million for the 1995 *Die Hard with a Vengeance*, an increase by four times what he received for the original 1988 *Die Hard*. The former took in $365 million in worldwide box office compared to $139 million for the original film. In between, Willis starred in *Die Hard 2: Die Harder*, which earned $237,500,000. The increasing successes of these ventures enabled Willis to command higher fees.

Because big sports are shown on television, outstanding athletes like Serena Williams, Tiger Woods, and Roger Federer can augment their winnings by endorsing products in television commercials that earn them far more than their prize money. Forbes Magazine declared Maria Sharapova the top-earning female athlete in 2005. Of her reported

$23,000,000 in income, only about ten percent accrued from winning checks at tennis tournaments. The remainder came from endorsement deals.

Producers and studio executives can also face compensation challenges. In *Ladd v. Warner Bros. Entertainment,* 184 Cal.App.4th 1298 (Cal.App. 2 Dist. 2010), producer Allan Ladd, Jr. was among the plaintiffs challenging Warner Brothers' practice of "straight-lining" the allocation of licensing fees to movies in a package for re-broadcast on television and cable networks. With "straight-lining," Warner Brothers allocated the same share of the licensing fee to every movie in a package, regardless of its value to the licensee. Ladd claimed this deprived him of a fair allocation of the licensing fees to which he was entitled as a profit participant for 12 motion pictures that included *Blade Runner*, *Body Heat*, and *Chariots of Fire*.

The trial court awarded Ladd and his co-plaintiffs nearly $3.2 million in damages for the unfair licensing practice, and Warner Brothers appealed. The court noted that every contract in California contains an implied covenant of good faith and fair dealing, which Warner Brothers breached with its "straight-lining" practice. The court affirmed the award of $3,190,625 to Ladd, and granted him his appeal costs.

It was Walt Disney Company shareholders that challenged the $130 million severance package paid to Michael Ovitz after he served only 18 months of a contracted five-year term as president. The shareholders brought a derivative action alleging that directors and officers of the company breached their fiduciary duty and committed waste claims when they fired Ovitz without cause and gave him a $130 million golden parachute. The Delaware Supreme Court disagreed.

It held that Ovitz did not breach any fiduciary duties when he negotiated his employment agreement with Disney and accepted the $130 million severance payout. Further, it found sufficient evidence to establish Disney's CEO, officers, and Board of Directors did not violate their fiduciary duties in this matter. It also concluded that Disney's payment of the severance package did not constitute waste of its corporate assets.

In short, the different components of the entertainment industry compensate their members in a variety of ways.

1. FILM AND TELEVISION COMPENSATION

Two aspects of compensation that are peculiar to the film and television industries are "pay or play" and net compensation. Both issues are discussed in detail below.

a. Pay or Play

Actors with clout and who are in demand negotiate to include "pay or play" provisions in their contracts. If for any reason the project is cancelled, these clauses require producers or studios to compensate the artists or provide a comparable substitute. These clauses recognize that actors turn down roles in order to accept a producer's or studio's project. The following is a "pay or play" provision from an international contract, which is reprinted with permission from Marc Vlessing of Trendraise Company Limited:

This Agreement is on a "pay or play" basis (as this term is understood in the UK film industry) PROVIDED THAT:

...the financier(s) providing the majority of the funding for the Film and the completion guarantor bonding the Film shall have gone on risk in relation to the Film, i.e. become so legally obligated without unfulfilled conditions precedent, within 3 weeks of the date hereof:

...the Artist shall mitigate the Producer's liability under this pay or play provision, whereby the liability hereunder shall be reduced to the extent that the Artist be remunerated for any services rendered to any third party during any period that would or could have constituted any part of the Rehearsal Period and/or the Shooting Period.

Vlessing used this contract to produce *The Gambler*, a film based on a book of the same name by Dostoyevsky. This pay or play clause states the obligations of the producer kick in once the financing is secure and an insurance company has guaranteed the film. Note also that the clause obligates the artist to look for work should the provision kick in. The actor is not permitted to sit around and wait for work but, rather, he should actively seek to find other work.

In 1970, Academy Award-winning actress Shirley MacLaine litigated the true meaning of this provision in *Parker v. 20th Century Fox Film*, 118 Cal. App.3d 895 (Cal.App.2 Dist. 1981). She sued Twentieth Century-Fox Film Corp. after it cancelled the musical "Bloomer Girl" and offered her the western "Big Country, Big Man" in its place. While the compensation was to remain at $750,000, MacLaine argued that the two were not the equivalent as required by her contract. "Bloomer Girl" would allow her to employ her song and dance talents and would be filmed in Los Angeles, whereas "Big Country, Big Man" was a straight dramatic role to be filmed in Australia. The new contract also eliminated her right to approve the director of the film and the screenwriter. The court agreed that the two films were not equivalent, and thus MacLaine was entitled to receive the $750,000 even though she had rejected the substitute film.

In a phone interview, MacLaine said that she "had turned down a year and a half of pictures to do 'Bloomer Girl'." She advises talent to "get the contract down and get it signed by everyone involved." [Author Interview with MacLaine.] Neither "Bloomer Girl," which had opened October 5, 1944, at the Shubert Theatre and ran for 654 performances on Broadway, nor "Big Country, Big Man" were ever made into feature films.

Actress Raquel Welch sued MGM after it fired her from her starring role in the film *Cannery Row*. A jury found that MGM had breached its contract, which contained a "pay or play clause," and ordered MGM to pay $2 million in compensatory damages and over $8 million in punitive damages. In affirming, the Court of Appeals noted in *Welch v. MGM*, 254 Cal.Rptr. 654, 663 (Cal.App. 2 Dist. 1988), that Welch was harmed by the loss of reputation and revenue from the additional film roles she would have obtained but for the firing. The *Welch* case was subsequently vacated and transferred to the Court of Appeal for reconsideration in light of a ruling in another employment case. With no further case history, the parties most likely settled their dispute.

Actress Cicely Tyson sued Elizabeth Taylor and her production company for violating the "pay or play" provision of her theatrical contract. Tyson agreed to play the lead role in the Broadway production of "The Corn is Green," which was to be taped for television. She was to receive $750,000 in a "pay or play guarantee," which reflected that Tyson, at the height of her career, would have to turn down other film, television, and stage opportunities to commit a year to "The Corn is Green." After a short run, the play was cancelled and never filmed for television. Regardless, the court found in *This is Me, Inc. v. Taylor*, 157 F.3d 139 (2nd Cir. 1998) , that Taylor and her production company owed Tyson the balance on her contract.

b. Net Compensation

Film and television artists often receive three types of compensation: guaranteed, deferred, and contingent. The first two are fairly easy to calculate. Guaranteed compensation is fixed and must be paid according to the contract schedule. Deferred compensation refers to that which is delayed until the happening of a specified event. Contingent compensation can be based on gross or net revenues.

Gross compensation is paid based on the revenue generated at the box office. An actor who has contracted for gross participation points will receive a percentage of all box office and other revenues. Net compensation is paid after a number of subtractions, which leave the film or television show in a negative balance. Actors, writers, and other talent who have contracted to receive net participation points rarely receive additional compensation beyond guaranteed and deferred payments.

For example, Leonardo DiCaprio earned $1.8 million plus 18% of net compensation to star in *Titanic*, which earned $600,000,000 domestically as part of a global box office of nearly $2 billion. Like all movies, *Titanic* never earned a profit because of the studio's accounting system. DiCaprio received guaranteed compensation of $20,000,000 for his next picture *The Man in the Iron Mask*, which was released in 1998 and earned $57 million in the U.S. and $126 million globally, for a total of $183 million. [Movie Box Office Figures, *available at* http://www.ldsfilm.com/box/box.html.]

On August 31, 1992, The Hollywood Reporter published an accounting of the picture *Rain Man*, which had earned $228,112,545 as of May 31, 1992. The studio subtracted distribution fees, distribution expenses, and gross participation payouts, which left a balance of $16,582,814. Only then did it subtract $45,870,506 in production costs, which included direct costs, an overhead charge representing 15% of the production budget, and interest. The result was that *Rain Man* was in the hole.

TABLE 8-1: FILM ACCOUNTING	
ITEM	*AMOUNT*
Box office revenue	$228,112,545
-Distribution Fee	$ 79,330,738
-Distribution Expenses	$ 54,649,361
-Gross Participation Payouts	$ 77,549,632
=*Preliminary Balance*	*$ 16,582,814*
-Production costs	$ 29,098,523
-Direct-Overhead Charge (15%)	$ 4,364,779
-Interest	$ 12,407,204
=Final Balance	**($29,287,692)**

Based on this type of accounting, those individuals expecting net profit payouts on a picture that cost $29 million to make, yet earned $228 million at the box office, were out of luck.

Net profits are also referred to as backend profits. In an interview, screenwriter Walon Green said, "To obtain backend profits on my projects, I'd have to hire a forensic accountant. The cost of hiring the accountant and an attorney would probably exceed what the accountant found." [Author Interview with Green.] Art Buchwald discovered the truth of this statement the hard way.

Once Buchwald and his co-plaintiff Alain Bernheim won their initial lawsuit to have Buchwald credited with providing the idea and Bernheim with being a producer for *Coming to America*, they found themselves in the uncomfortable position of having to enforce a contract that was based on net profits. In the second phase of the case [Art Buchwald v. Paramount Pictures Corp., Second Phase, No. C706083 (Cal. Superior. Ct. Dec. 21, 1990)], Judge Schneider found Paramount's definition of net profits unconscionable.

Judge Schneider declared that following seven provisions of Paramount's net profit formula were unconscionable: (1) the 15% overhead on Eddie Murphy Productions Operational Allowance; (2) 10% advertising overhead not in proportion to actual cost; (3) 15% overhead not in proportion to actual costs; (4) charging interest on negative cost balance without credit for distribution fees; (5) charging interest on overhead; (6) charging interest on profit participation payments; and (7) charging an interest rate of 20% to 30 %, which was not in proportion to the actual cost of the funds. [*Id.*] Schneider considered many of these items to be double charges and a method of hiding huge profits. [*Id.*]

In the third phase of the trial, Buchwald, Bernheim, and their attorney found out that even when you win, you lose. The court awarded Buchwald compensation of $150,000 for his idea based on his entitlement to 1.5% of net profits and his partner Alain Bernheim $750,000 based on his initial entitlement to a minimum of 17.5% (reduced from 40%) of net profits. Art Buchwald v. Paramount Pictures Corp., Third Phase, No. 706083 (Cal. Superior Ct. Mar. 16, 1992). To win this judgment, their attorney Pierce O'Donnell, a partner at the prestigious Kaye Scholer, Fierman, Hays, and Handler's Los Angeles office, ran up a $2.5 million legal bill and over $500,000 in costs to complete the three and one-half year case.

O'Donnell, a former Supreme Court clerk to Justice Byron White, had taken the case on a contingency fee arrangement that made Buchwald and Bernheim responsible only for the cost of the trial. In the end, O'Donnell and his team spent $3 million to reap a judgment of $900,000 for their clients. O'Donnell wrote the book *Fatal Subtraction: How Hollywood Really Does Business* (1992), detailing the inside story of *Buchwald v. Paramount Pictures*, in part to recoup some of his investment. O'Donnell left Kaye Scholer in 1996 to start his own firm, O'Donnell and Shaeffer LLP.

Net profit stories are a legend in Hollywood, and yet such lawsuits continue to be filed. Benjamin Melniker and Michael Uslan sued Warner Brothers after their 13% net profit deal on the *Batman* films, which earned over $1 billion in box office revenues, yielded no further compensation beyond their $1,100,000 in fixed and deferred fees. The court found in *Batfilm Productions, Inc. v. Warner Bros.*, No. BC 051653 and No. BC 051654 (Cal. Superior Ct. Mar. 14, 1994), that they were not coerced into signing a net profit deal. Melniker was a former

MGM general counsel and senior executive who, according to the court, "knew all the tricks of the trade." Melniker and Uslan argued that their contract was unfair to them because Warner Brothers and others earned millions of dollars on *Batman* and they did not. The court considered this argument irrelevant, determining that while the contract may have been unfair, it was not unconscionable. [*Id.*]

Matt Damon and Ben Affleck, the writers and stars of the 1997 film *Good Will Hunting*, found themselves in a position similar to the producers of *Batman*. Harvey Weinstein had invested between $15 and $20 million on *Good Will Hunting*, which returned a worldwide box office gross of $226 million, excluding network, cable, and video revenue. Damon was paid an acting fee of $650,000, while Affleck received a little less. Weinstein eventually gave them a bonus of $500,000 each. In an interview with Peter Biskind, Affleck said, "*Good Will Hunting* had done enormously well by then, but we had gotten an accounting statement that said the movie was $50 million in the red…. You had to have some great accounting to hide net profits on that movie." [Biskind, *Down and Dirty Pictures*, at 118.]

Affleck further indicated that he and Damon had made a Faustian bargain with the Weinstein brothers. "The exchange is," he said, "they'll spend money promoting the movie, they'll spend money on an Academy campaign, they'll win you an Oscar®, and their reputation is they make better movies. But they're a nightmare to work with . . . So, yeah, we kind of got screwed, but when it came right down to it, it worked out great for us." Affleck and Damon became highly paid actors, able to command $10 - $20 million per picture. [*Id.*]

Television writers, actors, directors, and producers experience the same problems trying to collect net profits on their hits. Anthony Yerkovich sued MCA and Universal for net compensation due him for writing the pilot teleplay that Universal subsequently produced as *Miami Vice*. [Yerkovich v. MCA, 11 F.Supp.2d 1167 (C.D. Cal. 1997)] The Court of Appeals affirmed the District Court's finding that even if it accepted Yerkovich's interpretation of his agreement, there was insufficient admissible evidence showing that he was entitled to additional money. [Yerkovich v. MCA, 211 F.3d 1276 (9th Cir. 2000)] The Supreme Court denied his petition for a writ of certiorari.

One of the problems talent confronts in pursuing claims for net profits is that studios tend to settle the suits they think they are going to lose. In the legal data bases, researches will find little information about former television star Fess Parker's litigation seeking his 40% net profits share of the $38 million Fox Studios received once it syndicated the 165 episodes of his show *Daniel Boone*.

Parker said that his lawsuit went on for 10 years and cost him over $350,000. He attended one motion hearing after another until a judge finally ruled in *Parker v. Twentieth Century Fox Film Corp.*, 118 Cal.App.3d 895 (Cal.App.2.Dist. 1981) that he was entitled to a trial. After that, the studio settled quickly. Parker had hired a young Santa Barbara attorney to represent him. Buried in the documents the lawyer received was a memo from a Fox accountant with a note that said, "Can we do it this way and screw old Fess?" [Author Interview with Parker.] After the lawsuit, Parker's 19-year Hollywood career came to an abrupt end, but he has no regrets. He owns the Fess Parker Winery, Inn, and Spa. The former is renowned for its Chardonnay, Pinot Noir, and Chocolate Chardonnay Raspberry Sauce. The lesson from Parker's story is that lawyers may have to dig deep to find the important document, and for talent that it might pay off to stick with the right lawyer.

After negative publicity denigrated the term "net profits," studios and production companies are more likely to use the phrases "adjusted gross profits" or "modified adjusted gross profits" in their contracts. The result may be same, however, unless the contract is clearly structured to yield a positive amount of profits, from which talent will receive a share.

2. MUSIC COMPENSATION

Musicians may earn money from composing songs, tour performances, merchandising their group name, and royalties on their records. Rolling Stone Magazine regularly releases an annual list of music's biggest moneymakers for the prior year. For example, in 2010 it declared that Bon Jovi was the world's top concert attraction, "despite a soft market for live music and weak sales for the band's most recent album. The New Jersey rockers sold $201.1 million worth of tickets through the year, with sales split almost evenly between shows in North America and the rest of the world. The tour currently ranks as the 9th highest grossing in the history of the North American market. AC/DC was the second biggest draw, grossing $177 million. U2 came in third for global sales, raking in $160.1 million for two overseas legs for their massive 360 Tour, which was the top worldwide tour in the previous year. Lady Gaga was the fourth-highest grossing act, taking in $133.6 million for her Monster Ball world tour. Gaga was clearly the hardest working act in the top 10, performing a whopping 138 gigs compared to Bon Jovi's 80, AC/DC's 40 and U2's 32." [Rolling Stone's Best of 2010, available at www.rollingstone.com]

Symphony conductors with top orchestras are among the more highly paid musicians who receive salaries for their services. The New York Times revealed on July 4, 2004, that the New York Philharmonic paid Lorin Maazel $2,280,000 during the 2002-03 concert year and the Chicago Symphony paid Daniel Barenboim $2,140,000 during the 2001-02 concert year. The Times reported that "[a]mong the 18 American orchestras with 52-week contracts, at least seven pay their music directors more than $1 million, and three pay their manager more than $700,000." [Tindal, *The Plight of the White-Tie Worker*.] The Times also stated, "[A]s pay increases for symphony leaders soared, the player's annual raises dropped from 3.9 percent in 1993 to 1.7 percent in 2003." [*Id.* at 24.]

Early in their careers, musicians who write and perform in other genres often find themselves in positions similar to beginning film and television stars whereby they accept bad deals in order to get their records made. Composers, as discussed above, receive royalties based on their copyright credits. Performers may receive a flat fee, a percentage of the box office revenues, or a combination thereof depending on how big they are. Merchandising revenue stems from trademarking the musician's or band's name and then applying it to products ranging from t-shirts and posters to programs and any other memorabilia that resonates with fans.

It is the record contracts that give musicians the most heartache, causing them to bargain for as much upfront payment as possible. The royalty payments, representing a percent of the sales revenue, often shock musicians when they receive their statements, particularly if they have produced a gold or platinum album and spent money in anticipation of a big payout. The problem is similar to the net profit scenario in film and television in that the key factor is to determine what is subtracted from gross revenues.

The contract may subtract recording costs, advances to producers and musicians, video production costs, excess mechanicals, royalties payable to the producer, packaging costs, promotional costs, and a percent for reserves against returns before paying any royalty to the musicians. This royalty rate decreases on mid-price and budget records by as much as 50%, although Peter Thall says that the rate can be increased to a two-thirds rate for budget records and a three-quarters rate for mid-price records. [Thall, *What They'll Never Tell You About the Music Business*, at 28.] Thall says that the royalty rate may also be reduced for singles, for foreign sales, and for record clubs. [*Id.* at 28-29.] Even when the record companies support the cost of tours, they deduct any money advanced from the royalties. [*Id.* at 33.] All these deductions can leave the musicians owing their recording company money or waiting for payments that may never arrive. This accounts for some of the bankruptcy problems discussed in Chapter 3.

Disputes can arise over foreign royalties and even royalties due after heirs after the musicians have long expired. In *Evans v. Famous Music Corp.*, 1 N.Y.3d 452 (N.Y.2004), a group of songwriters sought an interpretation of a provision in six music royalty contracts detailing the manner in which income from the exploitation of songs must be apportioned between themselves and Famous Music Corporation. Specifically, they questioned whether the contract obligated Famous to share with them certain tax savings resulting from foreign tax credits. The court answered the question in the negative because the contract did not require the sharing of any benefit resulting from defendant's use of the foreign tax credit.

In *MCA Records, Inc. v. Allison*, 2009 WL 1565037 (Cal.App.2 Dist. 2009), a dispute arose over the proper amount of royalties MCA Records, Inc. (MCA) should pay heirs for songs by rock and roll legends Buddy Holly and the Crickets (J.I. Allison and Joe B. Mauldin). The contracts were entered into in 1956 and 1957. Holly was killed in a plane crash in 1959. Following a court trial, Holly's heirs (his wife and others) and the estate of Norman Petty (the former manager of Holly and the Crickets) recovered a total of approximately $251,000 in additional royalties and prejudgment interest. The Crickets recovered approximately $234,000 in additional royalties and prejudgment interest.

The Holly heirs, the Petty estate, and the Crickets appealed the award, and MCA cross-appealed, contending that all the royalty claims were completely barred because the original contract dates in the 1950's and 1960's, rather than the periodic royalty payment dates, should have been used in determining the expiration of the contractual and statutory limitation periods (two and four years respectively).

The court disagreed with MCA's contentions. It modified the judgment to increase the amount of royalties awarded the heirs by eliminating the void packaging deduction, and remanded the matter to the trial court for calculation of that adjustment. It found all other contentions to be unavailing.

As new forms of compensation develop so too will the disputes over whether the resulting amounts are fair under the contracts.

CHAPTER 9

ENTERTAINMENT CONTRACTS

William Shakespeare's plays are in the public domain, which means any film, television, or theater company may reproduce or perform them without acquiring a contract, paying fees, or seeking permission. If, however, an entertainment company wants to perform a play that is protected by copyright or hire an actor, author, director, or other personnel, the company must seek permission, which is manifested in a contract.

All contracts in the entertainment industry should contain answers to the classic questions of who, what, when, where, and how much. Contracts may be oral or written, implied or expressed. The contractual terms should serve to guide the parties in their business interactions.

For example, consider the following simple contract to publish an article in a magazine. Author Gregg Levoy (*This Business of Writing*) received a letter agreement from Vogue Magazine on 10 February 1988 that read:

Dear Gregg,

As discussed, this confirms your assignment for a piece on self-defense courses. The piece will be 1500 words in length and we will pay you $1250.

It is due in mid-February. If it isn't published, I
will pay you half that amount.

The "who" are the parties to the contract: Gregg
Levoy and Vogue Magazine. The "what" is an assignment to write an article on self-defense courses.
The "when" is the due date, by mid-February 1988.
The "where" is left up to Levoy who just has to produce the piece. The "how much" is clearly stated in
that *Vogue* will pay Levoy $1250 if they publish his
piece and $625 if they kill the piece. More common-
ly, this is called a "kill fee," which pays the author
for some of his or her time in researching and writing the article.

This letter agreement is not comprehensive. It is,
for instance, silent on the issue of copyright. When
nothing is said, the author retains all rights to the
copyright, with the exception of first publication
rights that he granted the publisher.

Written contracts endeavor to spell out precisely
what is expected of the parties involved. Oral contracts are also a staple of the industry. Personal
service contracts have always raised problems, particularly the question of when holding someone to a
contract may run afoul of the 13th Amendment to
the Constitution, which prohibits slavery. Nevertheless, entertainers do back out of deals. Sometimes,
they are better off honoring a commitment than
welching on a deal, as they may be sued and forced
to pay tremendous damages if someone has relied

on their commitment. Some entertainers discover, to their detriment, that they are bound by their oral agreements once another party has acted to secure financing based on the expectation that actors' words are their bonds.

A. FILM CONTRACTS

Whether oral or written, it is important for talent to understand the provisions of their contracts before they sign them. *Main Line Pictures v. Basinger*, 1994 WL 814244 (Cal. Ct. App. 1994), involved three types of contracts: an oral agreement, a deal memo, and a long-form agreement. In that case, the question became whether actress Kim Basinger had indeed contractually committed to star in the film *Boxing Helena*. After the trial evidence was presented, the jury concluded that Basinger and/or Mighty Wind, her loan-out corporation, had entered into oral and written agreements that they breached.

The California Court of Appeals observed that the jury found direct evidence that Basinger herself entered into a contract with Main Line. There was testimony that she personally discussed the project with her attorney, and she gave her agents the authority to bind her in the contract. The documents referred to Basinger's performance. Further, there was the evidence to support the contention that Mighty Wind entered into the contract with Main Line. The discussions took place at Mighty Wind's offices. There was also a written agreement between Mighty Wind and Basinger and the deal memos evidenced a contract with Mighty Wind. Basinger was ultimately held responsible for having breached a contract with Main Line Pictures.

In addition to the truism that entertainers are bound by their contracts, they must also be aware of standard practices that are inferred into contracts. Director Otto Preminger, for example, admitted that when he signed the agreement to have *Anatomy of a Murder* shown on television, he was aware that the practice in the television industry was to interrupt motion pictures for commercials and to make minor cuts. Although he was aware of the practice, the court found in *Preminger v. Columbia Pictures*, 49 Misc.2d 363, 267 N.Y.S.2d 594 (S.Ct. 1966), that Preminger did not specifically negotiate to change conditions prevalent in the industry. Industry practices may be altered, but they must be done so expressly in a written agreement.

1. INSURANCE CONTRACTS

Insurance contracts are also important to filmmaking as they guarantee that the picture will be completed. Problems arise when actors die, such as when the singer Aaliyah tragically perished in a plane crash before completing her role in *The Matrix: Reloaded*. Nona Gaye, the daughter of singer Marvin Gaye, replaced Aaliyah.

In *CNA Intern. Reinsurance Co. Ltd. v. Phoenix*, 678 So.2d 373 (Fla.App. 1 Dist. 1996), an insurance company sued an actor's estate to recover payments to the insured. At the time actor River Phoenix died after taking an overdose of drugs, he was committed to star in two films, *Dark Blood* and *Interview with the Vampire*. After Phoenix's death, *Dark Blood* was abandoned and *Interview with the Vampire* was completed with actor Christian Slater replacing Phoenix.

The insurance companies sued Phoenix's estate for breach of contract, alleging that he was "under a general obligation not to do anything that would deprive the parties to the agreement of its benefits." CNA argued that "by deliberately taking illegal drugs in quantities in excess of those necessary to kill a human being, Phoenix deprived the parties of his services and breached his obligation." [*Id.*] CNA also charged that Phoenix had signed a fraudulent medical certificate in which he denied having ever used "LSD, heroin, cocaine, alcohol in excess, or any other narcotics, depressants, stimulants or psychedelics whether prescribed or not prescribed by a physician." [*Id.*]

After the trial court dismissed the action with prejudice, finding that death excused performance of the contract, the Florida District Court of Appeal affirmed. It determined that "the parties to the agreements could have provided specifically for the contingent of loss due to the use of illegal drugs, as they provided for other hazardous or life threatening conditions." [*Id.*]

Insurance companies consider actors like Robert Downey Jr., who has been imprisoned for drug and alcohol problems, to be a high risk and increase rates accordingly. If the rates rise significantly or an actor becomes uninsurable, production companies and studios may forgo working with that actor. According to the *New York Times*, Downey was set to star in a Woody Allen project when producers dropped him after they "found out that there was no affordable way to resolve the cost of insuring him." [Udovitch, *The Sobering Life of Robert Downey Jr.*]

2. TALENT CONTRACTS

a. Actor Contracts

During her trial, Kim Basinger was asked under direct examination, "At what time can you breach an agreement?" She answered, "Anytime I want to." [Burr and Henslee, at 180.]

Ms. Basinger found out the hard way that contracts must be obeyed when the jury awarded a verdict of $9.8 million to Main Line Pictures, which was double their request. Unable to pay, Basinger declared bankruptcy and sold the town she had bought for $20 million for $1 million.

Actors give both oral consent and sign contracts to procure their services. Such contracts will state the term of the engagement (the number of weeks for rehearsals and principal photography); the remuneration (how much the actor is to be paid and in what installments); expense payments (for transportation, housing, and per diem); and the actress' services and obligations (specifying that the actress will complete the role and comply with all directions). A health provision requires the actress to indicate that she is not suffering from any physical or mental incapacity that would prevent her from rendering services. Other provisions may deal with copyright, dubbing, insurance, and force majeure. If the actress becomes incapacitated or fails to perform her services, the producer may suspend her services.

Shirley MacLaine, who has been acting for 50 years, advises her colleagues to "get the contract down and get it signed by everyone involved.... [W]hatever is in the contract should be observed." [Author Interview with MacLaine]

b. Writer Contracts

Author Tony Hillerman advises writers that when they receive Hollywood option money, "Tear open the envelope and run out and cash the check immediately. The writer's role in movies is to listen and nod." [Author Interview with Hillerman.]

Writers like Hillerman provide source material to Hollywood production companies. A producer will ask the author of a printed novel to sign an option agreement, which gives the producer a specified time period to pull together all the major components of the project—script, actors, directors, financing, and crew. With the option contract, the writer gives film rights in return for credit (usually a "based upon" credit) and a fee, but he retains the remainder of the copyright unless the contract says otherwise.

Hillerman told the author of this book about an incident early on when he accidentally gave up the rights to "Joe Leaphorn," his principal protagonist. His option contract said that when the final payment was made, the producer would own all rights to the book. Hillerman had to retain an attorney to retrieve the rights to his character.

Screenwriters use books like Hillerman's *A Thief of Time* and *Skinwalkers* to turn them into scripts for television or feature films. Screenwriters may also generate original material of their own. Screenwriters may be engaged for a particular period of time to pen a script, with delivery periods established to indicate when the drafts, re-writes, and the polished draft are due. The writer may receive sole or shared screenplay credit depending on how much of his words make it into the final draft. If there are several writers, the Writers Guild may arbitrate to determine who is entitled to credit.

The screenwriter's contract will also state the up-front compensation, which is set to delivery of material, payments for additional services, bonus, and deferred or contingent compensation. Some screenwriters' contracts attempt to tie the author in advance to a sequel. The screenwriters' contract may also set performance standards, requiring prompt, diligent and conscientious effort, and state the circumstances under which the screenwriter may be terminated. These contracts frequently state the producers' ownership rights, and that these rights can be assigned.

While writers should read their contracts in advance, too often they don't and are later surprised. Walon Green says some writers don't give their contracts to a lawyer "and they end up in trouble. They wait to find a lawyer when they haven't been paid. By then it may be too late." [Author Interview with Green.]

c. Director Contracts

Stephen Frears, who directed *Dangerous Liaisons*, *Dirty Pretty Things*, and *The Queen*, advises creators involved in the business not to take any money until they are sure they want to work with particular people. Frears was once sued by a producer after he orally agreed to do a film and the producer sent his agent some money before he had a chance to review the script. He says, "When I saw the script I realized it wasn't for me and I decided to back out." Frears says he learned, "Taking money creates a contract and expectations that you are really going to do the picture." [Author Interview with Frears.]

A contract to engage a director's service will specify the working title of the motion picture, the term of the engagement, and the services to be rendered. This kind of contract typically divides the time required for the director's services into pre-production (meetings, location searches, and rehearsals), production (principal photography), and post-production (editing, cutting, and final mix) periods. The compensation is divided into guaranteed or fixed, deferred, and contingent or net amounts.

Directors of a certain stature may have a "pay or play" provision, obligating the production company to pay the director or offer an alternate film if the one under contract falls through. These contracts specify the living, transportation, and other expenses to which the director is entitled to be allocated in advance or reimbursed.

The director may also be held to certain specified performance standards, which permit the production company to fire the director if he does not live up to them or becomes incapacitated. The director may have to warrant that he or she is not under any current disabilities or agreements that would affect his or her participation on the picture. With warranties come indemnities, requiring the director to compensate or reimburse the production company if the director breaches his guarantees.

Perhaps the most important advice for directors comes from Stephen Frears. He says he now makes certain that he wants to work with the particular people and their picture before he takes money or signs contracts. [*Id.*]

B. TELEVISION CONTRACTS

Contracts are important to every aspect of television production, from the idea stage to the final exhibition and licensing of material for distribution on videotapes or DVDs. As in film, TV contracts may be oral or written. If oral, the question becomes whether there was sufficient agreement among the parties to form a contract. Even when there are written pages available, the parties must clearly intend their words to form a contract.

The plaintiff in *Panizza v. Mattel*, 2003 WL 22251317 (S.D.N.Y. 2003), confronted the issue of how to enforce the use of an idea without an express contract. Like film plaintiffs before her, Panizza sought to have the law imply a quasi-contract because she gave the ideas in confidence. In doing so, she found herself in a bind once the defendants removed the case to federal court, which requires a federal question when the two parties are from the same jurisdiction. She properly brought the idea case in state court, but once it was removed to federal jurisdiction, she would have been better served if she had alleged copyright infringement as a first issue. She proved once again the difficulty of bringing an idea case based on quasi-contract theory.

Letters may also form the basis of a contract, if the parties manifested sufficient intent that they do so. In *Burr v. American National Theatre and Academy*, 103 N.Y.S.2d 589 (N.Y. Sup. Ct. 1951), Eugene Burr sued the defendants for breach of contract based on letters dated May 15, 1950. He alleged that the defendants had committed to pay him and his partner $1000 per show if they procured a sponsor. The court found that the plaintiffs had performed their duties but the defendants had not; therefore, it reversed the prior dismissal of the action.

Even when the contracts spell out precisely the obligation of all parties, disputes can arise as to whether they have been carried out. Sandra Furton Gabriel sued ABC for violating their contract to compensate her if they turned her idea and pilot for a talk show called *Girl Friends* into a full-fledged production. When *The View* premiered in August 1997, Gabriel thought they had done so. ABC maintained that *The View*, which featured Barbara Walters and four other female hosts of varying ages was created and produced by Walter's Barwall Productions, Inc. Inc. In *Girl Friends Productions v. ABC*, 2000 WL 1505978 (S.D.N.Y. 2000), the court agreed and granted summary judgment to ABC. It did not find any substantial similarity between the two shows. The Second Circuit affirmed. [20 Fed.Appx. 75 (2nd Cir. 2001)]

The terms of the contract may create a clash if one party argues that it gave them a right that the other party disputes. In *Wexley v. KTTV*, 108

F.Supp. 558 (S.D.Cal. 1952), the sole issue was whether the 1931 contract gave the purchaser the right to televise a motion picture. The third clause of the contract granted the purchaser "complete, entire, and exclusive motion picture rights in and to the said dramatic compositions." The court determined that the clause granted the right to televise motion pictures, "unless a limitation or reservation is expressly and clearly imposed." [*Id.* at 559.]

In this contract, Clause C reserved for the plaintiff "television rights unaccompanied by a visual representation of the play." The plaintiff contended that "a motion picture is not a visual representation of the play," but the court disagreed. While the uses of television in 1951 may not have been foreseeable in 1931, the parties did contemplate and convey television rights. A 15-year restriction was applied to "live television" only because it was considered the most serious competition to the exhibition of motion pictures, but they did not restrict all television. [*Id.* at 560.] The court granted judgment for the defendants.

Another important aspect of television contracts is that no party can give away more rights than he has. *Gilliam v. ABC*, 538 F.2d 14 (2nd Cir. 1976), involved a series of contracts between several parties. The British Broadcasting Corporation (BBC) contracted with the Monty Python group to require them to write and deliver 30-minute scripts for use in a television series. While BBC retained final authority to make changes to the scripts, only minor changes could be made without prior consultation with the writers. Nothing in the agreement permitted BBC to alter a recorded program.

BBC did have permission to license the programs to be shown in overseas territories. It contracted with Time-Life Films to distribute the Monty Python shows in the United States. BBC gave Time-Life the rights to edit the programs for insertion of commercials, applicable censorship, or governmental rules and regulations, although BBC did not have such rights in its own agreements with the Monty Python group.

Time-Life Films then sold to ABC the right to broadcast excerpts from various Monty Python programs. Monty Python objected to ABC's plans to broadcast two 90-minute specials comprised of three 30-minute Monty Python programs. Of the 90 minutes, ABC eliminated 24 minutes to devote to commercials. When Monty Python saw the first special, they were appalled "at the discontinuity and 'mutilation' that had resulted from the editing done by Time-Life for ABC." [*Id*. at 18.] They sought an injunction to keep ABC from broadcasting the second special.

The judge granted their request for an injunction, finding they would suffer harm to their reputation that would be irreparable from the showing of the special. The judge said, "ABC may obtain no solace from the fact that editing was permitted in the agreements between BBC and Time-Life or Time-Life and ABC." [*Id.* at 21.] Further, he noted, "BBC was not entitled to make unilateral changes in the script and was not specifically empowered to alter the recordings once made." [*Id.*] Monty Python had reserved to itself all rights it did not grant to the BBC. Thus, BBC's contract with Time-Life, and the latter's subsequent contract with ABC, to permit editing was a nullity. The court agreed that ABC had distorted Monty Python's work.

Perhaps because the Monty Python group was from a foreign country, the court did not infer into their contract with BBC and between BBC and Time-Life knowledge about the industry. In two prior cases, courts held that when the film artists authorized a television showing of their work, they were bound by industry standards that permitted a right to edit and cut for television. [Preminger v. Columbia Pictures, 49 Misc.2d 363, 267 N.Y.S.2d 594 (Sup. Ct. 1966), and Autry v. Republic Productions, 213 F.2d 667 (9th Cir. 1954)] Possibly, the difference is that editing for commercials was not the industry standard in Britain at the time. When Monty Python granted BBC the right to license production overseas, they expected the British television standards to prevail.

C. MUSIC CONTRACTS

The music industry employs a variety of contracts from band partnership agreements, which set up the formation of the band and how it will run, to band/management agreements that establish the relationship between manager and the band, to band/agent agreements that set out the expectation of the band's booking agent. The contract that musical groups sign with their attorney establishes the attorney's duties to the band. Their agreements with songwriters and producers set up mutual obligations.

1. BAND PARTNERSHIP AGREEMENTS

To create a band requires an agreement, which can be oral or written, between the parties. In *Holmes v. Smith*, 94 Fed. Appx. 905 (3rd Cir. 2004), Clarence Holmes sued Will Smith for breach of contract and quantum meruit based on an alleged recording contract between them. Sometime before 1986, Smith and Jeffrey Townes formed a musical group called "DJ Jazzy Jeff and the Fresh Prince," with Smith as the Fresh Prince and Townes as DJ Jazzy Jeff, and Holmes performing with the group under the pseudonym "Ready Rock C."

On July 26, 1986, Smith and Townes together signed a record agreement with a recording company, Word-Up Records Enterprises, Inc. Holmes claims that Smith later promised him that he would be an equal member of the group. Holmes asserts that, based on this oral contract and a purported written addendum, he was entitled a one-third share of the group's future income. The purported addendum, however, did not grant a one-third share of the group's profits to Holmes, nor was it signed by Smith or Townes.

To complicate matters, after Holmes experienced financial difficulties, between 1997 and 1998, Smith wrote several checks totaling $26,000 to him. Holmes claims that Smith was paying his debt under the contract while Smith counters that the payments were gifts.

The district court held that Holmes's claims were barred by the statute of limitations because he did not bring his action within four years of the alleged breach of the contract. Holmes appealed, arguing that his quantum meruit claim was not time barred because the statute of limitations should be tolled since his alleged contract with Smith was a "continuing one." The Third Circuit determined Holmes had waived that argument by failing to raise it in the district court, and affirmed the lower court ruling.

Another key component of the band partnership agreement concerns the name and who acquires use of the name in the event that the band dissolves. In *Kassbaum v. Steppenwolf Productions, Inc.,* 236 F.3d 487 (9th Cir. 2000), Nicholas Kassbaum was sued for referring to himself as "formerly of Steppenwolf," an "original member of Steppenwolf," or an "original founding member of Steppenwolf." The Court of Appeals reversed the District Court's grant of a permanent injunction to prohibit Kassbaum's use of the name.

Kassbaum conceded that his 1980 contract "absolutely precludes" him from "performing, sponsoring or endorsing a band entitled Steppenwolf." [*Id.* at 491.] In its review, the Court of Appeals considered that the ownership and control of the name was transferred from party to party through a series of contracts. It was the 1980 contract that effected the transfer of the trade name Steppenwolf from Kassbaum and The New Steppenwolf to SPI and SI and led to Kassbaum's discontinuing to perform under The New Steppenwolf. [*Id.* at 492.]

Nevertheless, the court considered too broad the contract clause permitting the band to use the name "for any purposes whatsoever." The court concluded that Kassbaum should be allowed to identify himself as a former member of the band as this was unlikely to create consumer confusion as to the source of the band's music. [*Id.* at 492-493.]

Bands also have to be careful to not lose the use of their name. In *Far Out Productions, Inc. v. Oskar*, 247 F.3d 986 (9th Cir. 2001), a dispute arose over the use of the band name "War." Harold Brown, an original member of the group, filed a direct action against Far Out Productions, claiming that it obtained the trademark fraudulently. The District Court disagreed and the Court of Appeals affirmed.

On April 1, 1987, Far Out Productions agreed in writing with each of the band members to reaffirm Far Out Productions' exclusive ownership in the name War. Thereafter, an incontestability affidavit was filed with the Patent and Trademark Office declaring that Far Out Productions owned the mark and that it had been in continuous use for five years. [*Id.* at 990.] The band lost its name through not understanding the full consequences of the contracts they signed.

2. BAND-MANAGEMENT AGREEMENTS

The right manager can assist in developing a band's career and taking them to the next level. Managers with contacts in the music business can get the band recording contracts and the right contacts. Managers ideally seek musicians who are professional and committed to their music. Once band members become famous or superstars, the manager's role evolves.

One manager of a famous band, who wished to remain anonymous, said his challenges include dealing with band members who hate each other and no longer enjoy performing together. The band members have also been inflicted with publicly documented personal problems ranging from collapsing marriages to ongoing abuse of drugs and alcohol. This manager cites that one of his principal jobs is arranging for lawyers to address legal problems and staging interventions to encourage the band members to take action on their personal problems. This band, which wrote dozens of songs that have been consistently recorded by other musicians, generates an ongoing stream of income from their publishing royalties.

Musicians and their managers have been known to dispute entitlement to royalties. When conflict arises, a court may review their contract. In *Ahern v. Scholz,* 85 F.3d 774 (1st Cir. 1996), a manager and a musician traded claims and counterclaims over which one owed the other money for breaching their agreements. Donald Thomas Scholz, a musician, composer, and record producer with the group Boston, accused the manager Paul Ahern of failing to render direct accountings every six months and to pay the appropriate royalties of $277,000 for a total of $459,000 with interest. While Ahern admitted at trial that he had failed to make some payments he owed Scholz, the jury did not consider his actions a material breach.

Ahern counterclaimed that Scholz owed him a share of the $6 million in royalties the third album earned from selling over 4 million copies. Scholz presented Ahern with an "Artist Royalty Statement," which, after deductions for a producer share and artists costs, fell to a net below zero. [*Id.* at 782-783.] Scholz maintained that he was excused from rendering an accounting to Ahern on the third album until Ahern had paid him on the first two albums. The Court of Appeals decided that Scholz was entitled to have this issue considered by a jury and remanded the case for further consideration.

This case illustrates the needs of both sides to keep on top of accounting issues. Both sides benefit when discrepancies are handled immediately rather than being permitted to fester and develop into further conflict.

Sometimes a disagreement can develop as to the nature of the manager's duties. Because managers are responsible for the band's overall career, their activities can overlap with those of agents.

Dave Park, for example, had a written contract to manage the Deftones in return for a 20 percent commission on all income earned from the employment he secured. Park also procured 84 performance engagements and a recording contract for them with Maverick Records without being a licensed agent. Under the California Talent Agencies Act, these activities require a license as a talent agent.

In *Park v. Deftones*, 71 Cal.App.4th 1465, 1469-1470, 84 Cal.Rptr.2d 616 (Cal.App. 2 Dist. 1999), the court observed that the job of personal managers is to "primarily advise, counsel, direct and coordinate the development of the artist career. They advise in both business and personal matters, frequently lend money to young artists and serve as spokespersons for the artists." Because Park would receive a commission from obtaining the recording contract, he was in effect acting as an agent. The court affirmed the Labor Commissioner's decision to void the management agreements. California subsequently amended its statutes to permit managers of recording artists to obtain recording contracts.

3. BAND-AGENT AGREEMENTS

Band agent agreements may similarly be voided if the agent fails to perform his or her duties in a customary fashion. Country singer Loretta Lynn's contract with the Wil-helm Agency required it to represent and advise her in the "radio, television, recording and personal appearances field" of the entertainment industry "throughout the world and in outer space for a period of [t]wenty years." The agency was obliged to procure employment, negotiate advertising and commercial tie-ups for using her name and likeness, and to counsel her on matters of professional interest. [Wilhelm Agency v. Lynn, 618 S.W.2d 748 (Tenn. Ct. App. 1981).]

This agreement was straight forward, but required professional individuals to properly implement it. Loretta Lynn initially worked closely with Teddy Wilburn who spent several hours almost daily with her, assisting her in rewriting songs and advising her on costumes, mannerisms, and lines. Loretta Lynn's career thrived during this period. Teddy Wilburn then left the firm after his brother Doyle began to consume excessive amounts of alcohol. Smiley Wilson then joined the firm and became Loretta Lynn's agent for a short while until Teddy was persuaded to return. When Teddy left again, Doyle began acting as Loretta Lynn's agent.

Doyle committed several acts of misconduct that reflected poorly on Loretta Lynn. He insulted the producer of the Johnny Carson Show during negotiations for Loretta Lynn to appear on the show. He disturbed Loretta Lynn during performances. While drunk, he once vomited on a dinner table at a post-performance party given for patrons, promoters, disc jockeys and their wives. He displayed public drunkenness during the London tour, while Loretta Lynn was taping the Ed Sullivan Show, and during every road trip. Loretta Lynn employed an attorney who alerted the agency that they were in breach of their duties and she was no longer bound by the contract.

The court agreed that the agency was in breach, finding Doyle Wilburn's conduct "entirely inconsistent with the duty owed the artist under the contract." [*Id*. at 751.] The court noted that each party owed the other obligations under the bilateral contract and were required to "restrain from doing any act that would delay or prevent the other party's performance of the contract." [*Id*. at 751-752.]

4. BAND-ATTORNEY AGREEMENTS

Relationships with attorneys are similarly important for bands to establish. Attorneys possess ethical obligations to perform their agreements with their clients in accordance with the law.

In *Croce v. Kurnit*, 565 F.Supp. 884 (S.D.N.Y. 1982), the widow of Jim Croce sued his attorney for fraud and breach of contract and sought rescission of the contracts between Croce and the company that represented him. Attorney Phillip Kurnit served as an officer of the publishing and managerial companies that signed Croce to recording, publishing, and managerial contracts. Kurnit never advised Croce and his wife to obtain outside counsel prior to signing the agreements on September 17, 1968. In the fall of 1968, Kurnit represented the Croces in connection with a lease agreement and by April 1969 was listing his firm as the party to whom all business related correspondence for Croces should be sent. He also executed a document as attorney in fact for them and became involved in a dispute between them and their managers. [*Id.* at 888.]

When Croce wrote Kurnit seeking to terminate his contracts, Kurnit relayed their concerns to the management company. After Jim Croce perished in a plane crash in 1973, Kurnit became the attorney for the estate. Later, Ingrid Croce sought another attorney to bring an action against Kurnit for breach of fiduciary duty.

The court found that in some instances, Kurnit did not act as their attorney, but nevertheless "a lawyer may owe a fiduciary obligation to persons with whom he deals," particularly when they have reason to believe they can rely on him. [*Id.* at 890.]

Kurnit had introduced himself to the Croces as "the lawyer" and explained the "legal ramifications" of the contracts to them. [*Id.*] He should have advised them to obtain outside counsel. Because he did not, he breached a fiduciary duty to them. [*Id.*]

Notwithstanding Kurnit's actions, Ingrid Croce was unable to obtain rescission of the agreements as unconscionable. The court considered the contracts to be "hard bargains, signed by an artist without bargaining power, and favored the publishers, but as a matter of fact did not contain terms which shock the conscience or differed so grossly from industry norms as to be unconscionable by their terms." [*Id.* at 898.] Due to uncertainty in the music business and the high risk of failure for new performers, the court said, "the contracts, though favoring the defendants, were not unfair." [*Id.*] While the contracts could not be rescinded, Ingrid Croce was entitled to the damages that resulted from Kurnit's breach of fiduciary duty for failing to advise the Croces to seek independent counsel. [*Id.* at 894.]

This case, which the Second Circuit affirmed in *Croce v. Kurnit*, 737 F.2d 229 (2nd Cir. 1984), indicates the importance of creating a contract between lawyers and clients. It should then be clear to the lawyer to whom he owes a fiduciary duty. Lawyers should never represent both sides of a contract without advising the other side that they should obtain independent counsel. If the other side chooses to forge ahead, the lawyer should have them sign a statement that they have been cautioned to seek another lawyer and chose not to.

5. SYMPHONY ORCHESTRA AGREEMENTS

The American Federation of Musicians negotiates symphony orchestra contracts on behalf of their members. Guillermo Figueroa, the conductor of the New Mexico Symphony Orchestra and an AFM member, says, "It was true that for a very long time that management was not favorable to players. With the advent of the unions, musicians have done much better." [Author Interview with Figueroa.] As a consequence, symphony orchestras are governed by a master agreement negotiated for a term of years. Figueroa says the disadvantage of such an agreement is "[i]t's hard to change things once the agreement is done, even when common sense tells you that you can break something if it is in everyone's best interest. However, both sides feel that if they open up a certain point that is not in the contract, the other side will want something in return." [*Id.*]

Symphony orchestras are, however, better off than in the era of conductor Leonard Bernstein, who "was known to fire musicians on the spot if they played off key one too many times," says conductor Sam Wong. Wong adds, "Artur Rodzinski, a former conductor of the New York Philharmonic...was reported to have carried a loaded gun when he rehearsed. And, of course, people didn't cross his path." [Author Interview with Wong.]

D. PUBLISHING CONTRACTS

Entertainers, who make their living in film, television, and music, often write books to tell their life stories or reveal their side of a major news event. Sometimes they write books themselves, but more often they are ghostwritten or heavily edited by the publishers. Others write books about entertainers.

Film actress Anne Heche wrote *Call Me Crazy* to discuss her various relationships with men and women and explain a well known episode where she acted bizarrely while high on ecstasy. In her memoir, television star Rosanne Barr divulged that she suffered from a multiple personality disorder. Scholars and producers continue to find material for their books and films in Mozart's life over two hundred years after his death.

Publishing contracts to produce articles and books range from simple one paragraph letters, as discussed earlier, to complex documents. In a contract to write an article on third world debt for a major magazine, author Gregg Levoy signed away the copyright to his work. The contract termed the relationship a "work made for hire," and noted that the magazine would retain the copyright.

The two-page contract also required Levoy to warrant that (a) he was the sole author of the work; (b) the work is original and does not infringe the copyright of another person; and (c) the work has not been previously published. Levoy would be required to indemnify the magazine if he violated any of these warranties. The magazine also retained the right to edit or make other changes to his work.

Book contracts can also be as short as two pages or lengthy documents. Most will contain some version of the clauses discussed below.

1. MANUSCRIPT CLAUSE

Many book contracts begin with a standard clause dealing with the specifics of the manuscript: the title, the name of the author, the length, the due date, how many copies the author must deliver in hard copy and on disk. Sometimes, in this clause the publisher reserves the right to reject the final manuscript as unacceptable or un-publishable.

While publishers have discretion to refuse a manuscript as un-publishable, they cannot arbitrarily reject a book for any reason. In *Harcourt Brace Jovanovich, Inc. v. Goldwater*, 532 F.Supp. 619 (S.D.N.Y. 1982), the District Court found an implied obligation for the publisher "to engage in appropriate editorial work with the author of the book." There needs to be some discussion "to allow the author the reasonable opportunity to perform to the satisfaction of the publisher." In the *Goldwater* case, the court found that because "there was no editorial work," HBJ breached its contract. The District Court dismissed HBJ's complaint seeking return of its advance.

What makes a manuscript un-publishable? The final draft may not be as well written as the initial proposal, it may contain information the publisher deems libelous, or the subject of the book becomes dated.

A savvy negotiator may be able to get the publisher to waive this clause, but this is rare. Instead, authors may insert that the publisher's right of rejection must be "reasonably exercised," but this is often implied in the contract. Publishers rarely reject a manuscript at the final stages unless they think that it is justifiably un-publishable.

In another high profile case, publisher HarperCollins sued actress/author Joan Collins for return of a substantial advance after she turned in a manuscript that it deemed un-publishable. A jury, however, decided that did she not have to return the advance even though HarperCollins found her manuscript unacceptable. Further, it required HarperCollins to pay the additional monies due on her contract. Ms. Collins won because her lawyer Irving "Swifty" Lazar negotiated an usual manuscript clause requiring her to produce a "completed manuscript" instead of the more standard "acceptable manuscript."

In another example, a change of circumstances caused a publisher to delay publication of a book. Documentary filmmaker Michael Moore was scheduled to have HarperCollins publish his book *Stupid*

White Men on September 11, 2001, the day that terrorists struck the World Trade Center. In a *60 Minutes* interview on CBS, he said on 27 June 27 2004 that HarperCollins called him and said because the world has changed, he needed to change the title and re-write 50% of the book, removing the negative references to President Bush. Moore read pages from the book to a group, and a librarian present started an e-mail campaign. After receiving numerous e-mails from librarians throughout the country, HarperCollins released *Stupid White Men* as originally conceived in the spring of 2002. [*Id.*]

The changing social climate that greeted Moore's book exemplifies why publishers insist on keeping an "out" clause in the contract. It permits them to cancel publication or request substantial changes to the book. If negotiations fail, they may return all rights to the author.

If a publisher does exercise its "out" clause or decides to "kill" the project, what happens to the author's advance? If the advance is tied to the production of an acceptable manuscript, and the publisher deems the author's book unacceptable, then the author must refund the advance. If the publisher kills the project for reasons that have nothing to do with the author's performance, the author has a strong case for keeping the funds. With magazine articles, contracts will specify the "kill fee" in advance, such as the one between *Vogue* and Gregg Levoy.

2. COPYRIGHT ISSUES

Depending on the type of publisher, the contract may require the publisher to register the copyright in the name of the author or in the name of the publisher. Most of the big publishing companies that sell to the publisher usually specify that the author will retain the copyright. Contracts from university, academic, and other small presses, however, often grant the publisher the right to register the copyright in the publisher's name. Since this clause may be negotiable, authors should ask. Casebook publishers seek to retain the copyright so that they can continue to publish editions even if an author dies, retires, or simply decides that he or she no longer wants to update his or her book.

The "Rights and Royalties" clauses are critical for authors. If a publisher has only the capacity to publish a book in English and distribute it in Canada and the United States, authors should be reluctant to grant the publisher the right to publish the book in any translation throughout the world. The author may be able to exploit this right with a separate publisher for more income. Authors can separate the rights by languages and by countries and, for example, sell Spanish language rights in Spain and Latin American countries.

Additionally, publishers may see audio, audiovisual, electronic, film, television, and digital media rights. Some contracts may specify all rights currently in existence and any other rights that may come into existence to take into account changing technology. Contracts that used to specify "world rights" are now being changed to refer to the "universe" because of satellite or Internet transmission.

Major conglomerates with movie, television, music, game, and other entertainment divisions have swallowed up many independent publishers. Highly connected publishers may seek film and television rights that they can shop to one of their divisions. Authors who consent may obtain a quicker sale, but perhaps with less revenue than if their agents sell these rights separately. Several New York literary agents, for example, maintain connections with Hollywood agents to service their author clients in this manner.

Rights are also intimately tied to compensation.

3. ROYALTY PROVISIONS

Trade publishers typically offer a royalty fee of 10 to 20 percent on the retail price for hardcover books, but less for paperback, and even less for mass-market paperback books. To fall into the latter category, publishers print 500,000 copies or more of a book, while offering authors a 5 percent royalty. They sell these deeply discounted books in markets like Costco, K-Mart, Wal-Mart, and Sam's Club. Some writers or their agents can negotiate a royalty schedule. After the first 10,000, 50,000, 100,000 or more in sales, the royalty fee increases according to an agreed-upon scale.

Smaller presses tend to be independent, university, and academic operations. They offer payment on net proceeds because they sell fewer copies and therefore receive less revenue. The royalty rate may range from 10 – 20% of net proceeds. The challenge for authors, their agents and attorneys, is to understand the publisher's definition of net proceeds.

Fortunately, the definition of net proceeds in the publishing industry is more likely to produce revenue than in the movie industry, where "net profits" may be termed a figment of some accountant's imagination. For example, one academic publisher defines net proceeds as "the actual price received by the Publisher from all sales whether retail or trade (wholesale) sales. The total of these sales shall be reduced by the amount of credits, actual returns, and a reasonable reserve for anticipated returns of 20%."

From this clause, the authors will receive higher royalties if the publisher sells the work at its retail price directly off its website or through mail order. The royalties will be noticeably less when the publisher wholesales the book to a bookstore or another website. The more aggressive the definitions of net profit, the more often authors try to negotiate a higher royalty payment of at least 15-20%.

When publishers purchase other rights, they may ask to split the film or television rights 50-50. Since the publisher is, in effect, acting as the author's agent, authors have been known to negotiate a more profitable (60-40, 75-25, or 85-15) split with the publisher.

Some authors, particularly of trade books, are able to secure advances against royalties. These advances may be as low as $1000 or exceed seven figures for high-profile celebrity authors like former President Bill Clinton. Once the advance is agreed to, it may be split into multiple payments. For example, former Arizona Senator Barry Goldwater and his co-author Stephen Shadegg signed an agreement with Harcourt Brace Jovanovich, Inc. for an advance of $200,000. HBJ contracted to pay them in three segments, with $65, 000 due on signing, $75,000 due on delivery of the manuscript, and $60,000 due on publication. [Harcourt Brace Jovanovich, Inc. v Goldwater, 532 F.Supp. 619 (S.D.N.Y. 1982)]

4. ACCOUNTING PROVISIONS

Accounting provisions indicate when authors can expect to receive royalty checks. The accountings may be monthly, quarterly, semi-annually, or annually. The smaller the press, the lengthier the accounting periods will be. The publisher will offer to send the payments within 30 to 90 days following the close of the accounting period.

These provisions may be difficult to negotiate because they often depend on the publisher's overall accounting practices. However, trade publishers have been known to provide shorter accounting periods for their best-selling authors who are generating a great deal of revenue. If the author docs not yet fall into this category, the agent or attorney can ask for a shorter period, but the publisher is likely to resist setting up a different system for a lesser-known author.

5. WARRANTIES

As discussed earlier, magazine and book publishers may require authors to warrant certain conditions about their manuscripts. Warranty clauses may require the author to guarantee to the publisher that:

* The author is the sole creator and owner of the work

* The work has not been previously published

* The work does not violate another work's copyright

* The work does not violate anyone's right of privacy

* The work does not libel or defame anyone

* The work does not violate any government regulation

If the author's work violates any of the above warranties, the publisher reserves the right to cancel the contract.

Warranty clauses are often accompanied by an indemnity provision, asking the author to indemnify, or repay, the publisher should the work violate a warranty provision. If the publisher is sued because of the author's work, the author must defend the lawsuit and reimburse the publisher for any of its related expenses.

6. EXPENSES, PERMISSIONS, AND FAIR USE

Publishers may grant authors a budget to cover certain expenses, such as those connected with travel, interviews, or obtaining permission to use other people's work. The type and amount of such expenses may be negotiated depending on the type of project.

Authors who quote substantially from other authors' copyrighted works should obtain permission from the copyright holder, who is usually the author or the publisher. Some copyright holders will grant the right to republish part or all of an article or book without payment. Others may request substantial fees for this right, although authors can always attempt to negotiate a lower rate than that initially quoted.

For some quotations and reprints authors may claim a fair-use privilege to use another's work. Uses of another's work that are considered fair include quoting the work to critique or comment it. In such a case permission is not required, as authors would rarely grant permission to use their work in a harsh manner. Determining whether or not the fair-use privilege applies requires authors to use their best judgment, while understanding the dictates of 17 U.S.C. 107, as discussed in Chapter 2. Authors using a work for educational purposes have more leeway than those who just plan to profit from another person's labor. Nevertheless, authors must keep in mind that if the copyright owner sues, the author may have to pay to defend both himself and his publisher.

7. EDITIONS, AUTHOR COPIES, OUT OF PRINT

A publishing contract may also specify that the publisher receive the first right to publish further editions of the work. Authors of a continuing series (such as mysteries) and textbook publications should be aware that such clauses give the publisher the right to name other writers to produce additional editions. This may be so even with newspaper columns. When Ann Landers died, her column expired with her. Yet when Dear Abby, Ann's twin sister, became too feeble to write, the column was passed on to her daughter to continue writing under the same name.

The author's copies clause specifies how many free copies of the book will be sent to the author, and the cost of any additional copies the author may want to purchase. Sometimes these clauses specify that the author cannot resell reduced-price copies. Other times, they are silent on this issue, which means that authors can resell such copies. Authors may attempt to elaborate on the circumstances where re-sales would be permitted, such as when selling copies at a lecture, conference, or book signing.

Publishing contracts often provide that when the book goes out of print, and the publisher refuses to print more upon written request, all rights will revert to the author. Some contracts permit the authors to buy back any remaining copies and the plates that were used to produce the manuscript.

8. ASSIGNMENT

A clause that has become standard in the era of mergers and acquisitions is the assignment clause, granting the publisher the right to assign the contract to another publisher. Authors may sell their book to Publisher A only to have Publisher Q purchase or merge with Publisher A soon thereafter. With an assignment clause, Publisher Q assumes the responsibility for publishing the book. The author remains protected because the book will still be available, although the publisher changes.

9. PRINT ON DEMAND, INTERNET, AND
ELECTRONIC BOOKS

In search of quick production at low cost, authors are turning to print on demand publishers and electronic book publishing. For reasonable set-up fees, iUniverse, Xlibris, Authorhouse, and many other Internet publishers will format authors' books and sell copies for them on an order-first/then-print basis. Authors who choose the POD route can purchase their own books at a 40% discount and they receive royalties when other people buy their books.

The POD publishing route is unlikely to produce significant revenue for writers. The Writer magazine reports that Xlibris has sold an average of 33 books of its 9,000 printed titles, and out of iUniverse's 17,000 titles, only 84 have sold more than 500 copies. Further, only about six of iUniverse's titles have made it on to the bookshelves of Barnes and Noble, which owns 25% of iUniverse. [Allen, *Measuring the value of POD*.]

When POD publishers sell books through an Internet reseller, like Amazon.com, authors receive a reduced royalty. Amazon.com has become a billion-dollar corporation by reselling new and used books, and other entertainment products, at discounts through its website. Jonathan Miller, the author of *Rattlesnake Lawyer*, says writers should "be aware that they will receive no royalties for used books resold through Amazon.com." He adds, "Writers also need to know that their ranking on Amazon.com is crucial. I know some unscrupulous publishers and authors who try to manipulate their ranking by urging their friends to buy books through Amazon.com."

The advantage to achieving the number 1 ranking on Amazon.com is that other publications use the Amazon.com numbers to compute their best-seller lists. Certain bookstores, like those found in airports, are much more likely to order books appearing on the New York Times or other major publications' best-seller lists.

Books have become accessible on multiple platforms, including laptops, cell phones, tablets, E-readers, and gaming systems. Among the most popular E-Readers are Amazon's Kindles, the iPad, and Barnes and Noble's Nook. E-Books are less expensive to produce than print books, and can be downloaded immediately. Individuals no longer have to travel to bookstores to find a book they desire if it is available electronically.

As a result, the publishing industry is in the midst of a sea change, with e-books sometimes outselling print books. In the 2nd quarter of 2011, Barnes and Noble sold $220 million worth of Nooks and digital content. Amazon sold over 1 million of six types of Kindles a week in December 2011.

This change in publishing presents advantages and challenges to writers. The e-book revolution makes it easier for them to obtain publication, but it may be more difficult to find a target audience. E-book rights are now part of negotiating a publishing package.

In conclusion, all contracts for entertainers offer their benefits and burdens. It's up to entertainers and their lawyers to discover what these are and proceed accordingly.

CHAPTER 10
CELEBRITY STATUS

Obtaining national and global eminence brings advantages and disadvantages to entertainers. This celebrity status blesses them with access to more resources. They can capitalize on their names and images by exploiting their right of publicity. Some celebrities use their prominence to run for political office or advance a social agenda. Other entertainers capitalize on the sudden availability of ordinary mortals seeking sexual relations with them. Sometimes they pay a price for their excesses in paternity suits or criminal actions brought against them. Some celebrities who are dissatisfied with their level of wealth have succumbed to greed, which has ultimately landed them in jail.

Taking on celebrity clients tests lawyers' abilities in a myriad of ways. A long-celebrated personality is more likely to view the lawyer as hired help and less likely to follow advice. This places attorneys in uncomfortable situations, particularly when clients seem determined to pursue unlawful activities. Some lawyers bite the bullet and fire clients. Others go along and may find themselves sent to prison along with their clients, although probably in a less comfortable facility.

This chapter addresses a number of issues associated with celebrity status. It first sets up the ad-

vantages and disadvantages that accompany celebrity status. This gives the attorney a broader sense
of the peculiarities associated with the accomplished
entertainer's life.

Second, this chapter highlights celebrities' rights
to privacy and publicity. The glitter of bright lights
fades as entertainers find their privacy constantly
violated by overzealous fans and a hyperactive media. Associated with the right to privacy is the right
of publicity, which permits celebrities to capitalize
on their names and images by endorsing products.
The right to privacy expires with the death of the
celebrity. The right of publicity survives the celebrity's demise and descends to his or her heirs at law
by intestate succession or by any person or entity
the celebrity chooses to designate by will or trust.

Because of the value attached to the rights of publicity and other forms of intellectual property, this
chapter concludes by briefly discussing estate planning issues for celebrities. More and more entertainers plan their estates to take advantage of their
income earning potential after their deaths. A number of celebrities earn more money after their demise than they did while living. This increases the
need for attorneys to explore estate planning issues
with their celebrity clients.

A. CELEBRITY ADVANTAGES AND DISADVANTAGES

Becoming a celebrity in this era of history generates economic rewards and fame where, to quote the Cheers theme song, "everyone knows your name." Several entertainers have used their fame to fulfill political ambitions, rising to become mayors of cities, governors in the states of California and Minnesota, congressmen, senators, and even president of the United States. The 1987 film Running Man, based on a Stephen King novel, was the first movie to feature two future governors, Arnold Schwarzenegger and Jesse Ventura, in a fight scene. The honorable governor of California won. Virginian John Warner married actress Elizabeth Taylor just prior to launching his senate campaign. The crowds came out in droves, he won, and the couple later divorced.

When Robert Redford first started discussing the environment in the 1960s, he was dismissed out of hand. "He's only an actor," was an often-uttered comment. "Then came Ronald Reagan, and Arnold," said Redford. "People began to take note." Now people flock to hear Redford bemoan the destruction of the environment. He told several hundred souls who assembled at the Randall Davey Audubon Center in Santa Fe, New Mexico, on July 14, 2004, "I'm here today to try to raise awareness, to try to stop this avalanche." He called for "responsible development, to get us into a sustainable future." His comments were greeted with sustained applause.

Some individuals who achieve wealth through the entertainment industry give away their money. According to lawyer turned television mogul Jim Rogers, "Once you've passed the buying and accumulating stage and you're not interested in pursuing contests of adding more commas and zeroes to your financial statement, all that's left is to give it away." Rogers says there "is no greater feeling than the joy that flows from giving."

Rogers donated $115 million to the University of Arizona in 1998, making national headlines as the largest gift ever to a law school. To express its gratitude, the institution renamed itself the James E. Rogers College of Law. Dean Toni Massaro said that Rogers' gift brought "hope, excitement, and a renewed commitment to acting on our better ideas."

With that gift, Rogers' status elevated from generous donor to philanthropist. In its July 24, 2000, edition, Time Magazine ran "The New Philanthropists" as its cover story and proclaimed Rogers as number 12 among the country's top philanthropists. This list included Bill and Melinda Gates who donated $22 billion to their foundation, and Ted Turner, founder of CNN, who gave a billion dollars to the United Nations Foundation.

From his office in Las Vegas in the fall of 2000, Rogers explained his simple philosophy of giving.

"You start with the premise that most great fortunes are earned by a group of people influenced by a convergence of circumstances, so that no one person can take 100% credit for creating it. Then you find that after you've accumulated so much, there are only so many cars, houses, boats, and planes that you can buy, and after you've bought them, you find you don't use them."

Rogers has also touched individual lives with anonymous small gifts. Sometimes his television station KVBC employees have dined at Las Vegas restaurants unaware that Rogers was present until they called for their check only to be informed that a Mr. James E. Rogers had already paid their tab.

Celebrities can also experience disadvantages when they become nationally prominent. Jon Moritsugu directed the 1999 film Fame Whore to challenge, he said, "a naïve view that once you're famous... everything will fall into place. Fame can be a particularly deadly drug." [Author Interview with Moritsugu.]

During their lives and immediately following their deaths, some celebrities have individuals come forth claiming to be related. After Marlon Brando achieved national prominence in the movie version of Street Car Named Desire, he told NBC executive Brandon Tartikoff what happened to him:

"For a year ... I never touched a door. I couldn't touch a door if I wanted to. People were opening

them for me. I could show up at the fanciest restaurant at the busiest hour and they'd say, 'Right
this way.' I'd sit up in my house in the Hollywood
Hills getting bombed, and I'd be watching the
news at ten p.m. and I'd see this blond woman doing the news and I'd call up the station. I'd ask to
get her on the phone, and I'd say, 'Hi, sweetheart,
this is Marlon Brando. I think you're real attractive. How'd you like to come over to my place
when you're done?' And sure enough, she'd be
over at my house about a half hour later, and I'd
be in bed with her. It was just like ordering Chinese food. That was Hollywood, and it was great."

[Tartikoff, Last Great Ride, at 23.] Brando's ability
to order up women was not without consequence.
After he died at the age of 80 on July 1, 2004, a
London paper reported that he might have had
eight illegitimate children in addition to the 11 he
acknowledged in his will. [Evans, Brando's Eight
Secret Children.] One sobbing 40-year-old actress
demanded to be let into the actor's home so she
could take her place among her siblings, but was
turned away by security guards. [Id.]

Tennis star Boris Becker was hit with a paternity
suit while still married to his pregnant wife Barbara. At a posh London restaurant, Becker dallied in a
broom closet with Russian model Angela Ermakova.
The result was a baby linked to Becker through a
DNA test. At trial, he claimed that the model was
hired to hold him down and steal his sperm. The

judge awarded the model $1.5 million to care for the child. Becker also paid his wife Barbara $14.4 million to settle their divorce. [Burr, Courts hear new angle on the law of sex]

Sports stars seem particularly vulnerable to the hordes of women who lie in wait after their games or in the lobby of their hotels seeking sexual relations with them. At least one woman claimed her sexual interactions with Los Angeles Laker Kobe Bryant were not consensual. He was charged with rape. More often, however, women with dollar signs dancing behind their eyes play the pregnancy game. They entice sports stars into sexual encounters in hopes of having a baby. As in the Boris Becker incident, the payoff can be huge. Women have filed paternity suits against basketball stars Larry Bird, Patrick Ewing, Jason Kidd, and Scottie Pippen. Shawn Kemp allegedly fathered seven illegitimate children, only to have their mothers hit him with millions of dollars in claims for support.

Sports stars and organizations have noticed this trend and taken action. Some basketball stars are known to mentor their younger brethren to urge them to avoid ensnarement with women seeking to have their children. The National Football League currently provides its rookies with a life talk during training camp to counsel them on this issue.

While paternity suits present challenges to lawyers, keeping some clients out of jail can be time consuming. Television host Martha Stewart convinced herself that she knew what she was doing when she spoke to federal prosecutors investigating her for securities fraud. Stewart thought she had nothing to hide. Along with her co-defendant Peter E. Bacanovic, she was convicted of conspiracy, obstruction, and lying to investigators. U.S. District Court judge Miriam Goldman Cedarbaum sentenced both Stewart and Bacanovic to five months in prison and five months of home confinement. The judge recommended that Stewart serve time in a minimum-security federal work camp in Danbury, Connecticut, which is situated 20 miles from Stewart's Connecticut home. She was permitted to remain free pending her appeal.

An argument can be made that Stewart was done in by greed, with karmic consequences. She saved $45,000 in the stock trade that brought the eyes of the prosecutors upon her. After she was indicted for lying about the trade to the SEC, her billion-dollar company lost half its value. Upon her conviction, Viacom cancelled her television show Martha Stewart Living, which had been on the air on stations covering 85% of the country since 1991.

Following her sentencing, bargain hunters bid up shares of Martha Stewart Living Omnimedia by 37% during heavy trading. After Stewart received a short prison term, some traders bet the company would rebound. Stewart served her time, and returned to the company and to television. Her original show was revived and she headed up The Apprentice: Martha Stewart during the fall 2005 television season.

When television stars like Robert Blake and O.J. Simpson are charged with murder, their attorneys must not only investigate their criminal cases but also augment their media skills to address the increased interest in their client's fate. Attorneys possessing such skills are in high demand. Thomas Mesereau Jr. represented Blake before they parted ways in a dispute. Mesereau was then hired by Michael Jackson to represent him on child molestation charges after Jackson released Mark Geragos. Geragos had represented movie star Winona Ryder on shoplifting charges. She was convicted.

Attorneys sometimes need to gag their clients for their own good. Instead of appearing at his arraignment quietly, Michael Jackson danced on top of a car and his family stoked the fans' interest by inviting them to his home for a picnic. Being charged with a crime brought an about face for Jackson who had jealously guarded his privacy and that of his children. He and his kids previously wore masks to prevent the media from obtaining full-faced photographs.

B. PRIVACY, PUBLICITY, AND DEFAMATION

1. PRIVACY RIGHTS

State law protects the right of privacy. Dean Prosser describes it as four distinct torts: (1) intrusion upon the plaintiff's seclusion or solitude, or into his private affairs; (2) public disclosure of embarrassing private facts about the plaintiff; (3) publicity which places the plaintiff in a false light in the public eye; and (4) appropriation, for the defendant's advantage, of plaintiff's name and likeness. [Eastwood, 149 Cal.App.3d at 416.]

Stardom and superstardom can bring a sudden and dramatic loss of privacy. Some overnight celebrities resort to shopping for the necessities of life at midnight where they are unlikely to be disturbed at their neighborhood grocery store. Reality television star Bob Guiney acknowledges that he cannot complain about the loss of privacy that accompanied his appearances on the ABC series The Bachelorette and The Bachelor. He says, "I did this to myself." [Author Interview with Guiney.]

When individuals agree to participate in a reality TV show, they usually sign a release agreement permitting producers to use their image. Ken Aronson authorized Michael Moore to use his video and song in the documentary Sicko. Even so, Aronson claimed Moore's production company Dog Eat Dog Films, Inc. violated his privacy rights by using

16 seconds of his image and voice within the 71 seconds of his footage in Sicko. In Aronson v. Dog Eat Dog Films., 738 F.Supp.2d 1104 (W.D.Wash. 2010), the District Court dismissed Aronson's privacy claim, noting that Sicko disclosed no facts of intimate details of Aronson's life that would be highly offensive to the ordinary reasonable person.

The release agreement must be tailored to the specific purposes related to how the person's image will be used to avoid violating a person's privacy rights. In Johnston v. One American Productions, 2007 WL 2433927 (N.D.Miss. 2007), the court denied a motion to strike a claim for misappropriation of likeness for commercial gain because the producers only obtained the plaintiff's explicit permission to be featured in a "religious documentary" that would be shown in a foreign country, not for Borat, a major motion picture shown across the U.S. and Europe.

The Johnston court did, however, dismiss the plaintiff's invasion of privacy claim. The plaintiff alleged that the production company invaded her privacy by using film showing her raising her hands in religious praise in response to the character Borat's apparent conversion to her religion. The district court decided that Johnston failed to state a claim for invasion of privacy based on intrusion upon seclusion and disclosure of private facts. Johnston was filmed at a church service, a public event, and the nature of the film Borat's use of her image was not highly offensive.

An individual can authorize the use of their private images their conduct. Steven Greenstein did not sign a release agreement before his image was captured on the New Orleans segment of Gene Simmons Family Jewels. Nevertheless, in Greenstein v. Greif Co., 2009 WL 117368 (Cal.App.2 Dist. 2009), the California Court of Appeal affirmed a motion to strike Greenstein's complaint for misappropriation of his image, noting that he acted as an escort for Simmons in New Orleans, wore a microphone, and was filmed. Greenstein also obtained signed release forms for everyone else participating in the segment.

In his complaint, Greenstein said he wanted to be paid for his appearance, yet he never communicated with the producers about his refusal to sign a release agreement or his request for compensation until more than a year after filming was completed. The court considered him to have consented by conduct to having his image used.

Individuals have also claimed they have had their privacy invaded on the Internet. In Boring v. Google Inc., 2010 WL 318281 (3rd Cir. 2010), Aaron and Christine Boring sued Google for invasion of privacy, trespass, injunctive relief, negligence and conversion after Google took color images of their home located on a private road, and uploaded the images

to its "Street View" program on "Google Maps." By
making the images available on the Internet, the
Borings claimed that Google disregarded their privacy rights, particularly since their road is clearly
marked with a "Private Road, No Trespassing" sign.

The Court of Appeals noted that to "state a claim
for intrusion upon seclusion, plaintiffs must allege
conduct demonstrating 'an intentional intrusion upon the seclusion of their private concerns which was
substantial and highly offensive to a reasonable
person, and aver sufficient facts to establish that
the information disclosed would have caused mental
suffering, shame or humiliation to a person of ordinary sensibilities'." The Court held that "[n]o person
of ordinary sensibilities would be shamed, humiliat-
ed, or have suffered mentally as a result of a vehicle
entering into his or her ungated driveway and photographing the view from there." It affirmed the
dismissal of the Borings' privacy and other claims,
with the exception of their trespass claim. It remanded that claim with instructions to the district
court to go forward.

The right of privacy expires upon death and cannot be evoked on behalf of the deceased by his survivors. In Maritote v. Desilu Productions, Inc., 345
F.2d 418 (7th Cir. 1965), the Court of Appeals said,
"It is anomalous to speak of the privacy of a deceased person." In Maritote, the widow and son of
mobster Al Capone claimed that Desilu Productions
violated his privacy right by exploiting his image for

commercial advantages when it produced a two-part drama and television series called The Untouchables. The court quoted Shakespeare, "the evil that men do lives after them." [Id. at 420.] It further added, "What a man does while alive becomes a part of history which survives his death." [Id.]

According to the court, deceased people do not possess privacy rights. Further, their relatives cannot sue for violation of their own privacy rights if they are not mentioned in a comment, fictionalization, or even distortion of a dead man's career. [Id.] The court thus refused to enjoin Desilu's use of Al Capone's name and image.

2. PUBLICITY RIGHTS

As mentioned above, the right to publicity is an outgrowth of a person's right to privacy. Dean Prosser describes the latter as an appropriation, for the defendant's advantage, of plaintiff's name and likeness. [Eastwood, 149 Cal.App.3d at 416.] The right of publicity is a property interest grounded in three separate legal sources: state statutes, common law, and the Federal Unfair Competition Act. When someone else profits from an entertainer's name, image, or voice, this affects the celebrity in a number of ways; most importantly, the entertainer loses some control over his image, particularly when the use presents false material.

In Zacchini v. Scripps-Howard Broadcasting Co., 433 U.S. 562, (1977), the United States Supreme

Court considered whether the First Amendment trumped the right of individuals to a commercial stake in their images. The court said it did not because the "human cannonball" entertainer was not seeking to enjoin the broadcast of his performance as news; rather, he simply wanted to be paid for it as entertainment. In this instance, the television had broadcast a film of Zacchini's entire 15 second-act. The Supreme Court found this broadcast infringed Zacchini's right of publicity, and was not immunized by the First Amendment.

The most commonly cited publicity rights' statute is California Civil Code Sec. 3344(a). This statute was amended in 1984 to prohibit any unauthorized use "on or in products, merchandise or goods" of celebrities' names and likeness. It provides that "Any person who knowingly uses another's name, voice, signature, photograph, or likeness, in any manner, or in products, merchandise, or goods, or for purposes of advertising or selling, or soliciting purchases of, products, merchandise, goods or services, without such person's prior consent ... shall be liable for any damages sustained by the person injured as a result thereof."

The right of publicity thus can be exploited during the celebrity's lifetime and after his or her death depending on the jurisdiction. The duration of the right of publicity is determined by statute. In some states, like New York, the right of publicity expires upon the celebrity's death. In other states, like California, it continues for fifty years following the celebrity's last curtain call.

Several television stars, including Johnny Carson and Vanna White, have successfully enjoined the commercial exploitation of their image. Johnny Carson was able to stop a company from marketing "Here's Johnny" portable toilets because that phrase was Johnny Carson's signature introduction on The Tonight Show. [Carson v. Here's Johnny Portable Toilets, Inc., 698 F.2d 831 (6th Cir. 1983)]

In White v. Samsung Electronics America, 971 F.2d 1395 (9th Cir. 1992), the Ninth Circuit held that the right of publicity extends to the name, likeness, voice, signature, and anything else that evokes the person's identity. For Wheel of Fortune star Vanna White, the latter category included a Samsung advertisement featuring "a robot, dressed in a wig, gown, and jewelry … consciously selected to resemble White's hair and dress. The robot was posed next to a game board which is instantly recognizable as the Wheel of Fortune game show set, in a stance for which White is famous." [Id. at 1396.] The Ninth Circuit held that White was entitled to pursue Samsung because the law protects the celebrity's sole right to exploit the value associated with his or her name that has been created with energy and ingenuity. [Id. at 1399.]

Cheers actors George Wendt and John Ratzenberger sued Host International to keep them from creating animatronic robot figures based on their likeness and placing them in airport bars modeled to resemble the Cheers' set without their permission. Having the robots emulate the Norm and Cliff characters meant they resembled Wendt and Ratzenberger who embodied those characters on Cheers. The Ninth Circuit ruled in Wendt v. Host International, 125 F.3d 806 (9th Cir. 1997), that the actors were at least entitled to a jury trial to determine whether Host International was commercially exploiting their likeness.

When singer Debra Laws claimed that Sony misappropriated her name and voice for commercial purposes, the Ninth Circuit held in Laws v. Sony Music Entertainment, 448 F.3d 1134 (9th Cir. 2006), that her Section 3344 were preempted by U.S. copyright laws. Laws objected to the sampling of her recorded song "Very Special" in the song "All I Have" performed by Jennifer Lopez and L.L. Cool J. However, her agent had sold a non-exclusive license to Sony to use a sample of the Laws' song in the Lopez-L.L. Cool J. recording. The Ninth Circuit said that if Laws wished to control the use of her performance, she should have retained the copyright or contracted for control over licensing. [Id. at 1145.]

Sports stars find their achievements magnified by television. Consequently, many can make more money from their endorsement contracts than from playing their respective sports. Protecting their trademark names and right of publicity is important to both unsuccessful and successful athletes. Anna Kournikova, who never won a tennis tournament during her short-lived career, earned millions of dollars from advertising endorsements that take advantage of her attractive looks. Her compatriot Maria Sharapova was able to make even more money from endorsements after winning the 2004 Wimbledon and 2006 U.S. Open tennis championships.

Basketball legend Kareem Abdul-Jabbar sued General Motors Corporation for using his birth name Lew Alcindor to advertise an Oldsmobile. In Abdul-Jabbar v. General Motors Corporation, 85 F.3d 407 (9th Cir. 1996), Abdul-Jabbar argued GMC's use of his birth name falsely implied that he had endorsed its products. GMC countered that Abdul-Jabbar had abandoned the name Lew Alcindor when he formerly recorded the Abdul-Jabbar name under an Illinois statute.

In reversing the District Court's grant of summary judgment for GMC, the Court of Appeals observed that because a birth name is an integral part of identity, it is not bestowed for commercial purposes and thus cannot be deemed "abandoned" when its possessor discontinues using it. [Id. at 408.] The court said, "California's common law right of publicity protects celebrities from appropriation of their identity not strictly definable as 'name or picture'." [Id. at 415.]

As noted earlier in the discussion of the Zacchini case, courts balance the right of publicity with the First Amendment right of freedom of expression. Professional golfer Tiger Woods sued the Jireh Publishing Company and artist Rich Rush for reproducing artwork that included his image and used his name to identify the work. In ETW Corporation v. Jireh Publishing, Inc., 332 F.3d 915 (6th Cir. 2003), Woods claimed that that the company violated his trademark "Tiger Woods" and his right of publicity. The Court of Appeals disagreed. It noted that "[a] celebrity's name may be used in the title of an artistic work so long as there is some artistic relevance." [Id. at 920.] In this instance, the court said that the "use of Woods' name on the back of the envelope containing the print and in the narrative description of that print are purely descriptive and there is nothing to indicate that they were used other than in good faith." [Id.]

The court was also careful to distinguish Woods' name as a valid trademark from his image, which is not protected as a trademark when it does not distinguish and identify the source of goods. As a general rule, the court said, "a person's image or likeness cannot function as a trademark." [Id. at 921.]

Nevertheless, a person's name and likeness can be used in news reporting. [Id. at 930.] The court noted that Woods' 1997 Masters victory was an historic event in the world of sports, and art "communicates and celebrates the value our culture attaches to such events." [Id. at 936.] The court found that Rush's artwork was "entitled to the full protection of the First Amendment.... Through their pervasive presence in the media, sports and entertainment celebrities have come to symbolize certain ideas and values in our society and have become a valuable means of expression in our culture." [Id. at 937.]

One final note on privacy and publicity rights is related to the growing crime of identity theft. Frank Abagnale, author of The Art of the Steal (2001), terms identity theft "the mother of all scams, because it steals everything, a person's very being." The Internet makes celebrities vulnerable because con artists can discover information about them through publicly available sources. Thieves seek to capitalize on the wealth associated with a famous name by stealing the person's credit cards and personal information. They then impersonate the person, using their identifying factors such as social security and driver's license numbers to buy clothes, furniture, cars, and real estate. Abagnale published the book Identity Theft (2004) to bring even more attention to the hazards of the crime.

On July 15, 2004, President George W. Bush signed the Identity Theft Penalty Enhancement Act, which adds two years to prison sentences for criminals convicted of using stolen credit card numbers and other personal data to commit crimes. "Like other forms of stealing, identity theft leaves the victim poorer and feeling terribly violated," Bush said.

"The criminal can quickly damage a person's life-long effort to build a good credit rating." [McGuire, Bush Signs Identity Theft Bill.]

3. DEFAMATION

While all individuals have a right to privacy, celebrities trade a measure of their rights for fame and thus what others can say about them is broader than for ordinary mortals. For example, there is no First Amendment protection of the media to publish defamatory statements about public officials and public figures with actual malice, "either with knowledge of their falsity or reckless disregard for the truth." [Eastwood v. The Superior Court of Los Angeles County, 149 Cal.App.3d 409, 424 (Cal.App. 2 Dist. 1983)] A private individual, however, can sue for defamatory statements published with negligence. [Id.]

After the National Enquirer published an article headlined "Clint Eastwood in Love Triangle," Eastwood sued the paper, claiming that it violated his right to privacy, particularly under Prosser's fourth category, as supplemented by the 1971 version of California Civil Code Sec. 3344(a). [Eastwood, 149 Cal.App.3d at 417.] Eastwood charged that the National Enquirer had placed him in a false light in the public eye by publishing an untrue article stating that he was caught in a love triangle between singer Tanya Tucker and actress Sandra Locke. The court agreed, concluding that the Enquirer violated his common law and Section 3344(a) rights when it "commercially exploited his name, photograph, and likeness." [Id. at 421.]

In considering Eastwood's case, the court examined the juxtaposition between the right of privacy and the public's right to know. Because Freedom of the Press is constitutionally guaranteed, the court observed, "a celebrity relinquishes a part of his right to privacy to the extent that the public has a legitimate interest in his doings, affairs, or character. The accomplishments and way of life of such persons may legitimately be mentioned and discussed in print." [Id. at 412.] Nevertheless, the court noted that First Amendment rights "do not require total abrogation of the right of privacy or the right of publicity." [Id. at 422.]

The distinction between the media's responsibility to investigate statements about public figures and ordinary citizens turned out to be an important one for Eastwood. He did not initially allege that the article was published with knowledge of falsity or with reckless disregard for the truth as required for media statements on public figures. The court granted him leave to amend his complaint to cure this defect. [Id. at 426.]

Celebrities can also defame others as well as be defamed. In Sommer v. Gabor, 48 Cal.Rptr.2d 235 (Cal.App. 2 Dist. 1995), the California Court of Appeal determined that negative statements made by one celebrity regarding the career of another celebrity were legally actionable when reported in the press. Actress Zsa Zsa Gabor and her ninth husband, Frederic Von Anhalt, gave an interview with a German journalist in which they claimed that actress Elke Sommer was financially ruined, had lost her hair, was living in a bad part of Hollywood, and associated with disreputable people. Sommer sued Gabor and Von Anhalt for defamation. The Court held that Gabor and Von Anhalt's statements were legally actionable, and ordered them to pay Sommer $4.6 million.

According to the court, these statements were not subjective opinions. Rather, they could be proven false as a matter of law. Sommer submitted evidence disproving the financial claims, her physical appearance, location of residence, and whether or not she frequented seedy bars.

In Agnant v. Shakur, 30 F.2d 420 (S.D.N.Y. 1998), the estate of rapper Tupac Shakur was sued by Jacques Agnant for libel because of lyrics in the Shakur song "Against All Odds". In 1993, Agnant, Shakur and a third man were arrested and indicted for sexual assaulting a woman in a New York City hotel. Agnant received a plea deal with lesser charges in exchange for cooperating with prosecution. Shakur went to jail. In 1996, he released his song "Against All Odds," which included the lyrics "a real live tale about a snitch named Haitian Jack, knew he was working for the fed…". Agnant alleged that as a result of the song lyrics, his employment prospects and reputation were damaged.

The Court held that the song lyrics were not libelous toward Agnant because his employment prospects were not damaged, and a claim of reputation damage is not actionable. Agnant was employed as a record executive at the time the Shakur song was released, and still employed in the same position when he filed suit. He did not experience any loss of income or negative impact on his career.

To claim defamation, the plaintiff must assert that the defendant used phrases capable of being proven false. In Seelig v. Infinity Broadcasting Corp., 97 Cal.App.4th 798 (Cal.App. 1 Dist. 2002), a contestant on Who Wants to Marry a Millionaire sued the producers of a radio talk show for defamation. After Seelig's appearance as was one of 50 contestants on "Who Wants to Marry a Millionaire", a morning radio talk show sought to interview her but she declined. During the show, hosts referred to Seelig as a "local loser", "chicken butt" and "skank". The Court held that these terms were "classic rhetorical hyperbole" and not defamatory because they cannot be reasonably interpreted as stating actual facts. They are too vague to be capable of being proven true or false.

By contrast, the court found the word "skank" actionable in Cohen v. Google, Inc. 25 Misc.3d 945, 887 N.Y.S.2d 424 (N.Y.Sup. 2009). Five different blogs titled "Skanks of NYC" included sexually suggestive images of Liskula Cohen with references such as "skanky", "ho" and "whoring". Cohen argued that the blogs constitute defamation per se, impugned her chastity, and negatively reflected on her business as a model. She requested that Google turn over the identity of the blog author(s) so that she could file a defamation suit. The Court held that Google must identify the authors of potentially actionable statements made on its weblogs. If the assertions are proved false, the Cohen has a legitimate defamation claim. The Internet does not shield wrongdoers who defame others and claim First Amendment protection.

C. ESTATE PLANNING

Forbes Magazine regularly publishes an annual list of top-earning deceased celebrities with their names, their principal occupation during their lifetime, and how many millions of dollars their estate made. Table 10-1 contains information for 2011.

TABLE 10-1: FORBES MAGAZINE'S 2011 TOP EARNING CELEBRITY ESTATES

CELEBRITY	DEATH YEAR	TALENT	ESTATE EARNINGS (in millions)
Michael Jackson	2009	Musician	$170
Elvis Presley	1977	Singer, Actor	$55
Marilyn Monroe	1962	Actress	$27
Charles Shultz	2000	Cartoon-ist	$25
John Lennon	1980	Musician	$12
Elizabeth Taylor	2011	Actress	$12
Albert Einstein	1955	Scientist	$10
Theodor Geisel	1991	Author	$9
Jimmy Hendrix	1970	Musician	$7
Stieg Larsson	2004	Author	$7 million

For many celebrities, their estates earn more than the celebrities did during their lifetimes. During her 36 years of life, Marilyn Monroe earned less than $1 million in total, yet her estate generated 27 times that amount between October 2010 and October 2011. Part of the increase was due to inflation, but a significant portion was due to her attainment of legend status.

When Michael Jackson met his untimely death in 2009, he was reportedly deep in death. His estate earned over $275 million during the year immediately following his death, and another $175 million between October 2010 and October 2011. By some estimates, in three years, the estate brought in over a billion dollars.

In 2003, Tupac Shakur made the top 10 list, earning $12 million. Since he perished from a gunshot wound in September 1996, Shakur has starred in five movies, including the 2003 feature documentary *Resurrection* produced with footage filmed before his death. Shakur has also released more albums after his death than before, leading to street rumors that he must still be alive.

Similarly the many "sightings" of Elvis around the world since his 1977 death from an overdose of drugs have only increased his allure and the revenue earnings of his estate. Presley's estate routinely makes the list of top earners.

A successful estate depends on the nature of the talent. When Whitney Houston passed away suddenly in 2012, her prior recorded albums became instant hits. However, the Huffington Post estimated that one of her biggest hits, "I Will Always Love You" will make more money for Dolly Parton, who wrote the song, than Houston. The Huffington Post quoted an insider who claimed that Houston lived primarily off of advances and probably owed her record company a great deal. [*See* Huffington Post, Whitney Houston's Death]

Because of the substantial earning potential of their estates after their death, some renowned figures carefully plan ahead. Dr. Martin Luther King, Jr. was known to copyright all his speeches. In 1963, he sued Mister Maestro, Inc. to restrain them from selling phonograph records of his "I have a Dream" speech. Dr. King delivered the speech on August 28, 1963, which he had just finished writing that morning. He mailed in the copyright registration form on September 30, 1963. [King v. Mister Maestro, Inc. 224 F.Supp. 101 (S.D.N.Y. 1963).] After his assassination in 1968, King's estate was valued at $66,492.29. It is now worth several million dollars and supports his surviving wife and children. [Burr, *Don't Leave Earth Without It*.]

To die intestate, without a will, or testate, with a will, is the celebrity's choice. The next sections examine the differences in outcome between the two choices for the celebrity's heirs.

1. INTESTATE SUCCESSION

In any given year, approximately two-thirds of all Americans die without a will. In the year 2000, the number of adults who had a will approached an all time high of 47%, but this number declined to 42% by 2004, according to legal publishers Martindale-

Hubble. [Chu, *Fewer Estates Exercise Will Power*.] The company cited procrastination as a common culprit for people not drafting a will, along with concerns about declining assets and estate tax uncertainties. [*Id*.]

Whatever the reason, the number of Americans dying intestate includes such luminaries as film financier Howard Hughes, movie star James Dean, and President Abraham Lincoln, who authored many memorable documents but not his own will. By dying intestate, individuals risk having their estate decided by the state or through a lawsuit.

After Howard Hughes' death in 1976, thousands of individuals claiming to be distant relatives and illegitimate children sought a share of his $6 billion estate. One fake will caused Hollywood to memorialize the tale surrounding its creation into the film *Melvin and Howard*. The brawl over Hughes estate was finally settled in 1996 with lawyers taking a hefty share, more than $20 million in fees. [Burr, *Don't leave Earth without it*.] The bizarre twists and turns of resolving Howard Hughes' estate are chronicled in James R. Phelan and Lewis Chester's *The Money: The Battle for Howard Hughes's Billions* (1997).

States allocate the deceased entertainer's remaining assets to their nearest relatives, unless there are none and then the assets will escheat or be consumed by the state. All states have adopted plans to distribute an estate in the event a person dies without a will. Eighteen states have adopted the Uniform Probate Code (UPC), which divides the estate among the nearest surviving relatives. The UPC gives the surviving spouse the deceased person's entire estate if no parents or descendants (children, grandchildren, etc.) survive the dead person, or if the surviving spouse and the deceased shared all the surviving children. The UPC also takes into consideration the decedent and the surviving spouse's prior and subsequent marriages that produced offspring.

If there are parents or descendants, then the surviving spouse may only receive the most significant part of the estate and the others may receive a share. When the deceased does not leave a surviving spouse, parents, or descendants, the UPC may give assets to siblings, grandparents, aunts, uncles, and cousins. Some states have laws that will look at the person's family tree as far as the great-grand parent level. To change the state's intestate default plan, the person must write a will to leave resources to foundations, friends, or more distant relatives.

2. WILLS

To write a valid will, the celebrity must meet three criteria. He or she must (1) be at least 18 years of age; (2) be of sound mind; and (3) sign and date the will according to the state's requirements. Several states permit a person to prepare holographic wills, which means the material provisions are entirely in the person's handwriting. If the will is typed, then there must be at least two witnesses (some states require three) who observe the decedent sign and date the will, and they must sign and date the will in the decedent's presence and in the presence of each other. In some states, the witnesses must be disinterested; that is, they will receive nothing from the will. Under the UPC, they may be interested or disinterested.

The requirements are simple and the advantages are important to the celebrity's family or other persons or entities the celebrity wishes to leave part of his or her estate. For example, Section 201(d) of the U.S. Copyright Act specifically provides that the ownership of copyright may be "bequeathed by will or pass as personal property by the applicable laws of intestate succession." The celebrity can give all of his copyrights to a particular family member or to a charity. The celebrity possesses the choice.

Estate planning preserves the rights of celebrities to continue to capitalize on their image and valuable intellectual property after their deaths. In 1616, Shakespeare crafted a will giving away his estate primarily to his wife, son, and daughter. Shakespeare penned his sonnets and plays before England passed the Statute of Anne, the world's first Copyright Law in 1710, and thus could not bequeath his copyrights to others.

Prior to committing suicide in 1962, Marilyn Monroe signed a two-page will leaving her estate to her mother, half-sister, and friends. While none of the specific gifts mentioned exceeded $100,000, the gift of her personal effects and clothing to her acting coach Lee Strasberg, who later left them to his wife Anna, turned out to be a goldmine. Valued at $3,200 at the time of Monroe's death, the items were auctioned off by Christie's New York in 1999 for $13.4 million after the death of Anna Strasberg. [Matthews, *Freudians Prefer Blondes*.]

During their lifetimes, both Strasbergs were careful to maintain Monroe's privacy by not disposing of her property or permitting media access to Monroe's letters or documents. In 1996, Anna Strasberg sued the heir of Monroe's former manager to keep him from auctioning off some of Monroe's personal effects. In *Strasberg v. Odyssey Group, Inc.*, 51 Cal.App.4th 906, 59 Cal.Rptr.2d 474 (Cal.App. 2 Dist. 1996), Strasberg claimed she was the present sole beneficiary of Monroe's personal effects under Monroe's will and sought a constructive trust over the items. The court agreed and ordered the items returned to Strasberg.

Currently, Monroe's estate receives its revenues primarily from licensing the use of her image and royalty deals. Monroe's image is used on posters, T-shirts, checkbook covers, Venetian blinds, cookie jars, Christmas ornaments, shoulder pads, camera straps, and stockings. [Mathews, *Freudians Prefer*

Blondes.] According to her estate's official website, http://www.marilynmonroe.com, Monroe's face has graced promotional campaigns for Mercedes Benz in the United States, Levi's jeans in Germany, and Nestlé in the United Kingdom. [*Id.*]

To what extent the Monroe estate could continue to exploit her right of publicity became an issue after it lost the case of *Shaw Family Archives Ltds. V. CMG Worldwide, Inc.*, 486 F.Supp.2d 309 (S.D.N.Y. 2007). The Marilyn Monroe, LLC sued the Shaw Family Archives and Bradford Licensing Associates for violating her right of publicity by using her name, image and likeness for commercial purposes without consent in violation of Indiana's Right of Publicity Act.

Although the case was initially filed in Indiana, the district court ordered it transferred to New York for consideration of whether Monroe had publicity rights in New York that survived her death since she had died domiciled in New York. The federal district court in New York determined that the state had not adopted post-mortem publicity rights, which made the Indiana matter moot.

In the subsequent case of *Milton H. Greene Archives, Inc. v. CMG Worldwide, Inc.*, 568 F.Supp.2d 1152 (C.D.Cal. 2008), a federal district court in California concluded that the estate was precluded by judicial estoppel from claiming that Monroe died a domiciliary of California after it had already received the death tax benefit of claiming that she was domiciled in New York at the time of her death. Although California does recognize such rights, and passed a law that extends them to celebrities for 50 years after death even if the celebrity died before enactment of the law, the California statute did not apply to Monroe who did not die domiciled in California.

Singers John Lennon and Elvis Presley left the bulk of their estates to their families. Lennon took into consideration tax issues in leaving his estate to his widow Yoko Ono. The second clause of the will establishes one-half of estate to qualify for the marital deduction. He named his wife and his friend Eli Garber as trustees of the remainder of the estate and appointed her as guardian of their children. Lennon did not make any references to his first-born son Julian Lennon, the product of his first marriage to Cynthia Lennon.

By writing a will, celebrities may add clauses that disinherit someone, either by name or by category. In his will, Elvis Presley left the remainder of his estate in a residuary trust for his "lawful children." He also directed his trustee to pay maintenance and support for his daughter "Lisa Marie Presley, and any other lawful issue I might have." When Deborah Delaine Presley came forward in 1989 claiming to be Presley' illegitimate child, the court held in *Presley v. Hanks*, 782 S.W.2d 482 (Ten. Ct. App. 1989), that Elvis Presley's will expressly excluded her because she was not born during Presley's marriage to her mother. Indeed, he never married her mother.

The issue of whether Deborah Delaine was actually Presley's daughter became irrelevant. In Tennessee, the court noted that words such as "children" in a will are construed to mean legitimate children and do not include illegitimate children. [*Id.* at 490.] To include illegitimate children in Tennessee, Presley would need to have expressly done so. Instead, he did the opposite. Thus, either way Delaine was left without a valid legal claim to a share of Presley's estate.

3. TRUSTS

Elvis Presley signed his will a few months before his death in 1977, leaving the bulk of his estate in support trusts for his daughter Lisa Marie Presley, grandmother Minnie Mae Presley, father Vernon E. Presley, and other relatives living at the time who may need emergency assistance while his father is alive. After the death of his father, these beneficiaries were eliminated from support. The trust for Lisa Marie terminated on her 25th birthday and she received all the assets outright.

The trusts that Presley created in his will are considered testamentary trusts. Trusts may also be set up during the person's lifetime. They are called intervivos trusts. Such trusts permit flexible management of assets during the person's lifetime. Because they often include payable-on-death provisions, they avoid the probate process. Because wills are public documents, many celebrities create trusts so that the public will not know, unless there is a lawsuit, how they chose to dispose of their assets.

There is, however, a mistaken assumption that intervivos trusts also avoid taxes. They do not. The IRS will calculate the celebrity's gross estate in deciding whether or not the estate tax is due.

The estate of a dead person will be exempt from paying taxes on the first $5,000,000 (adjusted for inflation) of assets. When the exemption applied to the first $3,500,000 of assets in 2009, the Brookings-Urban Institute Tax Policy Center estimated that only 4,500 estates paid estate taxes. In 2010, Congress eliminated the estate tax for a year. Thus, when New York Yankees' owner George Steinbrenner expired from a massive heart attack in Tampa Florida on 13 January 2010, his family saved an estimated $500,000,000 in estate taxes on a $1.4 billion fortune.

Since accomplished celebrities may die with considerable assets, they can benefit the most from planning their estates in advance.

CHAPTER 11

GLOBALIZATION OF ENTERTAINMENT

The United States entertainment industry is a global enterprise. All forms of music emanating from the United States are routinely sold and downloaded abroad. The MPAA, a trade association comprised of the leading film studios, estimates that U.S. films are shown in more than 150 countries worldwide and television shows can be found in over 125 international markets. For some films, like *The Da Vinci Code*, the foreign box office far exceeds the U.S. box office by a factor of almost 2.5 to 1. [Holson, *More Than Ever, Hollywood Studios Are Relying on the Foreign Box Office*]

Film industries vary across countries. India's Bollywood turns out approximately 800 pictures a year, more than any other foreign country's film industry, including Hollywood. Portugal, on the other hand, produces just a handful of films, mostly with support from its government agency ICA - *Instituto do Cinema e do Audiovisual* (Cinema and Audiovisual Institute). José Pedro Ribeiro, the director of ICA, says it gave 12 million Euros to Portuguese filmmakers in 2011, and anticipated giving 8 million Euros in 2012. [Author Interview with Ribeiro.]

Portugal is similar to many countries with low audience support for local films. Portuguese films account for 0.7% of the local box office. When most Portuguese films do not sell 1000 tickets, one of Portugal's most successful filmmakers, António-Pedro Vasconcelos, brings in an audience of 100,000 to 200,000 to view his films. He says a lot of Portuguese filmmakers "make films that only they and some of their friends understand. There is no story. There is no logic." As a consequence, "we lose the market. So we ask the government to protect artistic creativity." [Author Interview with Vasconcelos.]

Portugal's film industry also receives support from private entities. Paulo Pereira established the Algarve Film Commission as a nonprofit to promote the Algarve region as a place to make commercials, television, and films. [Author Interview with Pereira.] Miguel Valverde, the director of IndieLisboa--Portugal's International Film Festival, screened 30 Portuguese films, or 15% of the festival's 240 offerings in 2012 [Author Interview with Valverde.]

The Canadian government gives approximately 100 million Canadian dollars per year to Telefilm Canada, an agency which reports to the Department of Canadian Heritage, the ministry responsible, according to its website http://www.pch.gc.ca, "for national policies and programs that promote Canadian content, foster cultural participation, active citizenship and participation in Canada's civic life, and strengthen connections among Canadians." Telefilm manages the Canada Feature Film Fund, administers the Canada Media Fund, and promotes Canadian screen-based content internationally. An interview with Brigitte Monneau, Director of Telefilm's International Relations, revealed that Telefilm also administers co-production treaties on behalf of the Canadian Government once they are signed and recommends a film deal as an official co-production. [Author Interview with Monneau.]

Once a film or television project receives its co-production status, the producers can apply for selective funding and tax credits. As for 100% Canadian content programs, official co-productions can access the so called "production tax credits" that are higher than "services tax credits" usually given to foreign companies for location shooting in Canada. [*Id.*] The ministry of Canadian Heritages states that the credit is fully refundable and available at a rate of 25 percent of the qualified labor expenditure of an eligible production. [http://www.pch.gc.ca/eng/12687 52355851#a2]

Canada allocates its Feature Film Fund by language, with about one-third devoted to French language films and two-thirds devoted to English language films, which approximates the country's linguistic divide. [Author interview with Monneau.] Monneau estimates that $90 million of Telefilm's budget went directly to filmmakers and producers in 2010-11. Producers and distributors who are successful at the box office benefit from a performance component specified in the guidelines for the Canada Feature Film Fund. The performance component creates an envelope system whereby the CFFF earmarks resources back to the companies with the most distinguished track record of performance at the Canadian box office.

Like the United Kingdom, Canada recoups a portion of the revenues based on its contribution to the budget, which cannot exceed 49%. Monneau explained that Telefilm receives money pro-rata pari-passu with other financial contributions (producer investment, private fund, license fees...). When a project includes distribution advances/ minimum guarantees or presales, Telefilm negotiates on a case by case basis with the producer to find a fair recoupment schedule for all parties involved.

Globalization has affected other forms of entertainment as well. The London theater district sends plays to Broadway and vice versa. Russian and African dance troops are as likely to tour the United States as the Alvin Ailey troop is to perform in Paris. United States' citizens enhance the culture of others and are similarly enriched.

Perhaps a true testament to globalization can be found in the dual 2006 films about the 1945 battle of Iwo Jima that were directed by Clint Eastwood. He first released *Flags of Our Fathers*, based on a book by James Bradley who survived the battle and became one of six men to hold up the American flag, in the United States. He subsequently released *Letters from Iwo Jima*, which depicted the story of Japanese young men who were told they were being sent to Iwo Jima to die for the Emperor, in Japan. Eastwood wrote, "I found it fascinating to make *Letters from Iwo Jima* in a whole different culture and language. Sure I didn't understand what the actors were saying, but all those Italian movies I did in the 1960s taught me that acting is acting." [Eastwood, *We All Have the Same Fears*.]

Many foreigners have crossed oceans to participate in Hollywood productions. Australians Nicole Kidman and Mel Gibson have won Academy Awards for their participation in American films. Two Australian actors, Anthony LaPaglia and Poppy Montgomery, play FBI agents in the top-ten television show *Without a Trace*, which also features as their co-star Haitian actress Marianne Jean-Baptiste. Asian actors Jackie Chan, Jet Li, and Ken Watanabe have brought martial arts sensibility to films as diverse as *Rush Hour*, *Lethal Weapon IV*, and *Batman Begins*. The latter film was directed by Christopher Nolan and starred Christian Bale, both British nationals. Another British citizen, Stephen Frears directed French actress Audrey Tatou and a British actor of Nigerian parentage Chiwetel Ejiofor in *Dirty Pretty Things*. Peter Jackson, a New Zealander, directed four films (the *Lord of the Rings* trilogy and *King Kong*) that together generated more than $2 billion in global box office revenue.

This chapter addresses issues associated with the ongoing internationalization of the entertainment business and the legal consequences that flow there from. As companies expand their production venues and markets, other countries are feeling the pressure of declining control over local culture. Piracy continues to be a problem, as nations in the early stages of economic development have an incentive to encourage the pilfering of intellectual property creations like films, television shows, and music. Their citizens are enlightened without having to pay the full price, yet these events are not without legal consequences. This chapter concludes with a discussion of attempts to settle disputes between foreign nations over copyrights and other entertainment related issues.

A. FOREIGN PRODUCTION VENUES

This section discusses the globalization of film and television production, as foreign companies buy U.S. companies and companies like Viacom seek to expand venues for creating entertainment products. As producers seek to trim costs, they are generating films and television shows in places far beyond the traditional venues of California and New York. Several Hollywood producers and studios have shot films in countries like Australia, Canada, India, Japan, and on the continents of Africa, Asia, Europe, North America, and South America.

Foreign corporations have purchased or engaged in deals with Hollywood studios to expand their reach into the United States. Sometimes foreigners' Hollywood adventures result in rude awakenings.

The Japanese conglomerate Sony bought Columbia studios and eventually had to fire the two Hollywood producers it put in charge to run their investment. While Peter Guber and Jon Peters had produced the mega hit *Batman*, they proved inept at running a studio. Nancy Griffin memorialized Sony's tale of woe in her book *Hit and Run: How Peter Guber and Jon Peters took Sony for a Ride in Hollywood* (1996).

These foreign firms mistakenly expect studios to produce hit after hit. Yet, as screenwriter William Goldman said in his *Adventures in the Screen Trade*, "Nobody Knows Anything." [Goldman, *Adventures in the Screen Trade*, at 39.] In other words, the magic formula that produced a mega hit could easily produce 10 flops.

In 1996, German television giant, the Kirch Group, invested $2 billion in Universal Studios to lock up film and TV rights for its fledgling digital pay-TV systems, according to a Los Angeles Times article. Feeling duped after Universal released duds such as *Babe: Pig in the City* and *Meet Joe Black*, the Kirch Group sued Universal. [L.A. Times, *Universal Sued by Kirch*.] While Universal did release hits such as *Notting Hill* and *The Mummy*, it also cut back on film production to contain spiraling costs. The Kirch Group expected Universal to provide 20 to 30 films and ended up with a fraction of that number. [*Id.*] The Kirch Group also expressed concern that Universal had shifted its attention from film and television production to music. [*Id*.]

In 2002, Universal sued the Kirch Group after it stopped payments on their 1996 deal. At that time, Universal's international television co-president Phil Schuman proclaimed, "We're the studio of the moment." [Guider, *Mouse House springs passel of new deals*.]

Hollywood is not the only film industry to produce illusory financial success. Variety Magazine reported, "At first glance, the bottom line on Australia's film industry is simple. While sales agents and other investors might turn small profits, fewer than 10% of films ever fully recoup their entire production budgets and go into overall profit." [Variety, *Oz Bottom Line Shaky*.] Variety also said that of the 110 or so films that Australia's Film Finance Corporation invested in through June 1997, only about seven have gone into profit, including *Sirens*, *Green Card*, *Shine*, *Strictly Ballroom*, *Priscilla: Queen of the Dessert*, and *Muriel's Wedding*. [*Id*.]

To diminish the risk associated with film production and increase the potential for profit, Hollywood and foreign filmmakers seek to trim production costs. They search out locales that offer production, tax, and other incentives, which make films cheaper to create.

U.S. firms that produce films and television shows in foreign settings are sometimes termed runaway productions. A study released in 1999 estimated that the U.S. economy suffered a direct loss of $2.8 billion in 1998 from runaway productions. This was five times the 1990 figure of $500 million. [Waxman, *Location, Location*.] The study reported that of the 1,075 film and television productions released in the United States during 1998, 27 percent were produced abroad for economic reasons. [*Id.*] Eighty-one percent of these were filmed in Canada, whose government offers tax credits that can save 22% on labor costs. [*Id.*]

Canada is also a popular venue because its exchange rate against the U.S. dollar benefits Americans and because its cities can double for several American cities. For example, Toronto resembles New York, Chicago, and L.A., and it is cleaner than its American counterparts. Warner Brothers President of Production, Lorenzo di Bonaventura, said he was able to initially make *The Matrix* in 1999 for 30 percent less because the Canadian "rate of exchange is 62 cents on the dollar." [*Id.*]

Several other countries have followed Canada's lead by forming film commissions to solicit international entertainment dollars. Countries benefit from the direct investment, the multiplier effects that aids their economies, and from increased tourism. As mentioned in Chapter 1, over 300 film commissions belong to the Association of Film Commissions International (AFCI). These commissions actively promote their membership on their business cards and websites.

Cine Tirol, an Austrian Film Commission for the state of Tirol that is headquartered in Innsbruck, belongs to AFCI. Cine Tirol offers a limited amount of financing and provides free location scouting to assist filmmakers in finding appropriate locations to shoot their films. Cine Tirol commissioner Sabine Aigner says her organization has a small budget to finance films that are either entirely or at least partially produced in the Austrian state of Tirol. [Author Interview with Aigner.] She also takes pride in the ability of the Austrian state of Tirol to attract Hollywood productions such as Queen Latifah's 2005 film *Last Holiday*. Further, Cine Tirol has actively courted Bollywood producers to film their dream sequences in the mountains of Austria.

The Swiss government is similarly fond of having Bollywood producers shoot part of their films in Switzerland. The Bollywood filmmakers effectively advertise Switzerland's mountain beauty to Indian audiences. As a consequence, Switzerland experienced a five-fold increase in Indian tourists seeking honeymoon destinations. Cyril Jost, the head of Location Switzerland, says that Switzerland offers a scouting package to five Bollywood producers "of a certain importance" every year to survey Swiss locations. The packages include plane tickets, hotel, and other travel costs. "India is the only nation where there is a clear link between film movies and tourism increase," Jost adds. [Author Interview with Jost.]

Bavarian film commissioner Anja Metzger also has experience with Bollywood filmmakers. She prefers to have Indian producers work with a local producer to clear pathways and secure permits. Bollywood filmmakers are legendary in Europe for setting up shop and filming with no notice and lack of location permits. Rather than focus on encouraging foreigners to produce in Germany, the German government spends over 200 million Euros annually to support the growth of its internal film industry. According to Metzger, the government supports film students by giving them grants to shoot their first film. [Author Interview with Metzger.]

Similarly the United Kingdom plugs 100 million pounds into promoting and subsidizing the production of British Films, which showcase British culture. The British government receives a percentage of the copyright of the film based on the percentage of its contribution to the film's budget. The British government also funds a government agency that endeavors to attract foreign productions to the United Kingdom. One officer acknowledged that their success rate fluctuates with the value of their currency, the British pound. The higher the pound trades relative to other currencies, the more expensive it becomes to film in Britain and the more likely producers will seek other venues.

The Australian Film Commission strives to promote its film industry and cultural development. In the 1980s, Australia produced numerous pictures distributed into the international marketplace, including *Crocodile Dundee* and *Muriel's Wedding*. At that time, the Australian government was giving a 100% tax rebate on film expenditures within the country, guaranteeing that filmmakers would break even on their costs. The Australian government later increased the rebate to 150%, which assured that filmmakers would not only recoup their production costs, but also would earn a 50% profit. According to Stephen Boyle, a legal officer with the Australian Film Commission, the program got "rotted, quite rotted," as filmmakers started to make junk just to receive the tax rebate. [Author Interview with Boyle.] The government ended the program, and created the Film Finance Corporation to oversee the financing of local productions and co-productions that benefit Australian filmmakers.

By investing in their entertainment industries, foreign governments also aim for multiplier effects. Positive multiplier effects return some multiple (say 100% to 300%) of their initial investment back into the economy. Multiplier effects can also be negative. A 1999 U.S. study on runaway productions estimated that the multiplier loss to the U.S. economy was $10.3 billion. [Waxman, *Location, Location*.] This loss affected industries such as real estate, restaurants, clothing, and hotels, and cost 20,000 jobs.

The globalization of the film and television industries creates an odd paradox for the U.S. economy.
On the one hand, U.S. studios and producers benefit
when they can make films cheaper. It increases the
likelihood that they will recoup their initial investment and earn profits. Lowering costs also permits
them to absorb losses associated with the international piracy of their films. Yet, on the other hand,
when studios produce abroad, they take jobs and
revenue with them. It is for this reason that the
state incentive plans, discussed in Chapter 1, have
received a great deal of media attention. They permit studios and producers to cut their costs while
keeping jobs and revenue within the United States.

B. INTERCONTINENTAL MARKETS

Films, television, music, games, and other entertainment products regularly travel between continents through foreign distribution outlets or via the
Internet. Globalization creates advantages for producers in Hollywood, Bollywood, Europe, Asia, Africa, and South America because it increases the
number of individuals who experience their products. Travel to just about any foreign country and
you will see theaters headlining the films that you
could see in Los Angeles or New York, and listen to
radio stations playing all too familiar songs. Similarly, someone walking the streets of New York can
catch an African, Asian, or Latin American film.

Turn on the television in Munich and experience
the ladies of *Desperate Housewives* speaking Ger-

man. By October 2006, Germans could watch not only the occasional show, but a full night on a television station showcasing only American programs, thanks to RTL, a station owned by the German media conglomerate Bertelsmann. It offers German-speaking versions of *CSI: Miami*, *House*, *Monk*, and *Law & Order* concentrated into one night. [Pfanner, *As U.S. Is Reviled Abroad, American TV Charms*.] If one night is not enough, British citizens can watch a new television channel, Five US, that features only American programming. [*Id*.]

This internationalization of entertainment is not without detractors, as in some venues, foreign films, television, and other entertainment products have overwhelmed the domestic market. In doing so, they leave little room for local entertainment.

Mark Woods, the CEO of AusFilm which markets Australian tax incentives abroad and tracks foreign production down under, describes Australians as "big consumers of American content." [Author Interview with Woods.] He estimates the Australians' share of their own box office ranges in any given year from one to twelve percent. By comparison, the French contribute 30% and the Indians supply approximately 90% of their own films to their respective domestic box offices. Woods says that Australians "have both the gift and curse of the English language." [*Id*.] The gift permits them to easily view American produced content; the curse is that content is saturating their theaters and television airwaves. Woods believes that Australians should shift their focus from trying to compete with Americans and instead "promote Australia as a destination for footloose producers, post production, and games." [*Id.*]

Attorney Bruno Charlesworth asserts that Australian films have become "almost a negative to the Australian public. For an Australian film to be successful, it must sell into the European and American markets." [Author Interview with Charlesworth.] He decries "the Americanization of the Australian culture," which makes Australians "beholden to Americans." Charlesworth crossed from music lawyer to filmmaker when he produced the comedy *The Extra*. The film, which cost $6.5 million to produce and was supported in part by the Australian Film Finance Corporation, took in barely $1 million at the box office.

In Charlesworth's view, Australia lacks a strong domestic market. He says that in the 1980s, "people embraced Australian films. Now if people have a choice, they will not go because it's an Australian film." He compares Australia negatively to England and France where he says that "domestic audiences will go see their own products." [*Id.*]

Charlesworth took his film *The Extra* to Cannes where he screened it to potential foreign buyers, but did not enter it into the festival. He says that there were perhaps 50 films competing in the festival compared to 3,200 available for sale. He enlisted a foreign sales agent to assist him. His agent screened a total of eight films that year, but found no takers for his film. "It's very bleak when no one wants to see what you've got to sell." Charlesworth also contends that "Australian films go in and out of fashion."

Interviews with other Australian filmmakers confirm this tale of woe. Several lament the loss of the glory days of Australian filmmaking supported by generous government tax incentives. Documentary filmmaker Christine Gallagher works for Screen Tasmania, which is part of the Tasmanian Department of Economic Development and seeks to encourage producers to capture the beauty of Australia's southernmost island in their films. Gallagher says, "We were lucky in the 1980s because we could be on the dole and make films. The generation after is struggling." One of Gallagher's biggest concerns is "the globalization of the voice" or the "loss of voice" unique to Australia. [Author Interview with Gallagher.]

Filmmaker and lecturer Andrew Laurence shares Gallagher's concern. He worries about the decline of Australian-made television shows and commercials. He fears that because Australia buys cheap television from abroad, his child will grow up with an American accent. [Author Interview with Laurence.]

Australian director Dick Marks (*Sheer Will*) has a different view. He believes that the "downturn in film production is good for Australia because we will get back to making short Australian films." He spent most of his 30-year career making commercials and documentaries. He contends there will always be a market for local-content commercials and documentaries because people want to buy products from people who sound like them and relish the telling of neighborhood stories.

Although the glorious 1980s tax incentives may have vanished, the Australian government continues to pump money into supporting its film and television industries. The 2004-05 Annual Report of the Film Finance Corporation indicates that it contributed $87.9 million (Australian) toward creating a production slate worth $228.6 million (Australian). The FFC financed 14 feature films worth $101.3 million (Australian) and 37 documentaries worth $16.5 million (Australian).

C. DOMESTIC MARKET PROTECTION

Some countries seek to protect their domestic market through the use of film quotas. Table 11-1 illustrates this public policy practice by depicting the film quotas in five countries. This list is neither exhaustive, nor totally representative of all countries who protect their film and television industries with some form of quotas.

For example, Argentina requires exhibitors to show at least one local film in each quarter for each screen. Thus, according to a Terramedia report, "a 16-screen multiplex must show 64 Argentinean films a year." [http://www.terrameia.co.uk/media/film/quotas_and_levies.htm] Austria, on the other hand, has used a film quota of 1 Austrian film for every 20 foreign films since 1926. [*Id.*]

Table 11-1: Country Film Quotas	
COUNTRY	*QUOTA*
Argentina	Exhibitors must show at least one local film in each quarter for each screen
Austria	Exhibitors must show one domestic film for every 20 imported films
Brazil	Exhibitors must show Brazilian films for a number of days every year that is defined by yearly presidential decree
China	Exhibitors are limited to screening 34 foreign films per year
South Korea	73 days a year must be devoted to showing Korean films

The requirement that exhibitors show Brazilian films for a minimum number of days a year varies by year. In 1998 the quota was 49 days, and in 2004 it was 63 days. [*Id.*] Similarly, South Korea requires exhibitors to devote 73 days per year to showing South Korean Films. Rather than impose a quota by days, China imposes one by number of films. In February 2012, China raised its quota from 20 to 34 films per years. Chinese exhibitors wanted to show *The Dark Knight Rises*, which Chinese authorities initially censored, but eventually relented according to Variety. [Coonan, *China Clears 'Dark Knight*.]

D. GLOBAL PIRACY

Prior to World War II, the United States was a net *importer* of intellectual property and its citizens actively pirated works produced in other countries. Charles Dickens avidly promoted the adoption of stronger copyright laws in the United States. On his tour of the country in the 1840s, he was greeted as a hero of the common man until he complained about American booksellers routinely printing and selling his books without paying him royalties. The press criticized him, but he exacted revenge with unflattering portraits of the United States in *American Notes* and *Martin Chuzzlewit*. [Burr, *The Piracy Gap*, at 248.]

Mark Twain also advocated the United States adopt more stringent copyright laws. He became upset after a boy tried to sell him a pirated version of *The Adventures of Tom Sawyer*. He sued several booksellers for printing his books in other countries and importing them into the United States. After one of his lawsuits failed, Twain wrote, "A Massachusetts judge has just decided in open court that a

Boston publisher may sell not only his own property in a free and unfettered way, but also may as freely sell property which does not belong to him, but to me—property which he has not bought and which I have not sold. Under this ruling, I am now advertising that the judge's homestead is for sale and if I make as good a sum out of it as I expect, I shall go out and sell the rest of his property." [*Id.* at 249.]

There is no evidence that Twain ever carried out his threat. It would take nearly a century before the United States joined the Berne Convention, the major international copyright treaty designed to prevent the kind of theft that Dickens and Twain experienced on a grand scale.

The United States began to change its position on copyright piracy after it became a net *exporter* of intellectual property creations following World War II. Only then did legislators see the advantage to strengthening U.S. copyright laws. By the 1980s, the U.S. had become one of the principal providers of intellectual property to the rest of the world. Reagan Administration officials campaigned vigorously to have developing countries like China, Brazil, and Thailand curtail theft. The Reagan Administration came to view protecting intellectual property rights as critical to the continued growth of the U.S. economy.

The L.A. Times reported in 1993 that in Thailand, "pirates control 90% of the video market ... and reportedly cost the U.S. film industry about $30 million.... Total U.S. losses due to piracy in Thailand were about $123 million in 1992, including $49 million on computer programs and $20 million on books, according to industry officials." [Los Angeles Times, *International Trade.*]

More than a decade after the L.A. Times article ran, the problem with international theft of films, television shows, and music produced in the United States has expanded rather than contracted. Music piracy, for example, has reached a global epidemic, hitting countries as diverse as Italy and Egypt.

The International Federal Phonographic Industry (IFPI), whose 1500 members come from 76 countries, reported that in 2001, Italy placed sixth worldwide in terms of piracy valued at $121 million. Jay Berman, the chairman and CEO of IFPI, said, "Italy has a rich and vibrant musical culture, but the value of this music is being undermined by piracy on a massive scale.... [P]irate CDs are ... sold everywhere in the streets. Even when prosecutions do reach the courts, pirates often get off much too lightly." [www.ifpi.org/site-content/press/ 20030707. html]

In Egypt, the police seized nearly two million counterfeit Arab language music cassettes on July 7, 2003. The IFPI reported that next to Lebanon, where the piracy rate is almost 70%, Egypt has one of the highest piracy rates in the Middle East region at about 50%. [*Id.*]

The Property Rights Alliance, a Washington Advocacy group, ranked Latin American countries as among the world champions of illegal reproduction of movies, music, books, medicines and other goods subject to royalty. The Alliance ranked Mexico 55th, Nicaragua 92nd, Bolivia 94th, Venezuela 99th and Paraguay 102nd out of 115 countries in terms of respect for intellectual property rights. Federico de la Garza, general manager of the Motion Pictures Association's Mexico Office, said "Ninety percent of the videos sold in Mexico are pirated." Because Mexico has the world's fifth-largest market of movie-goers, the MPAA estimated nearly $600 million is lost every year in unpaid intellectual property rights. Mexican pirates sell DVD versions of films like Slumdog Millionaire for about $1.25 even before they appear in movie theaters. [Openheimer, Intelectual Piracy Hurts.]

Technology has made it easier to steal with impunity. Films appear on the Internet the day of their release, sometimes with a laughter track that indicates they were surreptitiously taped in front of a theater audience. To discourage this form of piracy, Japanese theaters prohibit by contract, printed on the back of tickets, potential thieves from taping films in their theaters.

Other times, bootleg copies of movies become available for purchase before the film appears in the theatre. Producers of the 2004 film *Soul Plane* blamed the bootleg copies for its poor performance at the box office. Gabriel Snyder wrote that the film "crashed with critics, but ... was a huge hit with bootleggers." [Snyder, *Was 'Plane' hijacked*] Snyder noted that for years "in overseas markets, Hollywood has had to contend with bootleg copies of their films being sold on the street well before their theatrical release.... But this incident marks the earliest pirates have gotten hold of a major movie ahead of its U.S. release." [*Id.*] *Soul Plane* was available on the black market two months before it showed up in theaters.

Bootleggers enable their customers to avoid trips to the theater to see films or to stores to purchase copies. Ultimately, they may undermine production and creativity. *Soul Plane* cost $16 million to produce and recouped only $13,957,242 during its 30-day box office run. When considering whether to do another film like *Soul Plane*, the producers must mull over whether they can keep the film under wraps long enough to recoup their investment.

In the summer of 2005, the Tom Cruise film *War of the Worlds* was available for purchase on the streets of Spain the same weekend that it premiered at the box office there. The introductory credits, which appeared in the Russian language, indicated that this Cruise film was probably stolen from a

Russian source and then copied for foot-traffic distribution throughout Europe. Nevertheless, the film took in nearly $400 million in global box office.

In 2010, IDC Research Iberia released a study, finding that Spaniards pirated online contents worth an estimated E5.1 billion ($6.3 billion) in the second half of 2009. IDC polled 5,911 Spaniards, and uncovered that piracy accounted for 83.7% of all online movie consumption and 95.6% of music. IDC estimated that pirates cost the Spanish digital content industries more than $12 billion a year and the Spanish government $1.7 billion in lost taxes in 2009. [Hopewell, Piracy ravages Spain]

After considerable debate, Spain's parliament rejected anti-piracy regulations that would have created an Intellectual Property Commission run by Spain's Ministry of Culture. The Commission would have been able to recommend blocking or closure of websites that facilitate unauthorized movie and music downloads for commercial gain. Variety reported that the film industry reacted furiously when the law failed to pass. [*Id.*]

E. INTERNATIONAL DISPUTE FORUMS

This section addresses issues associated with global dispute resolution. As studios and producers internationalize their operations, inevitably disputes arise with their foreign partners and other companies. Similarly, big name talent such as singer Madonna and author Dan Brown have been hauled into courts in Belgium and Britain, respectively, and charged with copyright infringement. Shopping for an appropriate forum to defend or resolve a dispute becomes a source of concern for talent and companies.

In *London Films v. Intercontinental Communications*, 580 F.Supp. 47 (S.D.N.Y. 1984), a British corporation sued a New York Corporation for infringement of British copyrights that occurred in Chile and other South American countries. London Films alleged that Intercontinental was showing its motion pictures on television in South America. Intercontinental sought to dismiss the suit by claiming the court lacked jurisdiction. It expressed concern that none of the wrongdoings constitute violations of U.S. law.

While the court acknowledged that London Films did not allege that Intercontinental violated U.S. laws, the court determined that it possessed jurisdiction over whether an American corporation has acted in violation of a foreign copyright. The court noted that it was the only forum in which the defendant is the subject of personal jurisdiction. The court concluded that where "the balance does not tip strongly in favor of an alternative forum it is well-established that the plaintiff's choice of forum should not be disturbed." [*Id*. at 50.]

In some cases with individuals from different countries, courts endeavor to balance the private and public interest in deciding whether a plaintiff's choice of forum should be rejected on grounds of *forum non conveniens*. In *Overseas Programming Companies, Ltd. v. Cinematographische Commerz-Anstalt*, 684 F.2d 232, (2nd Cir. 1982), Judge Newman wrote that among a litigant's private interests to be considered are: (1) the relative ease of access to sources of proof; (2) the availability of compulsory process for attendance of unwilling witness and cost of obtaining willing witnesses; and (3) other matters affecting the cost, speed, and ease of litigating a suit in a particular forum. [*Id.* at 234.]

Further, the judge observed that a court must also evaluate the enforceability of a judgment rendered by it; weigh relative advantages and obstacles to a fair trial; and determine whether the plaintiff has instituted suit in a particular forum with the intent to vex or harass the defendant. [*Id.*] The judge said the public interests to be considered include (1) the administrative burdens imposed on already congested courts by suits that are properly centered elsewhere, and (2) the burden of jury duty on members of a community with no real relation to the dispute. [*Id.*] The court applied these factors to reverse the District Court, and ordered that the case be tried in the United States because England was not a more convenient forum.

The Second Circuit applied similar factors and affirmed the dismissal of an action against the British Broadcasting Corporation on *forum non conveniens* grounds. In *Murray v. BBC*, 81, F.3d 287, (2nd Cir. 1996), both the plaintiff and the defendant were British nationals and the plaintiff asserted claims based on copyright infringement under both U.S. and English law.

Another important issue concerns whether the U.S. copyright laws can be extended extraterritorially to actions that take place in other countries. In *Subafilms, Ltd. v. MGM-Pathe Communications Co.*, 24 F.3d 1088, 1096 (9th Cir. 1994), the Ninth Circuit held that it lacked jurisdiction when the infringing conduct occurred abroad. The Court of Appeals noted that Congress had declared "the unauthorized importation of copyrighted works constitutes infringement even when the copies lawfully were made abroad." The Court of Appeals said there is a presumption against the extraterritorial application of U.S. Copyright Law, and thus United States copyright laws do not reach acts of infringement that take place entirely abroad. [*Id.* at 1098.] Indeed, to extend U.S. copyright laws would "disrupt the international regime for protecting intellectual property that Congress ... described as essential to ... protecting the works of American authors abroad." [*Id.*]

The *Subafilms* case is consistent with the longstanding proposition that copyrights are territorial, and must be enforced within the jurisdiction of creation. Nevertheless, in *Richard Feiner v. BMG Music Spain*, 2003 WL 740605 (S.D.N.Y. 2003), the District Court said an exception exists "where the defendant commits a predicate act of infringement within the U.S." BMG Music Spain produced compact disc recordings of the soundtrack from the movie *Marjorie Morningstar* in Spain and sold the discs in Europe. Feiner alleged that BMG Spain first copied a master copy of the recordings in the New York offices of co-defendant Bertelsmann Music Group, Inc., which it then used in Spain. There was also some question as to whether a portion of the Spanish production found its way into the United States. These were issues that the court felt should go to a jury to determine the extent of a U.S. connection to the infringing acts.

Golan v. Holder, 132 S.Ct. 873 (2012), involved orchestra conductors, musicians, and publishers who challenge Congress' enactment of §514 of Uruguay Round Agreements Act (URAA) that granted copyright protection to certain preexisting works of Berne member countries that were protected in their country of origin, but lacked protection in the United States. The Supreme Court held that Congress did not violate the Copyright Clause by enacting §514 of URAA, and that the First Amendment did not inhibit the restoration of copyright protection authorized by §514 of the URAA.

Courts are thus willing to take cases where there is a defined U.S. connection to the infringing acts. They are less willing to dismiss cases if it means that the plaintiff will not receive his day in court.

In conclusion, the entertainment industry will continue to globalize. Hollywood studios will persistently seek out cheaper production venues, be it Bollywood or Canada, and new markets for their products as they saturate old ones. Talent will migrate from across the globe to where the jobs are. Hopefully, the biggest beneficiary will be worldwide audiences who will experience better stories that amuse the funny bone, calm the soul, and lift the human spirit.

INDEX

References are to Pages

ATTORNEYS (See Lawyers)

AUTHORS (Literary)

BANKRUPTCY

BERNE CONVENTION

CABLE TELEVISION

CENSORSHIP